Numerical Computing
with Modern Fortran

Numerical Computing with Modern Fortran

Richard J. Hanson

Albuquerque, New Mexico

Tim Hopkins

University of Kent
Kent, United Kingdom

Society for Industrial and Applied Mathematics
Philadelphia

Library of Congress Cataloging-in-Publication Data

Hanson, Richard J., 1938-
  Numerical computing with modern Fortran / Richard J. Hanson, Albuquerque, New Mexico, Tim Hopkins, University of Kent, Kent, United Kingdom.
    pages cm. -- (Applied mathematics)
  Includes bibliographical references and index.
  ISBN 978-1-611973-11-2
1. FORTRAN (Computer program language) 2. Numerical analysis--Computer programs. 3. Science--Mathematics--Computer programs. I. Hopkins, Tim, author. II. Title.
  QA76.73.F25H367 2013
  518'.0285--dc23   2013030887

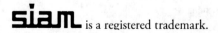 is a registered trademark.

Contents

Introduction   **ix**

   0.1   Getting Started ix
   0.2   Using a Reference Book x
   0.3   Become Familiar with the New x
   0.4   Moving to Interesting Topics xi

1   The Modern Fortran Source   **1**

   1.1   Introduction 1
   1.2   Source Code Formatting and Labels 2
   1.3   Comments in Source Code 2
   1.4   Continuation Lines 3
   1.5   Statements Separated by ';' 4
   1.6   Relational Operators and Related Symbols 4
   1.7   Introducing Derived Types 5
   1.8   Basics on Modules 6
   1.9   Optional Arguments 8
   1.10   The Include Line and Preprocessor Directives 9
   1.11   New Timing Routines 10

2   Modules for Subprogram Libraries   **13**

   2.1   Introduction 13
   2.2   Running a Fortran 77 Program 14
   2.3   Develop with Modules 19

3   Generic Subprograms   **29**

   3.1   Introduction 29
   3.2   Illustrations with Airy Functions 30
   3.3   Writing the Module Procedures 31

4   Sparse Matrices, Defined Operations, Overloaded Assignment   **35**

   4.1   Introduction 35
   4.2   Representing Sparse Matrices 36
   4.3   A Simple Sparse Representation 37
   4.4   Overloaded Assignment 39

4.5   User-Defined and Overloaded Operators   42
4.6   Sums and Transposes of Sparse Matrices   42
4.7   Sparse Matrix, Dense Vector/Matrix Products   45
4.8   Documentation and Error Processing   45

5   Object-Oriented Programming for Numerical Applications   47
5.1   Introduction   47
5.2   Inheritance and Polymorphism   49
5.3   Encapsulation   50
5.4   Using Classes for Passing Information to User-Written Routines   51
5.5   Summary   55

6   Recursion in Fortran   57
6.1   Introduction   57
6.2   Basic Quicksort   58
6.3   Generalizing Using Type-Bound Procedures   63
6.4   Using Abstract Data Types and Interfaces   66
6.5   Efficiency Considerations   69

7   Case Study: Toward A Modern QUADPACK Routine   71
7.1   Introduction   71
7.2   Converting Source Form   74
7.3   Transformed Interface   74
7.4   A One-Dimensional Integration with User Data   77
7.5   Two-Dimensional Integration Using Extended Types
       and Recursion   81
7.6   A Complex Line Integral   85

8   Case Study: Documenting the Quadrature Routine qag2003   89
8.1   Introduction   89
8.2   The PUBLIC Symbols and Base Class   90
8.3   The Arguments for qag2003   92
8.4   Example: Three Ways to Package the User Function   94
8.5   Documenting Internal Working Variables   98

9   IEEE Arithmetic Features and Exception Handling   101
9.1   Introduction   101
9.2   Example Problem   103
9.3   Using the IEEE Features from Fortran   107
9.4   Denormalized Numbers and Underflow Modes   113

10   Interoperability with C   117
10.1   Introduction   117
10.2   Characters and Two-Dimensional Arrays   121
10.3   Sharing Data Structures and Global Data   124
10.4   Function Pointers   125

10.5   System Calls 127
10.6   Some Names Are Still Not Allowed 129

11   Defined Operations for Sparse Matrix Solutions   131
11.1   Introduction 131
11.2   Ascended Harwell–Boeing Sparse Matrices 132
11.3   C Wrappers Calling SuperLU Functions 134
11.4   The Overloaded Assignments and Defined Operators 137

12   Case Study: Two Sparse Least-Squares System Examples   141
12.1   Introduction 141
12.2   Data Fitting with Continuous Linear Splines 141
12.3   Airy's Equation with Boundary Values 145

13   Message Passing with MPI in Standard Fortran   151
13.1   Introduction 151
13.2   Two Examples 152
13.3   MPI Implementations 153
13.4   Fortran Standard Code Violations 157
13.5   A Core Suite 158

14   Coarrays in Standard Fortran   163
14.1   Introduction 163
14.2   A Core Suite of Coarray Intrinsic Functions 164
14.3   A Coarray Alternative for Computing π 166
14.4   Matrix-Vector Products Using Coarrays 167

15   OpenMP in Fortran   169
15.1   Introduction 169
15.2   Examples 171
15.3   Tips on Writing Thread-Safe Routines 176
15.4   A Mention of More General Threading Models 180

16   Modifying Source to Remove Obsolescent or Deleted Features 181
16.1   Introduction 181
16.2   On Replacing Obsolescent Features 182
16.3   On Replacing Deleted Features 187
16.4   On the Removal of **GO TO** Statements 187

17   Software Testing   193
17.1   Introduction 193
17.2   What Constitutes a Test? 194
17.3   When to Start and Stop Testing 194
17.4   Other Types of Testing 196
17.5   Problems with Constructing Test Data 198
17.6   Equivalence Partitioning and Boundary Value Analysis . . . 198
17.7   Final Word 202

18   Compilers   **205**
   18.1   Introduction 205
   18.2   Commonly Available Checks and Options 206
   18.3   Other Useful Commonly Available Options 208
   18.4   Optimization 209
   18.5   My Code Doesn't Run Fast Enough! 212
   18.6   Dealing with Dusty Decks 212

19   Software Tools   **215**
   19.1   Introduction 215
   19.2   Application Building Using *make* 216
   19.3   Source Code or Text Control Systems 219
   19.4   Source Code Documentation Systems 219
   19.5   Debuggers 220
   19.6   Profiling 221
   19.7   Sample Output and Run-Time Error Processors 222
   19.8   Source Code Stylers 223
   19.9   Other Software Tools 225

20   Fortran Book Code on SIAM Web Site   **227**
   20.1   Downloading the Software 227
   20.2   Topical Headings for the Software 227

Bibliography   **231**

Index   **239**

Introduction

0.1 Getting Started

This book represents our approach and prejudices toward writing computer software for numerical computing and applications. Both of us have served as editors of the Collected Algorithms (or CALGO) from the ACM [2]. This experience and our personal application development and programming histories have convinced us that Fortran is currently the best computer language for numerical software. We present our views and practices primarily in the form of a tapestry of meaningful examples along with exercises for the reader to work through. We do this because writing or modifying an algorithm or application may involve several elements of the Fortran language, and, while these elements are individually defined in the standard sources, they tend to be organized from a language standpoint, and therefore they appear sprinkled throughout the text.

Constructing software often involves combining ideas with a variety of language constructs. Integrating these ideas, checking for conformance to the current standard, and recalling the syntax of the language elements all place significant research demands on the programmer. We emphasize our preferences for combining these constructs to accomplish the goals of performance and maintainability, as well as the righting of out-of-date practices.

Other aspects of software development are cost and the need to save both time and money. Toward this end, if an existing C function or application can provide some required functionality, then we should consider using it rather than implementing an equivalent Fortran code. We provide examples of integrating C functions into Fortran software even when these functions are available only as precompiled libraries. The same tactic may be used by C programmers when a useful component is available in Fortran by making an interlanguage call from C to Fortran.

In the past, doing this was highly dependent on the C and Fortran compilers being used and was, thus, a high maintenance strategy. The Fortran 2003 standard specifies a mechanism for performing this interoperability between consenting compilers, thus making it an effective option.

In this book we present a set of problems and their solutions that we believe will be of common interest to both Fortran programmers and those who must maintain or interface to existing Fortran software.

We have tried to anticipate many of the common questions that programmers face as they write codes that use the algorithms of numerical analysis and scientific computing. In our choice of illustrative examples we emphasize the new features of the language that help with the writing and maintenance of this type of software. We will dispel the common myth that Fortran is an out-of-date language that does not conform to modern programming requirements. Fortran is no longer your father's or grandfather's language; rather, it is a modern and vibrant language consistently being updated with new standards that respond to the needs of new computing hardware. In addition, a significant effort has been made with each new standard to ensure that existing standard-complying codes continue to compile and execute correctly.

The spelling of the "FORTRAN" language name used all CAPS prior to the introduction of the Fortran 90 standard [47] when it was agreed to use the name "Fortran."

Most of the chapters in this book make reference to a complete program that illustrates the practical use of features of the newer Fortran standards. For space reasons, within the book we have generally avoided including complete listings. Essentially all the software has been made available for downloading from the SIAM web site, www.siam.org/books/ot134, and details are given in Chapter 20. We encourage you to study and modify these codes in order to reinforce your understanding of the material we are presenting. We also urge you to attempt the exercises provided within each chapter, many of which require compilation and execution of the software.

We begin chapters with a *Synopsis* section giving the main features covered so that you may quickly ascertain the content without further reading.

All the code we have provided within the book is copyrighted by SIAM, but there is no restriction on the use of the software for any purpose. The only requirement is that, if use is made of our codes, our book and SIAM are referenced in any derived work.

0.2   Using a Reference Book

Throughout the book we frequently refer to two texts that describe the Fortran 2003 language: Metcalf, Reid, and Cohen [65] and Adams et al. [4]. We strongly recommend that you have access to one of these while reading our book. Finally, there is the full standard, ISO/IEC [48], which is the authoritative reference but is no easy read for the humble coder! While a comprehensive discussion of the language elements can be found in these references, our goal is to illustrate the use of the Fortran 2003 language with helpful and nontrivial examples.

0.3   Become Familiar with the New

If you are acquainted with Fortran only up to the Fortran 77 standard [46], you will need to gain some understanding of the basic new features that were introduced with Fortran 90 [47]. These include the formatting of source code, use of comments, and new system functions, along with a number of the newer constructs, including derived types, elemental functions, and the use of modules. We discuss these further in Chapter 1. As a guide for study, the top ten features added to Fortran since the 1977 standard are, in our prejudiced order,

1. The Fortran Module

2. The Derived Type and Classes

3. Allocatable Objects

4. Optional Arguments

5. IEEE Exception Handling

6. Interoperability with C

7. Support for Recursion

8. Array Operations

9. Machine Constants

10. Generic Typing of Routine Names

0.4 Moving to Interesting Topics

Every chapter in this book was included for a reason. What follows is a "road map" from topics to their discussion in the chapters that follow. Reasons for including these chapters come from our experiences as editors and our work in application development.

0.4.1 Leading to QUADPACK

One aim is to present Fortran software technology in the role of interfacing numerical codes with user routines. The demands of modern hardware and application requirements give compelling reasons for using extensible derived types—designated as class arguments—passed to user routines. A meaningful example is developed in Chapter 7 for numerical quadrature, a modernized version of QUADPACK, described in Piessens et al. [72].

This example illustrates an essential design element of Fortran numerical software that is missing from many popular codes, and getting comfortable with it requires study. Here are guidelines to topics that we believe will help lead to such an understanding.

Qpack: new source formats, logical operators, comments, and optional arguments; see Chapter 1.

Qpack: derived types, module organization; see Chapter 2.

Qpack: generic names; see Chapter 3; type extension, classes, information passing; see Chapter 5.

Qpack: recursion for multiple integrals; see Chapter 6.

Qpack: using parallelism; coarrays and OpenMP; see Chapters 14 and 15.

Qpack: the QUADPACK Fortran source; see Chapter 20.

Qpack: documenting the use of the revised QUADPACK; see Chapter 8.

0.4.2   Leading to SuperLU

The use of SuperLU [see 59, 58] for solving sparse matrix systems of linear equations may often be a critical part of a Fortran application code. However, many developers may shun the use of this function library because of the integration and maintenance problems perceived in integrating their application code with software only available in C. With older versions of the Fortran standard this would have involved a compiler-dependent solution, but the introduction of interlanguage calls in the newer standards alleviates many of these problems. Furthermore, we do not need to make any changes to the source code of the C application library to allow Fortran access to the underlying functions; indeed, we may only have a compiled version of the library available. To allow interlanguage calls we only need to study the calling sequences of the C functions; the objective then is to make things simple for the Fortran programmer while still retaining flexibility.

There are other preliminary algorithmic steps that are part of sparse matrix linear algebra: building the data structures, forming transposed matrices, computing matrix-vector or matrix-matrix products, adding sparse matrices, accumulating entries, and preprocessing a matrix to ensure that every row or column contains at least one nonzero entry. We show how to implement these by using defined operators that make interlanguage calls to existing C functions. Finally, we provide two practical applications, a data fitting problem and a linear boundary value problem for Airy's equation, to illustrate how all these components act together.

SupLU: building data structures, accumulating entries, user-defined operations, addition of sparse matrices; see Chapter 4.

SupLU: interlanguage calls to C; see Chapter 10; sparse solves with user-defined operations; see Chapter 11.

SupLU: sparse matrix defined operations in sample applications; see Chapter 12.

0.4.3   IEEE Arithmetic Exceptions

In many applications there are situations where a computation may encounter an exceptional operation. This may be a divide by zero, an overflow, a significant underflow, or an operation with a NaN—an unspecified floating-point value. Modern software will typically include code to protect against program crashes or the wasteful discarding of results by trapping such conditions and taking appropriate action.

However, even a relatively small amount of testing for exceptional arithmetic operations will almost invariably lead to an inefficient use of the floating-point processor. If such events are rare, an alternative strategy may be to try a simple approach and use the Fortran standard IEEE intrinsic modules to detect any arithmetic problems. Only if the simple approach has an exception do we resort to a more careful but less efficient means of performing the calculations. If this method also fails, we may need to bow out gracefully after printing an explanatory error message.

IEEE: computing the l_2 norm of a vector, BLAS function *DNRM*2 [56]; see Chapter 9.

IEEE: managing exceptions during an OpenMP parallel construct; see Chapter 15.

0.4.4 Quicksort and Recursion

Conventional thinking regards the use of recursion as inefficient, but this is certainly not the case with large scale data sorting. Using the Quicksort algorithm (see [85, Chapter 7]) we illustrate how the software development is best presented using recursion. The practical requirements of sorting are varied, for example, sorting data of different precisions or data types; sorting data into increasing or decreasing order; sorting a subset of the data or returning a permutation vector rather than sorted data. We illustrate how, by using specialized derived types, we may produce very general purpose software.

QuickS: recursion, type-bound procedures, abstract data types and abstract interfaces; see Chapter 6.

0.4.5 Generic Names of Subprograms

Numerical software is easier to use if the routine names are easily recalled. For example, since the introduction of Fortran 77, users have been able to use intrinsic functions like $SIN(x)$ to compute the expected result for x of real or complex type, regardless of precision. Later standards extended this to return an array of values when the argument is an array. Such functions are termed *generic,* and modern Fortran also allows users to define their own generic subprograms. This is a welcome design feature and we illustrate its use by constructing an interface to some existing software for Airy functions [26].

Gener: generic naming, real and complex arguments, arguments that are arrays; see Chapter 3.

0.4.6 MPI, Coarrays, and OpenMP

MPI, or the Message Passing Interface, is used in applications where the size of the problems and/or the execution times requires the use of more than one process executing the same program simultaneously. These parallel running executables typically interact with one another by communicating partial results (message passing).

Fortran 2008 introduced an alternative approach using *coarrays* which extend Fortran to provide a more natural way for executables to interchange data. This approach leads to many of the calls used by MPI to send and receive data from one process to another being performed via an assignment operator. A good introduction to coarrays may be found in Reid and Numrich [79].

We present examples that perform the same computations using both MPI and coarrays.

OpenMP, or Open Multiprocessing, describes a technology that enables each executable to use its internal CPUs, or "cores," for improved performance.

These software methodologies require study and practice in order to understand and use them successfully in applications. Our coverage of MPI and OpenMP is brief and resources other than just a Fortran compiler may be required to run the sample codes. We do not discuss in detail the use of MPI in numerical software.

Excellent tutorials on MPI and OpenMP are available (see, e.g., Barney [10, 11]).

ParL: a standard-conforming interface to MPI, examples to compute π and compute parallel matrix-vector products; see Chapter 13.

ParL: use of *coarrays,* examples of duplicate MPI computation of π and matrix-vector products; see Chapter 14.

ParL: some guidelines and tips for using OpenMP; see Chapter 15.

0.4.7   Getting the Bugs Out

A developer of numerical software will often spend more time removing bugs or achieving accuracy and performance than writing the source code in the first place. We offer some topics that may help to improve productivity in this area. But the human capacity for error and unfortunate choice is unlimited! There is no fix for this fact of life.

Obsol: identify and remove obsolescent features from source code; see Chapter 16.

Tests: what testing is, types of testing, constructing test data; see Chapter 17.

CompL: using compiler options for optimization, run-time checks, clutter removal; see Chapter 18.

Times: portable timing for CPU use, elapsed time; see Chapter 1.

Tools: using *make,* version control with *SVN*, documentation systems, debuggers, profilers, pretty printers, sample output and error processors; see Chapter 19.

0.4.8 Getting to the Source (Code)

A primary intent of this book is to provide program units for use by the reader that illustrate the lessons we have learned. To use this material a developer can turn directly to Chapter 20. There one can find the URL to the SIAM web site that has these files available for download. The subdirectories for the code suites are listed in Chapter 20 with a longer description of their contents.

Chapter02 Packaging for collections of Fortran 77 codes.

Chapter03 Generic packaging of Airy functions.

Chapter04 Defined operations and overloaded assignment for sparse matrix operations.

Chapter05 Class objects, interior to a numerical code.

Chapter06 A framework and packaging for the Quicksort sorting algorithm.

Chapter07 Modernizing QUADPACK routine qag to use Fortran 2003.

Chapter08 Documenting the use of the modernized QUADPACK routines.

Chapter09 Computing the l_2 norm of a vector using the IEEE intrinsic modules for handling exceptions.

Chapter10 Demonstrating standardized interlanguage calls between Fortran and C.

Chapter11 Defined operations and overloaded assignment for solving square, sparse matrix linear systems with SuperLU.

Chapter12 Defined operations developed for sparse matrices, illustrated with two applications.

Chapter13 Direct interface to a core suite of the C library of MPI routines, with two examples.

Chapter14 The two examples using MPI are repeated using coarray Fortran.

Chapter15 Program units that illustrate usage of OpenMP directives.

Chapter16 Before (Fortran 77) and after (Fortran 90) versions of a simple Newton method program.

- ▶ *Statements separated by ';'*
- ▶ *Relational operators and related symbols*
- ▶ *Introducing derived types*
- ▶ *Basics on modules*
- ▶ *Optional arguments*
- ▶ *The include line*
- ▶ *Preprocessor directives*
- ▶ *Provided timing routines*

1.1 Introduction

This chapter introduces a number of basic changes that have occurred in the Fortran language since the Fortran 77 standard and discusses how they affect the way modern Fortran source code is written. This is not intended to be a comprehensive description of all the newly introduced features and will primarily be of assistance to programmers who have gained most of their coding experience with Fortran 77; more specific details of all the language changes may be found in Metcalf, Reid, and Cohen [65] and Adams et al. [4].

1.2   Source Code Formatting and Labels

Fortran 77 used a fixed format for source code; each source line was limited to 72 characters and consisted of 4 fields:

1. the first five characters were designated the *label* field;

2. the sixth character was for specifying a *continuation line*;

3. characters 7–72 were for the Fortran statement;

4. characters from 73 onwards were ignored by the compiler.

This format dates back to the earliest versions of Fortran when programs were input using 80 column punched cards. Several of the earliest IBM machines were wired to read the first 72 columns, and columns 73–80 were often used for ordering the deck of cards.

Starting with Fortran 90, and with subsequent releases, the standards have recognized two source code formats: the fixed format described above for backwards compatibility, and a new free format. In the new format there are no predefined fields and each source line may be up to 132 characters long.

The first five characters in the fixed format were reserved for labels. These were effectively integers in the range of 1–99999 and were necessary because, prior to Fortran 90, the language required their use, either explicitly or implicitly, to implement a number of common logical constructions. For example, a *case* statement was implemented via a "computed-**GO TO** statement," and an exit from a loop required an explicit **GO TO** statement using an associated numeric label.

Fortran 90 is semantically rich enough that programmers should not need to use labels in constructing their code. Should they need to include old code, which was originally in fixed format, then labels in free format need to be the first non-blank characters on the line or following a semicolon in multiple statement lines (see Section 1.5 for more details).

The only restriction on the use of the two formats is that they may not be mixed in the same source file. Most compilers require the user to distinguish between the two formats either by the use of compiler directives (for example, *-fixed* or *-free*) or via the source file names. Typically the compiler expects a *.f* or *.for* suffix for the fixed format source and *.f90* or *.f95* for the free format. Such flags and file name suffixes are not part of the standard and are compiler dependent.

1.3   Comments in Source Code

In Fortran 77 a comment was a separate line of text with a maximum length of 72 characters and having either of the characters "C" or "*" in the first position. To conform strictly to the Fortran 77 standard, all letters used in a program needed to be in uppercase [see 46, Section 3.1.1]; this meant that only an uppercase C could be used as a comment character. We have chosen to largely ignore these requirements when presenting fixed format code since all of the modern compilers we have experience with allow the use of mixed cases for fixed format Fortran.

```
C234567
C Fortran 77: fixed format source code.
* Only complete lines can be comments in Fortran 77.
* The comment character at the start of the line may
C be mixed, use * or C at your pleasure.
```

In free format, a comment begins at the first "!" character in a line and this may appear anywhere within the first 132 characters of the statement. The ! character and all following characters are ignored by the compiler. This added flexibility allows for in-line comments, i.e., comments appended to executable statements, for example:

```
!234567
! Fortran 90: free format source code.
  ! The comment character does not have to be in
  ! the first position ...
  y = x**2  !  ... and an in-line comment is allowed
  IF (y <= 1) THEN
       ...
  END IF ! for the test:  IF (y <= 1) THEN
```

1.4   Continuation Lines

In order to accommodate statements that would not fit into the 66-character statement field, Fortran 77 allowed up to 19 continuation lines providing a maximum statement length of 1320 characters. These lines were signaled by using any non-blank standard character, excluding the digit zero, in column position 6 (the continuation line field) on each of the extra lines required. For example:

```
C Fortran 77: fixed format source.
C Blanks  after the '-' are included.
C Blanks before the '+' are not included.
      y=2.0*x**2 -
     +     66.0*x
C234567
```

With free format source, continuation lines are indicated by the appearance of the ampersand character "&" at the *end* of each line that is to be continued.

```
! Fortran 90: free format source code.
! Blanks  after the '&' are not  included.
! But the blanks before '66' count as source.
! The source in the next two non-comment lines
! may start anywhere in the line
      y=2.0*x**2 -&
           66.0*x
```

The new standard allows for a maximum of 39 continuation lines giving a maximum statement length of 5280 characters, although this does include continuation characters which are provided for separately with Fortran 77. (Note: the number of continuation lines was increased to 255 in the 2003 standard.)

The actual characters that make up the complete statement may be controlled by adding another ampersand as the first nonblank character of the continuation line. This is especially useful when splitting strings to avoid including superfluous blanks, for example, in **FORMAT** statements.

```
! Fortran 90: free format source code.
! The source in the two non-comment lines may start
! anywhere in the line.
! The blanks after the '&' in the next line are not included.
      aSplitString = 'There will be no space in the mid&
                     &dle of a word split across a continuation'
! The blanks before the leading '&' in the line above
! are not treated as source.
```

1.5   Statements Separated by ';'

Starting with Fortran 90, multiple statements, separated by semicolons, were allowed to appear on the same line of source text. This may be confusing when reading source code and is a practice that should usually be avoided because it is easy to miss critical source statements when reading a listing.

```
!234567
    ! Lots of short statements on a line can be hard to read
    y=2.0*x**2 + 66.0*x; y=SQRT(y); z=a; a=b; b=z;
```

1.6   Relational Operators and Related Symbols

Fortran 90 introduced a number of alternative relational operators (see Table 1.1) intended to improve readability by appearing more like the equivalent and common mathematical relation symbols. Both forms are valid, but we strongly recommend the use of the new notation rather than the clumsy Fortran 77 style of operators.

```
!234567
    ! Test if the value computed is in the range [0,1]
    IF (y >= 0.0 .AND. y <= 1.0) THEN
    ...
```

To improve readability of source code we suggest leaving a space on both sides of all relational operators. However, we note that multicharacter symbols are sensitive to internal spaces, so the operator `<=` becomes undefined if written with a space separating the two characters.

We also note that Fortran defines a symbol which might easily be confused with `<=` or `>=`. The symbol `=>` is used for pointer assignment (for example, `p => q` makes the pointer p point to the target q) and for the **ASSOCIATE** construct where, typically, a simple name temporarily represents a variable or object having a lengthy name. An example of this is a complicated or nested subscripted variable, or a component of a derived type. Chapter 7 contains practical examples of both usages; a simple example of the latter may be found in Section 1.7. Another helpful

Table 1.1. *Some relational operators.*

Logic	Fortran 90	Fortran 77
less than	<	.LT.
not greater than	<=	.LE.
not equal	/=	.NE.
equal	==	.EQ.
greater than	>	.GT.
not less than	>=	.GE.

use of the symbol => is resolving ambiguous names of objects that are use-associated from modules. Examples are mentioned below; see Section 1.8.

1.7 Introducing Derived Types

When writing software it is often convenient to group logically connected data together. The idea of a user-defined record or structure was introduced in Fortran 90 and is known as a *derived type*. We make extensive use of this construct throughout the book, so we confine ourselves here to a simple illustration which shows how to define a new type and how to access its components. Consider a record of a member of an organization which consists of four fields: surname, age, salary, and sex. We define a user-defined type *personal* with the four components, each represented by a simple intrinsic variable.

```
TYPE personal
   CHARACTER (LEN=32) :: surname
   INTEGER :: age
   REAL :: salary
   CHARACTER :: sex
END TYPE personal
```

Derived types can also contain other derived types as components, for example:

```
TYPE branch_office
   TYPE (personal) :: people(100)
   CHARACTER(LEN=64) :: location
END TYPE branch_office
```

To reference an individual component of a derived type we use the component selector symbol % to separate the name of the type from a component. We use the **ASSOCIATE** construct to abbreviate the components of the derived type.

```
      TYPE (personal) :: mygroup(10)
! Initialize components of a derived type
      mygroup(1) = personal('K. H. Haskell', 39, 60300.0, 'F')
! Access the salary component
      mygroup(1)%salary = 60400.0
! Use symbol association to make things easier to read.
```

```
ASSOCIATE(surname => mygroup(1)%surname, &
          Wage => mygroup(1)%salary)
write(*,*) 'Employee ', TRIM(surname), &
           'has a yearly salary of ', Wage
END ASSOCIATE
```

The Fortran-provided function *TRIM()* removes trailing blanks in the character variable *surname*.

1.8   Basics on Modules

Modules, also added in Fortran 90, provide a means of

1. grouping subroutines and functions,

2. typing and packaging data,

3. defining derived types and procedure interfaces, and

4. controlling access to the contents of a module.

The following is an example of a very simple module that defines a user-defined type *personal* along with an accessor-mutator routine that controls user access to the *salary* field.

```
MODULE peopleData
  IMPLICIT NONE

  TYPE personal
    CHARACTER (LEN=32) :: name
    INTEGER :: age
    REAL, PRIVATE :: salary
    CHARACTER :: sex
  END TYPE personal

CONTAINS

  SUBROUTINE salaryAccess(key, person, wage)
    INTEGER, INTENT(IN) :: key
    TYPE(personal), INTENT(INOUT) :: person
    REAL, INTENT(INOUT) :: wage
    ASSOCIATE(pay => person%salary)
      IF(key == 1) wage = pay   ! Get current salary
      IF(key == 2) pay = wage   ! Set current salary
    END ASSOCIATE
  END SUBROUTINE salaryAccess

END MODULE peopleData
```

The accessible content of a module is *use-associated* with another program unit by means of a **USE** statement of the form

```
USE peopleData
```

In the case of our *peopleData* module, this allows the program unit associating the module to access the definition of the *personal* derived type and the subroutine *salaryAccess*. All module content, by default, has the **PUBLIC** attribute and is thus directly accessible by any use-associating program unit. We may restrict access within a module by making the items have the **PRIVATE** attribute as with the *salary* component in our example. This means that another program unit cannot use *personal%salary* to access the salary component directly but rather has to use a call to the subroutine *salaryAccess*. By restricting access in this way we may build in extra checks within the *salaryAccess* routine to ensure that only validated data is stored in this component.

```
PROGRAM people_manage
USE peopleData ! The use-association of peopleData

TYPE(personal) :: khh = personal('K. H. Haskell', 39, 0., 'F')
...
CALL salaryAccess (2, khh, 60400.0) ! Salary changed.
```

By default the simple form of the **USE** statement provides access to all the public entities within the named module regardless of whether or not they are used in the associating program unit. We can restrict the items available by adding an **ONLY** clause followed by a list of all the names we wish to import; for example,

```
USE peopleData, ONLY: personal
```

would allow access to the derived type name but not the subroutine *salaryAccess*. Use of the **ONLY** clause improves the readability of the code by explicitly linking names appearing within a program unit with the particular module where they are defined.

It is sometimes necessary or useful to be able to change the name on an item being imported from a module. This may be because data of the same name is being imported from two different modules, or the user has already used a name locally that would clash with an imported name, or the readability of the code would be improved by making the imported name more obviously linked to the application being developed. This is generally known as *name transformation* and uses the composite symbol => to perform the renaming; note that this is the same symbol that is used in pointer assignment and for name simplification in **ASSOCIATE** statements. The following code snippet demonstrates a number of illustrative examples:

```
! The name used in the imported module has already been
! earmarked for use locally
  USE modA, newName => alreadyUsed

! Two data items need to be imported from two different
! modules but their names clash, i.e., in the example both
! modB and modC use clashName
  USE modB, modBName => clashName
  USE modC, modCName => clashName

! In the above the USE statement will allow all public names
! to be accessible to the USEing program unit. We can combine
! the use of ONLY with name transformation
```

```
     USE modD, ONLY: modDName => clashAgain
     USE modE, ONLY: modEName => clashAgain
   ! whence only the data clashAgain is imported (and renamed) from
   ! the two modules
```

1.9   Optional Arguments

Numerical algorithms typically contain parameters that need careful tuning to produce efficient and accurate computation solutions. Often we find that most of a problem coverage may be solved using a default set of values for these parameters, although in some cases we may need, for example, to trade optimum efficiency for ease of use. Giving subprogram arguments the **OPTIONAL** attribute allows the programmer to provide default values for particular variables while, at the same time, allowing the caller of the subprogram to override these values as required.

Developing routines that have optional arguments as module subprograms relieves the user of having to provide an explicit interface and improves the readability of the code.

To illustrate how this works in practice, consider a subroutine that calls the intrinsic subroutine *complexRandomPairs* to generate an array of random complex pairs. By default the code will use the size of the complex array argument to determine how many random complex pairs to produce. Should the user want less then the default number, an optional argument, *nPairs*, may be passed giving the exact number required. In the routine *complexRandomPairs*, note the use of the **LOGICAL** intrinsic function *PRESENT* which has the value **.FALSE.** for the first call from the main program and **.TRUE.** for the second and third calls.

```
MODULE complexRandom
  IMPLICIT NONE
CONTAINS

  SUBROUTINE complexRandomPairs(z, nPairs)
  COMPLEX, INTENT(OUT) :: z(:)
  INTEGER, OPTIONAL, INTENT(IN) :: nPairs
  REAL :: x(SIZE(z)), y(SIZE(z))
  INTEGER :: m

  ! Generate SIZE(z) random complex pairs unless the user
  ! has provided the optional argument, nPairs.
  ! Don't trust the user! Test that there is room to store
  ! the requested number of pairs and silently return to
  ! the default if there isn't.
  IF (PRESENT(nPairs)) m=MIN(SIZE(z),nPairs)

  CALL RANDOM_NUMBER(x(1:m))
  CALL RANDOM_NUMBER(y(1:m))
  z(1:m)=CMPLX(x(1:m),y(1:m))

  END SUBROUTINE complexRandomPairs
END MODULE complexRandom
```

```
PROGRAM getComplexPairs
! Use associate the module complex_random
! which provides two ways of calling
! the routine complexRandomPairs
  USE complexRandom , ONLY: complexRandomPairs
  COMPLEX :: z(100)

! Get all the complex numbers that z(:) will hold.
  CALL complexRandomPairs(z)

! Now get just 50 numbers using the key word nPairs=.
  CALL complexRandomPairs(z,nPairs=50)

! Or perhaps just 25:
  CALL complexRandomPairs(z,25)

! Of course we could also get the same effect using
! array slices, for example,
!   CALL complexRandomPairs(z(1:50))
! will also generate 50 random complex pairs


END PROGRAM getComplexPairs
```

An alternate—and, in this case, simpler—way of generating a complex vector of random numbers is with the *TRANSFER* intrinsic function. Use of this function allows data to be cast as an alternate type if there is no difference in the required storage space. No change in the physical representation occurs in the transfer. Thus to generate a random complex vector of length n, we could first create a random real vector of length $2n$ and use the *TRANSFER* intrinsic:

```
PROGRAM getComplexPairs_Transfer
REAL :: x(200)
COMPLEX :: z(100)

CALL random_number(x)
z=TRANSFER(SOURCE=x, MOLD=z)

END PROGRAM getComplexPairs_Transfer
```

1.10   The Include Line and Preprocessor Directives

A nonportable extension to many earlier Fortran compilers was the **INCLUDE** line. This was standardized in Fortran 2003 and takes the form INCLUDE 'filename'; note that this is defined as a compiler directive and is not, technically, a Fortran statement.

Prior to compilation, this directive substitutes the contents of the file *filename* in place of the line. The contents of *filename* may contain other **INCLUDE** directives, although the maximum level of nesting is not specified by the standard and is, therefore, processor dependent. For obvious reasons, nesting must not be ultimately recursive.

The format of the file name is not specified by the standard but, for portability, it should not contain any path information. Typically the contents of *filename* do not appear in compiler produced listings of program units that contain an **INCLUDE** line. In our experience, debuggers usually allow breakpoints and printing to be monitored within included files (see Chapter 19 for more on debuggers).

The use of **INCLUDE** lines can be of great help in producing, for example, sets of routines implementing the same algorithm in different precisions and data types, by requiring just one copy of the executable statements. It can also be used to insert groups of comments, symbol associations, and processor-dependent text. By avoiding the need to reveal or repeat text explicitly within program units, its use can greatly improve software maintenance.

Preprocessor directives are a commonly used feature of the C programming language and are often used for conditionally compiling Fortran source (see [83, pp. 238–248]).

Our experience is that the vast majority of Fortran compilers support the C preprocessor, although this is not part of the standard. While each compiler has its own particular way of defining macros, this is normally achieved via command line arguments to the compiler, or the inclusion of a directive in the Fortran source file, or using a separate preprocessor or software tool.

1.11   New Timing Routines

This is one instance of many where the new standard helps to improve the portability of Fortran software. One historical reason for nonportable codes and their associated maintenance headaches was the lack of any standardized, timing-related intrinsic functions in Fortran 77. The current standard defines three timing-related routines:

1. *DATE_AND_TIME:* retrieves date and time information from the wall clock in a variety of different formats.

2. *SYSTEM_CLOCK:* provides access to data from the system clock. This could be used for timing segments of code but, in practice, is more useful for ascertaining how accurate the system clock is.

3. *CPU_TIME:* allows access to the processor time in seconds.

The first two of these are described in more detail in [65]. The routine *CPU_TIME(t)*, which is likely to be the most useful in applications, takes a single, default **REAL** argument, t, which is used to return a processor-dependent approximation to the processor time in seconds. A segment of code may then be timed using two calls to the routine:

```
REAL :: timeStart, timeEnd, cpuTimeUsed
...
CALL CPU_TIME(timeStart)
... Code segment being timed
CALL CPU_TIME(timeEnd)
cpuTimeUsed = timeEnd - timeStart
...
```

The intrinsic subprogram *CPU_TIME* measures the amount of time that an executing program has been using machine resources. On multiuser systems, where processors swap between jobs, this may differ considerably from the total time that the job actually takes to complete (the elapsed time). To measure elapsed time we use the *SYSTEM_CLOCK* intrinsic function which, like *CPU_TIME*, needs to be called at the start and end of the segment of code being timed. The subprogram *SYSTEM_CLOCK* measures time in a processor-dependent unit, with the current value being returned via the *COUNT* optional integer parameter. The additional optional parameter, *COUNT_RATE*, returns the number of processor-dependent units per second for a given processor and may be used, with *COUNT*, to provide a portable means of obtaining the elapse time of a section code:

```
INTEGER :: istart, iend, irate
REAL :: elapsed_time
...
CALL SYSTEM_CLOCK(COUNT=istart, COUNT_RATE=irate)
... Code segment being timed
CALL SYSTEM_CLOCK(COUNT=iend)
elapsed_time=REAL(iend-istart)/REAL(irate)
...
```

Chapter 2

Modules for Subprogram Libraries

Synopsis:

▶ *Program units: main programs, routines, modules, include files*

▶ *Using codes from precompiled Fortran libraries*

▶ *Use of kind type parameters*

▶ *Packaging Fortran libraries: separate program units or module routines?*

▶ *Using interface blocks for library routines*

▶ *Importing and renaming symbols with use-association*

▶ *Exercises*

2.1   Introduction

Modern Fortran provides three compilation units:

1. Main programs;

2. Subroutines and functions; and

3. modules.

The first two have been part of Fortran since before the Fortran 66 standard, and it will be assumed that the reader already has a detailed knowledge of them. Fortran 90 [47] added a completely new programming unit, the **MODULE**, and Fortran 2003 [48] standardized the **INCLUDE** line (see Section 1.10).

The *module* is one of the most useful features of modern Fortran and, throughout this book, we will routinely pose problems and provide their solutions using modules.

2.2   Running a Fortran 77 Program

We review the different ways in which Fortran allows us to package together sub-programs for use as building blocks for application software and how these affect the way in which we generate executable files. We also consider how changes in the Fortran language have affected how we write Fortran code and provide data space. Some of the practical details of using these methods are outside the Fortran standard and, therefore, compiler dependent; however, all compilers we know provide a means of obtaining the desired effect.

To illustrate the practicalities of each of these mechanisms we give the commands required by *gfortran*, an open source Fortran compiler [33], running on Linux systems. In Chapter 19 we take a more detailed look at what facilities compilers offer and how to ensure that, during development and maintenance, executables are always kept up to date while minimizing the number of files that need recompiling.

We assume that files with suffixes *.f* and *.f90* contain fixed and free format Fortran source code, respectively. We show the various methods of compilation and the way in which we construct an executable file using an example that calls routines from LAPACK [5] to solve a linear system of algebraic equations. This involves two LAPACK routines. The first, *dgetrf*, computes the LU factorization of a square nonsingular matrix A; then *dgetrs* uses this factorization to solve the linear system for a given set of right-hand side vectors. In order to check how accurately the routine computes a solution, we take a known vector y, compute the matrix-vector product $b = Ay$, and then solve the system $Ax = b$. We should have $x = y$, and the quality of this approximation determines whether the routines are working. The example files we provide for downloading contain just the routines and dependencies from the LAPACK and BLAS collections necessary to run the example and not the complete libraries. Our check for an accurate approximation to the solution vector y does not consider issues of matrix conditioning, arithmetic accuracy, and backward error analysis. We avoid these complications (in the vast majority of cases) by using a simple error test that is good enough to detect program bugs but cannot be regarded as a stringent test of the underlying linear solver. More details of acceptable error bounds on y can be found in Golub and Van Loan [34, pp. 80–81]. The results obtained from backward error analysis depend on the numerical algorithm being used. For more details on Gaussian elimination with partial pivoting (the underlying algorithm used by the LAPACK routines *dgetrf* and *dgetrs*) see Stewart [88, pp. 150–152].

2.2.1   Fortran 77 Solutions

Prior to the release of Fortran 90, the language was designed to allow one or more complete subprograms to be stored in a file and for each source file to be independent of any others to the extent that the order of compilation was irrelevant. For our example the two source files *lapack.f* and *blas.f* contain the required subsets of the library routines to solve our linear system. We construct the main program using the following computational algorithm:

1. Choose a maximum problem size and declare static arrays A, y, b, and *ipvt*.

2. Fill the matrix A and vector y with random data.

3. Compute the matrix-vector product $b = Ay$.

4. Compute an LU factorization of the matrix A using a call to *dgetrf* and check that A is nonsingular.

5. Solve $Ax = b$ using the LU factorization from the previous step using a call to *dgetrs*.

6. Compute the relative difference in the two vectors x and y.

In Fortran 77 it was necessary to choose a maximum problem size that the program could solve, and declare static arrays to reflect this maximum size. Having to declare all array space as a fixed size at compile time was a real restriction with Fortran 77, and this has been removed with the newer standards (see Section 2.2.2 below for more details).

A complete example Fortran 77 driver program is given in Listing 2.1.

Listing 2.1. *Example Fortran 77 code calling LAPACK routines.*

```
C This code extract is part of the accompanying software
C that supports Chapter 2. It may be found in the file
C exampleLapack77.f
C
      PROGRAM example
C This program is (almost!) a Fortran 77 code that uses
C a pair of Lapack routines (dgetrf and dgetrs) to solve
C a randomly generated system of linear equations. The
C order of the problem to be solved is input by the user.

C First we need to reserve array space for a maximum
C size of problem because Fortran 77 did not allow
C dynamic array allocation. If problems arise that
C are larger than this maximum the parameter maxdim
C must be increased, the driver program recompiled and
C the whole code relinked.
      DOUBLE PRECISION one, zero
      PARAMETER (one = 1.0d0, zero = 0.0d0)
      INTEGER maxdim
      PARAMETER (maxdim=10000)
      DOUBLE PRECISION a(maxdim, maxdim), b(maxdim,1),
     +                 y(maxdim)
      INTEGER ipvt(maxdim)
C Declare the user-defined system size (n) and an error
C flag (info) as well as a couple of loop control variables
      INTEGER n, info, i, j
C Declare a variable for the relative error calculation and
C declare the return type of the BLAS Euclidean norm routine
      DOUBLE PRECISION relerr, dnrm2
C We cheat in the code and use the Fortran 90 intrinsics for
C timing the execution of the program.
C Note: these are defined as default REALs
      REAL tstart, tend
C Loop until an input value of n<0 is obtained. Also exit
C if an illegal input value is detected.
10    CONTINUE
      WRITE(*,'(A)')'Input the system dimension: '
```

```
      READ(*,'(I5)',IOSTAT=info)n
      IF (n .le. 0 .or. info .ne.0) GO TO 50
C Fill the coefficient matrix A and the solution vector
C y with random numbers. This uses the Fortran 90 intrinsic
C for generating random numbers because it is easier!

      DO 30 j = 1, n
        DO 20 i = 1, n
          CALL RANDOM_NUMBER(a(i,j))
20        CONTINUE
        CALL RANDOM_NUMBER(y(j))
        b(j,1) = zero
30    CONTINUE
C Compute the matrix-vector product B = A*Y.
      CALL dgemv('No',n,n,one,a,maxdim,y,1,zero,b,1)
C Start timing the solution computation.
      CALL CPU_TIME(tstart)
C Factor the A matrix into its LU form using Gaussian
C elimination with partial pivoting.
C The flag info is zero if there was no diagonal term == 0.
C This is not a good test for ill-conditioning.
      CALL dgetrf(n, n, a, maxdim, ipvt, info)
C Check that the Lapack routine has been successful
      IF (info .lt. 0) THEN
        WRITE(*,'(''Argument '',i3,'' has an illegal value'')')
     +          -info
      ELSE IF (info .gt. 0) THEN
        WRITE(*,'(''Zero diagonal value detected in upper ''//
     +            ''triangular factor at position '',i7)') info
      ELSE
C If there are no errors in the factorization stage then
C proceed to solve the linear system
        CALL dgetrs('n', n, 1, a, maxdim, ipvt, b, maxdim, info)
C Check that the Lapack routine has been successful
        IF (info .lt. 0) THEN
          WRITE(*,'(''Argument '',i3,'' has an illegal value'')')
     +            -info
        END IF
C Stop the timer
        CALL CPU_TIME(tend)
C Compute the difference between the solution vector returned by
C Lapack and the vector used to generate the right hand side.
        DO 40 i = 1, n
          b(i,1) = b(i,1) - y(i)
40      CONTINUE
        relerr = dnrm2(n, b, 1)/dnrm2(n,y,1)
C Write out relative errors and timings
        WRITE(*,'(A,1PD12.6)') 'The relative error  Y - '//
     +           'inverse(A)*(A*Y) = ', relerr
        WRITE(*,'(A,I5,0PE12.4, I5)') 'The compute time (S) for '//
     +             'solving a system of size = ',n, tend-tstart
      END IF
      GO TO 10
50    STOP
      END
```

We may now compile the complete program using a simple command of the form

```
gfortran -o driver example.f lapack.f blas.f
```

to generate an executable file named *driver*, assuming that there are no compilation errors.

Here the compiler actually performs two steps in a single command:

1. All the source files are partially compiled to form object files (defined as *.o* files on Linux systems).

2. All the *.o* files are linked together to form the complete executable, *driver*.

Because of the independent nature of the source files, we could minimize the cost of recompiling by saving the *.o* files and then only applying step 1 above to the source files that have been changed, followed by step 2. In the case of a large software project, this could substantially reduce the time taken to rebuild a system following a minor source change.

In order to generate the *.o* files we use the *-c* flag with *gfortran*; thus

```
gfortran -c example.f lapack.f blas.f
```

will generate files *example.o*, *lapack.o*, and *blas.o* which may then be linked together using

```
gfortran -o driver example.o lapack.o blas.o
```

Following a change to, say, the file *example.f*, we would then use

```
gfortran -c example.f
```

to refresh the file *example.o* and then relink to form the executable. (See Chapter 18 for more detail on using compilers.)

This approach to generating an executable is still far from perfect. The complete LAPACK and BLAS libraries consist of many hundreds of routines and tens of thousands of lines of code, and having the complete source code in a single file could cause maintenance problems. First, we have the cost of recompiling. Second, we potentially obtain an executable, which is unduly large due to the inclusion of many LAPACK and BLAS routines that are not required. To prevent this *code bloat*, all compiler systems offer some form of library mechanism that allows sets of *.o* files to be grouped together in a way that the linker can just extract those it needs to build the executable. The building and use of libraries is outside of the standard's remit and therefore depends on the compiler and platform being used to develop the software. On Linux systems we use the command *ar* to build a library file out of a set of individual *.o* files. Each subroutine is partially compiled as shown above and, typically, placed in a separate file with the same name as the routine it contains. The operating system command *ar* may then be used to generate an *archive library file*, *lapack.a* using

```
ar rv Lapack.a *.o
```

On some systems it may be necessary to use a second command

```
      ranlib Lapack.a
```

to provide additional information for the linker within the *.a* file. A library of BLAS routines, *Blas.a*, may be generated in a similar way.

We may now compile our driver program

```
      gfortran -c example.f
```

and link with the libraries using

```
      gfortran -o driver example.o Lapack.a Blas.a
```

The order of the library files may be important since they are often searched only once in the given order for missing routines. We need to place the BLAS library after the LAPACK library because the LAPACK routines make calls to BLAS routines. Different platforms have alternate ways of dealing with libraries—for example, dynamic link libraries, or DLLs, under Windows, and dynamic shared object libraries, under Unix or Linux. We refer to Petzold [71] and Levine [57] for additional insight.

EXERCISE 2.1.

Download the files associated with the LAPACK *example above from the repository at http://www.netlib.org/lapack/.*

Discover the commands and flags required for your Fortran system to compile and run the Fortran 77 example program using both the source files lapack.f and blas.f and by generating suitable library files.

Check to see if your system provides precompiled versions of the complete LAPACK *and* BLAS *object code libraries. If so, build an executable by linking against these libraries.*

2.2.2   Improvements Using Fortran 90

Before we take a detailed look at the new methods of packaging provided by Fortran 90, we will use the new dynamic array allocation features, as well as free format source code and new declaration forms, to improve our example program.

The main improvements are in replacing the statements at the start of the code in Listing 2.1 with those in Listing 2.2.

Listing 2.2. *Improvement to Fortran 77 example LAPACK code.*

```
!! This code extract is part of the accompanying software
!! that supports Chapter 2. It may be found in the file
!! exampleLapack90.f90
!!
   PROGRAM example
     USE set_precision , ONLY : wp
! This program is a Fortran 90 code that uses
! a pair of Lapack routines (dgetrf and dgetrs) to solve
! a randomly generated system of linear equations. The
```

```fortran
! order of the problem to be solved is input by the user.

! Declare allocatable arrays so we may reserve the correct
! amount of space for the particular problem being solved
      REAL (wp), ALLOCATABLE :: a(:,:), b(:,:), y(:)
      INTEGER, ALLOCATABLE :: ipvt(:)
! Declare the system size (n) and an error flag (info)
! as well as a couple of loop control variables
      INTEGER :: n, info, i, j
! These are values for relative sizes and errors.
      REAL (wp) :: relerr, dnrm2
! These are values for the elapsed time of solving.
      REAL :: tstart, tend
      REAL (wp), PARAMETER :: one = 1.0E0_wp, zero = 0.0E0_wp

! Loop until an input value of n<0 is obtained also exit
! if an illegal input value is detected.
      DO WHILE (.TRUE.)
        WRITE (*,ADVANCE='no', &
            FMT='(''Input the system dimension: '')')
        READ (*,'(i5)',iostat=info) n
        IF (n<=0) THEN
          STOP
        ENDIF
        IF (info/=0) THEN
          WRITE(*,'(''Illegal value given for argument '', i3)') &
              info
          STOP
        END IF
! Allocate array space
        ALLOCATE (a(n,n), b(n,1), y(n), ipvt(n), STAT=info)
        IF (info /=0) THEN
          WRITE(*,'(''Error attempting to allocate array space ''// &
                  ''for system of order '', i6)') n
          STOP
        END IF
```

Here we define a, b, y, and *ipvt* to be allocatable arrays (i.e., the data space for these will be provided at run time when the required size is known). This provides us with two efficiency improvements:

1. We use just the amount of memory necessary to solve each particular problem rather than using a portion of the space reserved for a maximum problem size.

2. The code is now completely independent of problem size; with the Fortran 77 version, if the problem size exceeded our precompiled maximum size, we needed to change the size parameters in the source code and recompile.

2.3   Develop with Modules

The use of a module allows us to perform operations such as

- calling a Fortran subroutine or function from Fortran,
- calling a C function from Fortran (see Chapter 10)

- defining special operations with abbreviated code (see Chapters 4 and 11), and

- passing data to a function evaluation routine in a numerical software code (see Chapter 7).

2.3.1 Using Kind Type Parameters

We present a simple helper module whose use allows us to change the precision of a software package by editing a single line of code and then recompiling the whole package. First, we note how the declaration of floating-point data has changed.

Standard Fortran 77 recognized two floating-point real types, **REAL** and **DOU-BLE PRECISION**, although there was no specification of how much precision each should provide and no mechanism to specify or use any extended precision which may have been available on the processor. In addition, Fortran 77 defined only a single precision floating-point complex type.

With Fortran 90 each of the five intrinsic data types (**INTEGER**, **REAL**, **COM-PLEX**, **LOGICAL**, and **CHARACTER**) has a default *kind* along with a processor-dependent number of additional kinds. In the case of the **REAL** data type, a processor must provide at least one extra kind with more precision than the default. This is equivalent to **DOUBLE PRECISION** in Fortran 77 although, as we shall see below, the use of **DOUBLE PRECISION** declarations is now redundant and may become obsolescent in future revisions of the standard.

Modern floating-point hardware generally supports a small number of formats. For example, IEEE arithmetic processors must support single and double precision types as defined in [45] but may also provide an extended precision with more precision and range than double precision. Each supported **REAL** kind is associated with a compiler-dependent nonnegative integer value known as a *kind type param-eter*. As an example, *gfortran* uses the number of memory bytes employed for each representation. This is 4 for the default real type and 8 for the extended precision real type, while the NAG compiler uses 1 and 2, respectively.

The **KIND** inquiry function returns the kind type parameter of its argu-ment; for example, KIND(0.0) would return the parameter for the default real, and KIND(0.0D0) would return the parameter for the mandatory extended precision. Vari-ables may be declared using either specification:

```
      REAL(KIND=kindTypeParameterValue) :: x, y, z
```

or the abbreviated form

```
      REAL(kindTypeParameterValue) :: x, y, z
```

For portability reasons, *kindTypeParameterValue* should never be an explicit integer value. Rather, the **KIND** function should be used to generate the required internal value. Thus the declaration

```
      REAL(KIND=KIND(0.0d0)) :: x, y, z
```

Table 2.1. *Decimal precision and maximum exponent for IEEE standard formats.*

	Decimal precision	Maximum exponent
Single precision	6	37
Double precision	15	307
Quad precision (Nag)	31	291
Quad precision (gfortran)	18	4931

would define x, y, and z to be double precision real variables, and this form is independent of the compiler being used. To generalize this we could define a parameter, say, wp, and use this in the declarations

```
INTEGER , PARAMETER :: wp=KIND(0.0d0)
REAL(wp) :: x, y, z
```

Before we extend this further, within a module, we mention the intrinsic function **SELECTED_REAL_KIND(p, r)** which returns, as a default integer, the kind type parameter of an available real data type with at least decimal precision, p, and decimal exponent range $[-r, r]$. If multiple kinds are available, then the one with the least decimal precision is returned. A negative value is returned if

- the requested precision is not available (-1),

- the requested range is not available (-2), and

- both the requested precision and range are unavailable (-3).

The numerical inquiry functions **PRECISION** and **RANGE** may be used to determine the actual decimal precision and range of a real data type; these functions are covered in [65, Chapter 8].

In Table 2.1 we give the values of the range and precision defined in the IEEE standard [45] for single and double precision floating-point data, along with the extended precision available from two compilers on the same hardware and under the same operating system.

2.3.2   A Simple Helper Module

Our first module is a very simple, but extremely useful, example. It allows us to discuss how the contents of a module may be accessed by other components of a software package and the effect that the use of modules has on creating an executable.

In applications we often need to maintain software in several different precisions, for example, single and double precision or double and quadruple precision. To do this efficiently it is convenient to have a helper module, *set_precision* (see Listing 2.3), that provides the working precision via an integer parameter value wp (an abbreviation for *working precision*).

Listing 2.3. *Module for defining precision in a program.*

```
!! This code extract is part of the accompanying software
!! that supports Chapter 2. It may be found in the file
!! set_precision.f90
!!
! Module set_precision provides the kind type parameter needed
! to define the precision of a complete package along
! with values for all commonly used precisions
    MODULE set_precision
! ..
! .. Intrinsic Functions ..
    INTRINSIC KIND
! .. Parameters ..
! Define the standard precisions
! For IEEE standard arithmetic we could also use
!       INTEGER, PARAMETER :: skind = SELECTED_REAL_KIND(p=6, r=37)
!       INTEGER, PARAMETER :: dkind = SELECTED_REAL_KIND(p=15, r=307)
      INTEGER, PARAMETER :: skind = KIND(0.0E0)
      INTEGER, PARAMETER :: dkind = KIND(0.0D0)
! The next statement is required to run the codes
! associated with Chapter 10 on IEEE arithmetic.
! This is non-standard and may not be available.
! Different compilers set this value in different ways;
! see comments below for advice.
!       INTEGER, PARAMETER:: qkind = ...
! Set the precision for the whole package
      INTEGER :: wp = dkind
! To change the default package precision to single precision change
! the parameter assignment to wp above to
!       INTEGER, PARAMETER :: wp = skind
! and recompile the complete package.

! -----------------------------------------------------------------
! For the non-standard quadruple precision:
! IBM and Intel compilers recognize KIND(0.0Q0)
!       INTEGER, PARAMETER:: qkind = KIND(0.0Q0)
! -----------------------------------------------------------------
! If you are using the NAG compiler then you can
! make use of the NAG-supplied f90_kind module
!       USE, INTRINSIC :: f90_kind
!       INTEGER, PARAMETER:: skind = single ! single precision
!       INTEGER, PARAMETER:: dkind = double ! double precision
!       INTEGER, PARAMETER:: qkind = quad   ! quad    precision
! but note that this module is not part of the standard
! and is thus likely to be non-portable.
! -----------------------------------------------------------------

    END MODULE set_precision
```

Within any program unit that depends on a particular working precision we use an appropriate version of the module *set_precision* and invoke the module by use-association:

```
...
  USE set_precision
  REAL(wp) :: x
...
```

This form of the USE statement provides access to all the publicly available data and program units defined in the module. As detailed in Section 1.8, use of this general form can make it difficult to determine from whence individual names are being imported, especially when several modules are use-associated from a single program unit. For this reason we prefer (and recommend) the use of the more explicit form of the USE statement:

```
...
  USE set_precision , ONLY: wp
  REAL(wp) :: x
...
```

See Sections 1.8 and 2.3.5 for more discussions on USE statements.

To change precision, all routines that use *wp* need to be recompiled and the complete package either relinked or formed into a separate library. We note that different precision versions of the package produced in either of these ways will result in the same user-callable routine names. Constants used in arithmetic expressions are suffixed with the tag *_wp* to inform the compiler of the precision required for computing each expression. As an example, the expression x = 1.0/3.0 will result in a single precision value being computed and assigned to x; even if x is declared as double precision, the value stored will have only single precision accuracy. To ensure that the accuracy to which expressions are calculated changes in line with the defined working precision, we need to write x = 1.0E0_wp/3.0E0_wp.

The primary reason for suggesting this mechanism is that the editing required for a precision change is then restricted to the module *set_precision*. It is not necessary to hunt down and edit each type declaration within a package; we simply change *wp* to an alternate parameter value and recompile.

For routines that require specific precisions, we can directly use the appropriate kind value declared in the module *set_precision*. For example:

```
      USE set_precision , ONLY: skind , dkind
!     REAL(skind) :: x
! which is equivalent to
!     REAL :: x
!
!     REAL(dkind) :: y
! which is equivalent to
!     DOUBLE PRECISION :: y
```

The use of modules affects the way in which we build executables. Because a module contains information that cannot be obtained just from analyzing the program unit that accesses it, it is necessary to compile a source file containing a module before any use-association takes place with that module.

This requirement—compile a module before its use—also places restrictions on the way modules can be interrelated. For example, if MODULE a uses MODULE b, then MODULE b cannot use MODULE a. Furthermore, if more than one module is defined within a single source file, then the source for a module use-associated by another in the same file *must* appear first.

Thus assume that we have a file, *testPrecision.f90*, that uses our module *set_precision*. Then an executable may still be generated using the single command

```
        gfortran -o driver set_precision.f90 testPrecision.f90
```

Now the order of the source file names is important.

Using *.o* files means that we need to compile *set_precision* first using the command

```
        gfortran -c set_precision.f90
```

then generate *testPrecision.o* before finally linking with

```
        gfortran -o driver set_precision.o testPrecision.o
```

The order of the *.o* files in the link command above is irrelevant.

Some compilers generate additional intermediate files for each module (typically named *moduleName.mod*) which contain information used when compiling other source files use-associating that module. When a module source file is updated, not only do we need to recompile this file but we also need to recompile all program units that use-associate modules defined in that file. These files in turn can cause further files to need recompiling. Thus a simple edit to a single module file may cause a cascade of recompilations to occur. This provides a good reason for using tools like *make* (see Chapter 19) to ensure that the number of recompiled files is kept to a minimum.

2.3.3 Interfaces

Because each module is compiled before its use, the compiler is able to perform more extensive checks on any calls to module subprograms, and hence report errors such as misplaced or extra arguments, calls with arguments transposed, or the use of arguments with the incorrect data type. This is especially useful during code development.

A basic interface body associated with a subprogram can just be an exact copy of that program unit's header, argument specification, and, if applicable, function return type along with an end statement that includes the subprogram type and its name. Although including the name here is optional, it is recommended practice. Listing 2.4 shows the interface body associated with the LAPACK routine *dgetrf*.

Listing 2.4. *Example interface body.*

```
!! This code extract is part of the accompanying software
!! that supports Chapter 2. It may be found in the file
!! LapackInterface.f90
!!
        SUBROUTINE DGETRF( M, N, A, LDA, IPIV, INFO )
!
!    .. Scalar Arguments ..
        INTEGER            INFO, LDA, M, N
!    ..
!    .. Array Arguments ..
        INTEGER            IPIV( * )
        DOUBLE PRECISION   A( LDA, * )
        END SUBROUTINE DGETRF
```

Each interface explicitly defines how a routine must be called.

2.3.4 Packaging Calls to Routines from a Precompiled Library

For precompiled libraries for which the source code is not available for editing, it would be helpful in developing new software if we could still obtain compile-time checking of library routine calls. One way of achieving this is to provide a module containing interfaces to all the user-callable routines within the library and use this module to access the library routines. This requires some work but is certainly worthwhile for frequently used libraries.

We provide an example of an interface module in Listing 2.5 which shows the interface bodies required for calls to the BLAS routines that we use in our linear equation solution example. A similar module, *LapackInterface*, may be created containing the LAPACK routine interfaces.

Listing 2.5. *Module of interfaces for BLAS routines.*

```
!! This code extract is part of the accompanying software
!! that supports Chapter 2. It may be found in the file
!! BlasInterface.f90
!!
      MODULE BlasInterface
      IMPLICIT NONE
! This interface is for correctly calling codes in a
! complete library.  Each user-callable routine in
! the library has its calling parameters defined:
      INTERFACE
         SUBROUTINE DGEMV ( TRANS , M, N, ALPHA, A, LDA, X, INCX, &
                            BETA , Y, INCY )
!      .. Scalar Arguments ..
         DOUBLE PRECISION   ALPHA , BETA
         INTEGER            INCX , INCY , LDA, M, N
         CHARACTER*1        TRANS
!      .. Array Arguments ..
         DOUBLE PRECISION   A( LDA , * ), X( * ), Y( * )
         END SUBROUTINE DGEMV

         DOUBLE PRECISION FUNCTION DNRM2(N,DX,INCX)
!      .. Scalar Arguments ..
         INTEGER          INCX ,N
!      ..
!      .. Array Arguments ..
         DOUBLE PRECISION DX(*)
         END FUNCTION DNRM2
      END INTERFACE
      END MODULE BlasInterface
```

In particular, interface bodies provide a means for correctly matching assumed-shape arrays in calls to user routines that are written to perform operations on assumed-size arrays. Assumed-shape arrays are used in our main program and assumed-size arrays are used in the LAPACK codes. The use of the interface information in the module *LapackInterface* may not always be necessary but we recommend its use at all times to aid both portability and maintainability. This is our preferred way of packaging existing Fortran 77 codes in libraries.

Note that we have chosen to treat the interface modules as Fortran 90 rather than adhere to the fixed format style of the original application code. The editing required to do this is minimal, consisting mainly of replacing the Fortran 77 comment characters with a "!".

The driver program then imports the interface definitions using

```
!! This code extract is part of the accompanying software
!! that supports Chapter 2. It may be found in the file
!! exampleLapackInterface.f90
!!

    USE LapackInterface , ONLY : dgetrf , dgetrs
    USE BlasInterface , ONLY : dnrm2, dgemv
```

The only other important change to the driver program code is the removal of the explicit declaration of the return type of the BLAS Euclidean norm function, *dnrm2*. Because the name has been use-associated, its type is known; including a separate type declaration is an error and will usually be reported as an attempt to redeclare the type of an existing name.

2.3.5 Packaging Calls to a Fortran Library Subprogram Using a Module Subprogram Library

The final alternative packaging for libraries we discuss is to place the source codes for the library subprograms within modules. When doing this there is a requirement that each subprogram unit is terminated by either END SUBROUTINE or END FUNCTION; both statements can optionally include the name of the actual program unit, for example, END FUNCTION dnrm2.

In Fortran 77 it was considered good practice by some to declare all subprograms called from within a program unit as **EXTERNAL**. However, subroutines or functions intended to be called from within the module or by use-association to another module must *not* be declared **EXTERNAL**. Having such declarations present will result in the linker searching *elsewhere* for the routines and not using those defined in the desired module subprogram. That can be confusing! As described in the previous section, the declared type of the return values of functions use-associated within any program unit invoking them is known.

These changes usually necessitate some editing of the Fortran 77 source code. If this is not possible or convenient, for example, when only a compiled version of the library is available, then use of interface blocks is recommended.

In the new main program the symbols *dgetrf* and *dgetrs* are imported from the Lapack module along with *dnrm2* and *dgemv* from the BLAS module. The **USE** statements at the start of the program are

```
!! This code extract is part of the accompanying software
!! that supports Chapter 2. It may be found in the file
!! exampleLapackModules.f90
!!
```

```
! Import the precision parameter for declaring real data
    USE set_precision , ONLY : wp
! Import the names of the Lapack routines used to factorize
! and solve the linear system.
    USE LapackMod , ONLY : dgetrf , dgetrs
! Import the names of the Blas routines used by the main program.
! Other routines are used by the Lapack routines but these
! do not need to be mentioned here.
    USE BlasModule , ONLY : l2Norm=>dnrm2 , dgemv
```

In general both packaging methods described here will result in modules containing many application routine definitions. This means that, potentially, a large number of public symbolic names are visible to any use-associating program unit. We recommend importing only those names explicitly called by each program unit. The reasons for this are that

- name clashes will be largely avoided by importing only the needed symbols;

- name transformations can be used to improve readability; for example, in the code snippet above we have renamed the BLAS library routine *dnrm2* to the alternate name *l2Norm*;

- a minimal list of imported names or symbols provides information, at a glance, of what is needed in the routine or module; this aids in maintainability, documentation, and debugging; and

- the compiler has a symbol table that can use this list as an opportunity to minimize the size of the executable produced.

EXERCISE 2.2. *In the main program unit in the file exampleLapackInterface.f90, change the use-association name from the original LAPACK name dgetrf to DoublePrecLUFactorization.*

EXERCISE 2.3. *Temporarily introduce a deliberate error into a call to dgetrs by, for example, leaving out the last argument, INFO. Check that your compiler issues a suitable error message when attempting to compile this source file.*

EXERCISE 2.4. *By running the main program unit in the file exampleLapackInterface.f90 find the smallest system size, n, that takes at least one second to execute the factorization and solve steps.*

Chapter 3

Generic Subprograms

Synopsis:

> *Generic packaging:*
>
> ▶ *Reasons to use only one name*
>
> ▶ *Illustrations with Airy functions*
>
> ▶ *Writing the module procedures*
>
> ▶ *Exercises*

3.1 Introduction

This chapter presents an example of how to declare and use *generic* names for sets of subprograms. Most of the Fortran elementary functions have this generic characteristic, which allows us to use Fortran statements like $y=SIN(x)$ when x is either a scalar or an array of any of the intrinsic, floating-point data types and precisions, i.e., *REAL(skind)*, *REAL(dkind)*, *COMPLEX(skind)*, or *COMPLEX(dkind)*. If the compiler supports quadruple precision arithmetic, then *REAL(qkind) and COMPLEX(qkind)* will also be available.

Using a generic name usually makes it easier to maintain code that will be used with more than one precision or data type, and by an artful choice of the Fortran name, it can suggest the mathematical function on which it is based. This is also likely to improve the readability of source code.

Fortran 77 restricted the use of generic names to the intrinsic functions but, since Fortran 90, programmers have been able to define their own generic interfaces. We illustrate this technique by developing such an interface for a set of routines that compute the *Airy functions*, $Ai(z)$ and $Bi(z)$, and their first derivatives.

3.2   Illustrations with Airy Functions

The Airy functions, $Ai(z), Bi(z)$, are the elements of a matrix of linearly independent solutions to Airy's equation, $w'' - zw = 0$, given by Abramowitz and Stegun [1, Equation (10.4.1)]. We provide a module that computes these values and their first derivatives, $Ai'(z)$ and $Bi'(z)$, via a single generic function call for all data types. The source for these functions is based on the CALGO Algorithm 838 [26], with background development given by Fabijonas, Lozier, and Olver [27].

The package as submitted provides an interface to all the specific routines under a common name so, for example, we may compute the Airy function, $Ai(x)$, for a single or double precision, real or complex argument by calling the routine *airy_ai*. However, to obtain this "generic" behavior we have to use-associate a separate module for each type/precision we wish to use. Our first improvement to this package is, therefore, to write a short and simple module that provides true generic names in that only a single module, *airy*, needs to be use-associated to obtain access to all four type/precision combinations using the previously defined names. The code for *airy* is given in Listing 3.1.

Listing 3.1. *Improved generic access to Airy functions.*

```
!!  This  code  extract  is  part  of  the  accompanying  software
!!  that  supports  Chapter  3.  It  may  be  found  in  the  file
!!  airy.f90
!!
    MODULE airy
    USE airy_functions_real_single
    USE airy_functions_real_double
    USE airy_functions_complex_single
    USE airy_functions_complex_double

    PRIVATE
    PUBLIC :: airy_ai , airy_bi , airy_ai_zero , airy_bi_zero
    PUBLIC :: airy_info , airy_aux , airy_aux_info

    END MODULE airy
```

The fundamental matrix solution of Airy's equation is given by

$$\Phi(z) = \left(\begin{array}{cc} Ai(z) & Bi(z) \\ Ai'(z) & Bi'(z) \end{array} \right). \tag{3.1}$$

We aim to add convenience to the distributed code of Algorithm 838 by adding a new generic function, *abi*, which returns a vector

$$y(1{:}4) = [Ai(x), Ai'(x), Bi(x), Bi'(x)]^T .$$

The order of the results also allows us to form $\Phi(z)$ as a 2×2 array with a single function call.

For real values of x, Algorithm 838 provides a separate routine for $Bi(x)$ and $Bi'(x)$, but for complex values $x = z$ there is no routine for either function. The user must therefore employ the *connection formula* (Abramowitz and Stegun [1, Equation (10.4.6)]):

$$Bi(z) = e^{\pi i/6} Ai(ze^{2\pi i/3}) + e^{-\pi i/6} Ai(ze^{-2\pi i/3}).$$

Thus for each evaluation of $Bi(z)$ and $Bi'(z)$, we require three function evaluations of $Ai(z)$ and $Ai'(z)$ and use of the connection formula. By adding this facility we extend the usefulness of the package and, we hope, help to save time and avoid careless mistakes through users having to implement this extension themselves.

We provide an optional argument, *flags*, an integer array of length 2 for real arguments and length 3 for complex arguments. If present, this returns the error status flags from the underlying subprograms of Algorithm 838, and it is then up to the user to test these and decide on a plan of action if an error has occurred. If the *flags* argument is not present and an error occurs, the code prints a message.

3.3 Writing the Module Procedures

The Airy function subprograms, given in [26], are structurally similar in each supported precision within each data type. Van Snyder [92] shows how to write codes that obviate duplicating common blocks of source text—a concept related to *templates* in other languages.

Listing 3.2. *Outline of generic function.*

```
MODULE Ai_and_Bi
IMPLICIT NONE
...

INTERFACE abi
    MODULE PROCEDURE sairy, dairy, cairy, zairy
END INTERFACE abi

Contains
    FUNCTION sairy(x,flags) RESULT(abi)
...
    FUNCTION dairy(x,flags) RESULT(abi)
...
    FUNCTION cairy(x,flags) RESULT(abi)
...
    FUNCTION zairy(x,flags) RESULT(abi)
...
END MODULE Ai_and_Bi
```

Listing 3.3. *Single precision Airy function definition.*

```
!! This code extract is part of the accompanying software
!! that supports Chapter 3. It may be found in the file
!! Airy_Module.f90
!!
    FUNCTION sairy(x,flags) RESULT (abi)
        USE set_precision, ONLY : wp => skind
        USE airy_functions_real_single ! From ACM-TOMS/Calgo 838

!------Start BLOCK of common source for single and double precision.
        REAL (wp), INTENT (IN) :: x
        INTEGER, OPTIONAL :: flags(2)
        REAL (wp) :: abi(4)
```

```
        INTEGER :: ierra, ierrb
        LOGICAL :: modify_switch

        modify_switch = .FALSE.

! From ACM-TOMS 838:
        CALL airy_ai(x,abi(1),abi(2),ierra,modify_switch)
        CALL airy_bi(x,abi(3),abi(4),ierrb,modify_switch)
        IF (present(flags)) THEN
          flags(1) = ierra
          flags(2) = ierrb
          RETURN
        END IF
        IF (ierra==0 .AND. ierrb==0) RETURN
!------End BLOCK of common source for single and double precision.

        WRITE (*,'(A/A, 1PE16.8, 2I6)') &
          'Exception for single precision Airy', &
          'Values of X, flags for AIRY_AI, AIRY_BI', x, ierra, ierrb
      END FUNCTION sairy
```

To illustrate, we consider our generic function subprogram, *abi(...)*, outlined in Listing 3.2, which needs to be available in four versions depending on the type and precision of x. The real versions have the majority of their code in common; the only differences are in the setting of *wp*, the working precision, and the **USE** statement. By pointing *wp* at the separate **KIND** parameters for single and double precision (available from the module *set_precision* as *skind* and *dkind*, respectively) and having the common code access only *wp*, we may place the shared body of code into a file, say *sourceReal.txt*, and use the standard **INCLUDE** feature to insert the contents at the relevant points (see Listing 3.4 for an example).

Listing 3.4. *Use of include file for common source text.*

```
!! This code extract is part of the accompanying software
!! that supports Chapter 3. It may be found in the file
!! Airy_ModuleInc.f90
!!
    FUNCTION dairy(x,flags) RESULT (abi)
      USE set_precision, ONLY : wp => dkind
      USE airy_functions_real_double ! From ACM-TOMS/Calgo 838
!------Start BLOCK of common source for single and double precision.
      INCLUDE 'sourceReal.txt'
!------End BLOCK of common source for single and double precision.

      WRITE (*,'(A/A, 1PE24.16, 2I6)') &
          'Exception for double precision Airy' &
        , 'Values of X, flags for AIRY_AI, AIRY_BI', x, ierra, ierrb
      END FUNCTION dairy
```

This approach means that we have only two source files to maintain for the main body of code: one for the two real functions and one for the two complex functions. We find the idea of reuse in this way compelling. On the other hand, developing code with this technique may require having extra editing sessions: one for the common source file and others for the type-dependent text. Ideally this feature should be integrated into a code development environment.

EXERCISE 3.1. *The Wronskian of the Airy function is defined as* $\det(\Phi(z)) = Ai(z)Bi'(z) - Ai'(z)Bi(z)$, *where* $\Phi(z)$ *is defined by equation (3.1). We may test our implementation of abi by checking the identity (see Abramowitz and Stegun [1, Equation (10.4.10)])*

$$\det(\Phi(z)) - \frac{1}{\pi} = 0.$$

The program drive_airy.f90 (available online along with the code for Algorithm 838) computes the maximum relative error in the Wronskian for random arguments on the unit interval for the real functions and the unit square for the complex functions. For each precision and data type, the computed errors are scaled by the arithmetic precision, and we would expect that these scaled errors would not exceed five.

Run the program and verify this test using a number of different platforms.

EXERCISE 3.2. *Create versions of the routines sairy, dairy, cairy, and zairy that use the include feature. The included files of text will be in the two separate files sourceReal.txt and sourceComplex.txt. Run the driver program and check your modified code.*

EXERCISE 3.3. *If your Fortran compiler supports quadruple precision, create additional real and complex routines, qairy and wairy, using this extended precision. (Note: this will require editing the CALGO Algorithm 838 text to activate the quadruple precision versions of the Airy functions.)*

Chapter 4

Sparse Matrices, Defined Operations, Overloaded Assignment

Synopsis:

> *Defined operations in Fortran*
>
> ▶ *Sparse matrix representations*
>
> ▶ *Use of derived types for representing sparse structures*
>
> ▶ *Overloaded assignments*
>
> ▶ *User-defined operations*
>
> ▶ *Exercises*

4.1   Introduction

In this chapter we look at some of the ways the Fortran standard has been extended to include user-defined data types (data structures), overloaded assignments, and user-defined operations.

Fortran 77 provided a single data structure: a static array, i.e., an array whose size was fixed at compile time. This meant that programmers were not able to group together connected data items, typically of different types, as a single entity as in, for example, the employee record described in Section 1.7. The lack of allocatable data and pointers also meant that the implementation of dynamic data types such as linked lists and trees was convoluted, error prone, and often inefficient. In addition the need to declare array lengths at compile time removed one of the principal advantages of dynamic data structures, i.e., that they can grow as far as the available memory resources will allow.

The use of assignment overloading and defined operations lets an application programmer write more natural code. This is achieved by replacing sequences of subprogram calls by expressions; not only is this easier to read, it also removes the need to create and use temporary space to store intermediate results. The use of overloaded assignments between intrinsic and derived types also allows for the provision of easy-to-use data structure transformations.

In the rest of this chapter we look at how we may use these three features to produce a set of user-friendly functions for representing and manipulating sparse matrices of floating-point values.

4.2   Representing Sparse Matrices

A matrix is termed *sparse* if a large percentage of its elements are zero. This type of matrix occurs frequently in practice, for example in using finite element and finite difference methods to approximate systems of partial differential equations [31, 60], in structural engineering [19], and in air traffic control modeling [95]. We will return to the question of when a matrix should be considered sparse after we have looked at how we might store sparse matrices efficiently. Although many representations have been suggested [82, 25], we choose Harwell–Boeing (HB) [24] because it is both commonly used and accepted as input to a number of high quality sparse linear solver libraries, for example, SuperLU [59], which we use in Chapter 11 for a more complex example of defined operations.

Since the first Fortran standard, two-dimensional arrays have been defined as being stored within memory in column major order. Because of this, many sparse matrix formats are column-oriented, and HB is no exception. The HB structure represents a sparse matrix as a concatenation of the columns of the matrix stored as sparse vectors. The format also reflects the lack of any data structures, other than arrays, being available to Fortran programmers in the past.

As an example, consider the following matrix of order six with nine nonzero entries:

$$
\begin{pmatrix}
0. & -1. & 0. & 0. & 2. & 0. \\
5. & 0. & 0. & 0. & 0. & 0. \\
0. & 0. & 0. & 0. & -3. & 0. \\
0. & 0. & 0. & 0. & 0. & 1. \\
2. & 0. & 0. & 0. & 0. & -2. \\
0. & -3. & 0. & 4. & 0. & 0.
\end{pmatrix}
\tag{4.1}
$$

The nonzero values are stored in column major order in an array

        values = [5.0, 2.0, -1.0, -3.0, 4.0, 2.0, -3.0, 1.0, -2.0]

Now we want to be able to associate the row and column index with each value

        rowIndex = [2, 5, 1, 6, 6, 1, 3, 4, 5]

We provide the start position of each column within the *rowIndex* array in a second integer array *colStart*

        colStart(1:7) = [1, 3, 5, 5, 6, 8, 10]

Thus the row indices of the nonzero elements in column j are in elements *rowIndex(colStart(j) : colStart(j+1)−1)* with the associated nonzero values in elements *values(colStart(j) : colStart(j+1)−1)*. We note the following:

- The length of the *colStart* array is one more than the order of the sparse matrix so that the end row index may be identified. In Fortran 77 we would almost invariably be using a slice of a much longer array whose size had been fixed at compile time. To conserve memory we would obviously like to generate arrays *values*, *rowIndex*, and *colStart* of the exact length required for the particular sparse matrix being considered.

- It is not absolutely necessary to order the row indices in ascending order within each column, although this is normally done.

- Adding a new nonzero element into the representation is not trivial. If the matrix is being assembled by summing individual contributions in the form of small submatrices, then building the data structure by repeatedly adding elements in arbitrary locations is liable to be very inefficient, especially for the very large matrices found in practical applications.

- While the HB format is efficient for general computational use, it is not user friendly. In particular, it is not straightforward to identify the row and column indices associated with each *values* element, and hand coding a large problem is likely to be highly error prone.

- A column whose entries are all zero is signaled by `colStart(j) == colStart(j+1)`.

We now return to the question of when a matrix should be considered sparse. Our primary goal is to be able to solve larger problems by not having to declare two-dimensional arrays to store the full matrix. Thus, as a minimum, the matrix must be sparse enough so that the total amount of storage required for the sparse representation is less than the storage required for the equivalent full array. However, this is not the full story; arrays are very flexible data structures which allow a reasonably consistent speed of access to individual elements. Modern hardware provides different access speeds to blocks of array elements via a number of levels of cache memory [90, 35]. This is not the case with sparse storage, where access times to arbitrary element values may differ considerably depending upon row and column indices. More importantly, adding, removing, and altering data values are trivial and much faster with the array representation. Thus, the decision of when to choose a sparse matrix representation and the particular data structure to use depends heavily on both the algorithm being used to process the data and the problem size. If, due to its size, the only way of solving a problem is to use a sparse format, then the decision is clear. In other cases some preliminary analysis of algorithm performance and hardware characteristics is required to ensure efficiency in both storage and execution.

4.3 A Simple Sparse Representation

Recalling some of the points made in the previous section, we begin by considering a simple and more human readable representation of sparse matrices. First, we define a *triplet* type (see Listing 4.1 for details) consisting of the row and column indices along with the associated element value.

Listing 4.1. *Triplet definition.*

```
!! This code extract is part of the accompanying software
!! that supports Chapter 4. It may be found in the file
!! sparseTypes.f90
!!
! Define double precision triplets with three fields; the row
! and column index and value of each non-zero element.
    TYPE dpTriplet
       INTEGER :: rowIndex, columnIndex
       REAL (dkind) :: value
    END TYPE dpTriplet
```

A sparse matrix may then be represented as a list of *triplets*. For the example matrix given by (4.1) above this list would be

$$[(2, 1, 5.0), (5, 1, 2.0), (1, 2, -1.0), (6, 2, -3.0), (6, 4, 4.0),$$
$$(1, 5, 2.0), (3, 5, -3.0), (4, 6, 1.0), (5, 6, -2.0)]$$

We make the arbitrary decision not to impose any ordering on this list, and we accumulate the values of multiple triplets with the same row and column indices to give the final entry value, as this is typically the most useful interpretation in practice.

While this representation is not suitable for general computations involving sparse matrices, it is very efficient for assembling sparse matrices resulting from, say, finite element applications. For such problems it is convenient to assemble contributions to the matrix from each finite element and sum over all the elements in the mesh. Performing this prior summation analytically for all matrix entries can be an error prone process. Therefore, we aim to provide a set of robust and easy-to-use routines that allow the individual final matrix elements to be added or accumulated separately. To achieve this we define a second data type, *dpTripletList*.

Listing 4.2. *TripletList definition.*

```
!! This code extract is part of the accompanying software
!! that supports Chapter 4. It may be found in the file
!! sparseTypes.f90
!!
! Define a "list" of dpTriplets using arrays to allow
! efficient access and sorting.
    TYPE dpTripletList
! Define an expansion factor to allow extra free space to
! be allocated for efficiency reasons. The mutator function
! setExpansionFactor needs to be used to change this value
! to ensure that it is always at least one.
       REAL (dkind), PRIVATE :: expansionFactor = defaultExpansionF
! lastTriplet is the array index to the current end of data
       INTEGER :: lastTriplet = 0
! Status of the list; an allocation error has occurred if
! errFlag has been set to a non-zero value
       INTEGER :: errFlag = 0
! Arrays to store triplet data
       INTEGER, ALLOCATABLE :: rows(:), columns(:)
       REAL (dkind), ALLOCATABLE :: values(:)
    END TYPE dpTripletList
```

This is a dynamic list of *triplets*, which is used to accumulate a representation of a sparse matrix using the following algorithm:

1. Input: a set of *triplets*; no ordering of the row and column indices is required. This step uses overloaded assignment (see below for details).

2. If there is not enough free space available in the associated *dpTripletList*, allocate extended surrogate space to hold the combined lists. Copy the current list to the surrogate and rename the surrogate space back to the original. A sample code implementing this is given in Listing 4.5.

3. Add the new set of values to the end of the list.

4. Go back to step 1.

We could implement this using pointers to join the individual triplets together to form a linked list. Because we know we will need to sort the triplets on row and column indices, we choose to use three individual arrays to store the individual fields. These are declared as allocatable arrays, and we extend the size of them as necessary as new sets of triplets are added.

4.4 Overloaded Assignment

In earlier standards, prior to Fortran 90, an assignment was used solely to indicate that the result of an expression on the right-hand side of the equals sign was to be stored in the variable on the left-hand side. The Fortran 66 standard was extremely strict; for example, a floating-point real assignment required all variables and constants appearing in the statement to be of type **REAL**; i.e., mixed mode arithmetic of the form a = a+1 where *a* was of type **REAL** was not standard conforming. This restriction was relaxed in later standards to allow a variety of mixed mode expressions and implicit type conversions, although the rules still provide some traps for the unwary (see Exercise 4.1).

EXERCISE 4.1. *What are the results of the following intrinsic arithmetic assignments when a is double (extended) precision, b is real, c is complex, and i is an integer?*

```
b = 1.0/10.0
a = 1.0/10.0
a = ABS(a-b)
a = 1.0/10.0D0
a = ABS(a-b)
a = 2/5*a
c = 2
i = -5.9D0
```

Since Fortran 90, the standard has allowed assignment overloading where the types of the expression on the right-hand side (*rtype*) and the variable on the left-hand side (*ltype*) are different and, generally, not both intrinsic types. The assignment of a derived type to a variable of the same type results in a component-by-component copy.

An overloaded assignment defines a conversion from *rtype* to *ltype* and could be implemented by calling a subprogram; for example:

```
SUBROUTINE convertRtypeToLtype(ltype, rtype)
```

Or one could also use

```
FUNCTION convertRtypeToLtype(rtype) RESULT(ltype)
```

The ability to replace a subprogram call by an assignment statement is syntactic sugar that allows the conversion to be represented in a succinct way. This conversion can have a variety of meanings. We use it to convert one sparse representation to an alternate form and to deallocate internal working arrays.

To overload assignment we first need to define an interface block that associates an assignment to an *ltype* with one or more subprograms. Each associated subprogram must be a subroutine (it cannot be a function) and have two nonoptional parameters. The first is of type *ltype* and must be either **INTENT(OUT)** or **INTENT(INOUT)**, while the second is of type *rtype* and must be **INTENT(IN)**. Note that **INTENT(INOUT)** is not allowed for *rtype*.

No two procedures associated with an overloaded assignment may have identical dummy argument lists; i.e., at least one of the parameters must differ in type, kind, or rank. However, we are allowed to associate more than one distinct *rtype* with the same *ltype*.

As a simple example, we consider overloading assignment when the *ltype* is a *dpTripletList*. In two cases, where the *rtype* is either a single *dpTriplet* or a *dpTriplet* array, the data on the right-hand side is added to the *dpTripletList*. The third example, specified by the right-hand side being the integer value zero, clears the list and deallocates the arrays used to represent the list of triplets.

The required interface block is shown in Listing 4.3.

Listing 4.3. *Example of interface block for overloaded assignment.*

```
!! This code extract is part of the accompanying software
!! that supports Chapter 4. It may be found in the file
!! sparseAssign.f90
!!

      INTERFACE ASSIGNMENT (=)
! This defines the basic operations for building a list of
! triplets from individual triplets and for clearing a
! dpTripletList variable by reclaiming all the allocated space.

! TYPE(dpTripletList) = TYPE(dpTriplet)
      MODULE PROCEDURE a_triplet
! TYPE(dpTripletList) = TYPE(dpTriplet)(:)
      MODULE PROCEDURE list_of_triplets
! TYPE(dpTripletList) =  INTEGER (0)
      MODULE PROCEDURE clear_triplets
   END INTERFACE
```

As an example of an associated subroutine, we give the code to the routine *clear_triplets* in Listing 4.4.

Listing 4.4. *Example of associated routine for overloaded assignment.*

```
!! This code extract is part of the accompanying software
!! that supports Chapter 4. It may be found in the file
!! sparseAssign.f90
!!
      SUBROUTINE clear_triplets(sparse,iflag)
! The overloaded assignment TYPE(dpTripletList) = 0 clears the
! contents of sparse, reclaims allocated storage and sets
! lastTriplet=0.
      IMPLICIT NONE
      TYPE (dpTripletList), INTENT (INOUT) :: sparse
      INTEGER , INTENT (IN) :: iflag
! Note that only iflag=0 clears the list.
      IF (iflag==0) THEN
        IF (ALLOCATED(sparse%values)) &
          DEALLOCATE (sparse%rows,sparse%columns,sparse%values)
        sparse%lastTriplet = 0
        sparse%errFlag = 0
      END IF
      END SUBROUTINE clear_triplets
```

The other two subroutines both involve extending the list of triplets. We improve the efficiency of the code for list expansion in two ways. First, in preparation for further input and to reduce the number of calls to the **ALLOCATE** statement, a user settable extension factor is available to reserve more space than is necessary just to process the current right-hand side. Second, we use the Fortran intrinsic subprogram **MOVE_ALLOC** to reduce the amount of data being copied when extending the arrays. The **MOVE_ALLOC** subprogram is used to rename an allocatable object of any type by copying the data once rather than twice. The code in Listing 4.5 indicates how to extend the *rows* component in a *dpTripletList* variable.

Listing 4.5. *Expanding the available storage for triplet list data.*

```
INTEGER , ALLOCATABLE :: tempRows(:)
TYPE (dpTripletList) :: sparse
...
! Not enough space to store new set of triplets
  oldsize = SIZE(sparse%rows)
  newsize = expansion_factor * oldsize

! Expand the rows component of sparse to newsize from oldsize
ALLOCATE(tempRows(newsize), STAT=allocateStatus)
...
! Copy already stored data
tempRows(1:oldsize) = sparse%rows(1:oldsize)
! Rename without a further copy
CALL MOVE_ALLOC(TO=sparse%rows, FROM=tempRows)
! The surrogate array tempRows(:) is deallocated automatically.
```

Further examples of overloaded assignment are provided in the module *sparseAssign* for converting between *dpHBSparseMatrix* and *dpTripletList* types and for clearing a *dpSparseMatrix* derived type by reclaiming all the allocated array space and reinitializing the other components.

4.5   User-Defined and Overloaded Operators

Both unary and binary user-defined operators are allowed. Such operators may be formed either by overloading existing operators like **.EQ.** and + or by generating new ones using standard Fortran names enclosed within periods.

We illustrate how to implement and use overloaded and defined operators by generating code to sum a pair of HB sparse matrices, to transpose an HB sparse matrix, and to compute the product of an HB sparse matrix with both a dense vector and a dense matrix. Such functionality could be provided via user-callable subprograms, but providing operators allows the user to write more natural and more readable code.

In order to illustrate the various types of operators, we use **.t.** for the unary operation of array transpose, an overloaded + for the summation, and **.p.** for the matrix-vector product. While overloading the * operator might appear more natural for the product, this may cause confusion due to its use for the element-by-element multiplication of arrays.

Before we turn our attention to coding details we should mention the rules of precedence for defined operators and how these may cause errors that are difficult to uncover. Defined operations, or overloaded operations between differing types, have the lowest precedence in the compiler parsing order. Thus, suppose H is of HB sparse matrix type and x and y are double precision, floating-point, rank-1 arrays. The vector subexpression H .p. x + y without parentheses will compile but will be incorrect if the meaning, mathematically, is intended to be $Hx + y$. What is computed, because of the rules of precedence, is $H(x + y)$, which would result in a legal call to the associated subprogram but not the expected computation. On the other hand the subexpression y + H .p. x, intended to mean $y + Hx$, will give a compilation error, as the precedence rule will attempt to generate y + H, which is an undefined and therefore illegal operation. It is essential to use parentheses to force the correct combination of operands, for example, (H .p. x) + y or y + (H .p. x).

4.6   Sums and Transposes of Sparse Matrices

As with overloaded assignments, defined operators need to be specified in an interface block. Unlike overloaded assignments, the interface block links each operator with a user-defined function (not a subroutine) that implements it.

Listing 4.6 provides an example of the interface blocks required for the $.t.$, $+$, and $.p.$ operators.

Listing 4.6. *Example of interface block for defined operators.*

```
!! This code extract is part of the accompanying software
!! that supports Chapter 4. It may be found in the file
!! sparseOps.f90
!!
! Define procedure name for unary defined operation (.t.),
! the transpose of a Harwell-Boeing matrix.
      INTERFACE OPERATOR (.t.)
        MODULE PROCEDURE transpose_dhbc
      END INTERFACE
```

```
! Define the procedure name for the user-defined operation +,
! the sum of two Harwell-Boeing matrices.
      INTERFACE OPERATOR (+)
         MODULE PROCEDURE sum_dhbc_plus_dhbc
      END INTERFACE

! Define procedure names for defined operation (.p.), the product of
! a Harwell-Boeing matrix and dense array, i.e. y = H * x, or y = x
! * H. An error occurs if SIZE(x) is incompatible with the dimensions
! of H. The * operator is not overloaded to avoid confusing it with
! element by element multiplication.
      INTERFACE OPERATOR (.p.)
         MODULE PROCEDURE sparse_matrix_times_vector, &
            vector_times_sparse_matrix, sparse_matrix_times_matrix, &
            matrix_times_sparse_matrix
      END INTERFACE
```

The associated functions have a single parameter for a unary operator and two parameters for a binary operator. The result of the operation is returned via the function. In the case of a binary operator, the left-hand operator maps into the first parameter and the right-hand operator into the second. All parameters have to be **INTENT(IN)** so that the implementing code may not change any data associated with the operands which may be user-defined types. An example of where this is an annoyance is found in Chapter 11, where defined operations .ip. and .pi. are developed for solving sparse linear systems.

It is recommended that the interface blocks specifying defined operators and assignments along with their associated subprograms be contained within the same module. Defined operators may then be accessed via use-association; a short example is given by the code snippet in Listing 4.7.

Listing 4.7. *Fragment for overloaded sum of HB matrices.*

```
USE SparseOps, ONLY: OPERATOR(+), OPERATOR(.t.)
USE SparseTypes, ONLY: dpHBSparseMatrix
TYPE (dpHBSparseMatrix) :: h, k, s
...
s = h + k ! Compute sum of sparse matrices
h = .t. k  ! Assign the transpose of k to h
```

To compute the sum of sparse matrices we have made the following assumptions:

- The dimensions of the matrix sum are determined by the maximum dimensions of the operands. This is a convenience that avoids requiring the terms to have the same dimensions.

- The data for both terms on the right-hand side is sorted by row indices within columns. This result may be obtained using overloaded assignment of lists of triplets to HB sparse matrix type.

- The sizes of the component arrays are determined during the operation.

In Listing 4.7 the assignment $s = h + k$ generates a call to the function subprogram *sum_dhbc_plus_dhbc* from the module *SparseOps*. Both arguments to this function, h and k, are **INTENT(IN)** and of type *dpHBSparseMatrix*, as is the result.

This sum operation involves "uninteresting" but complicated code that depends on the nonzero entries in either operand. The suggestive + operator matches the mathematical computation being modeled and avoids the need for the application programmer to remember the associated subprogram name and calling sequence. This speeds up code development and assists with maintainability.

The code of Listing 4.8 provided for the transpose operation is succinct (but not efficient!) since we are able to reuse procedures we have already developed for our overloaded assignments. We first transform the HB matrix into an array of triplets using overloaded assignment using the function *list_of_triplets_eq_dhbc*. We then exchange the row and column indices of each element to define the transposed matrix and finally use two overloaded assignments to transform the array of triplets back to an HB sparse matrix via a list of triplets. These steps are, respectively, implemented with the functions *list_of_triplets* and *dhbc_eq_list_of_triplets*.

Listing 4.8. *Function implementing transpose operation.*

```
!! This code extract is part of the accompanying software
!! that supports Chapter 4. It may be found in the file
!! sparseOps.f90
!!
      FUNCTION transpose_dhbc(b) RESULT (a)
! This function constructs the transpose of a
! Harwell-Boeing sparse matrix, A=B^T. It supports the
! overloaded operation .t. B.

      IMPLICIT NONE
      TYPE (dpHBSparseMatrix), INTENT (IN) :: b
      TYPE (dpHBSparseMatrix) a

! Local working arrays of triplets
      TYPE (dpTriplet), ALLOCATABLE :: bb(:)
! Local list of triplets
      TYPE (dpTripletList) aa
! Local integers for indexing and swapping indices
      INTEGER itemp, k
! Convert Harwell-Boeing terms to list of triplets
      bb = b
! Interchange row and column indices to get a list
! of triplets corresponding to the transpose
      DO k = 1, SIZE(bb)
         itemp = bb(k)%rowIndex
         bb(k)%rowIndex = bb(k)%columnIndex
         bb(k)%columnIndex = itemp
      END DO
! Convert array of triplets to a list
      aa = bb
! Convert list to output Harwell-Boeing matrix form
      a = aa
      END FUNCTION transpose_dhbc
```

4.7 Sparse Matrix, Dense Vector/Matrix Products

Products of a sparse matrix and a dense vector or matrix occur frequently in numerical linear algebra. Mathematically we wish to implement $y = Hx$ and $Y = HX$, where H is a sparse matrix; x, y are dense vectors and X, Y are dense matrices of the appropriate sizes. To accommodate both dense vectors and matrices, we associate the functions, *sparse_matrix_times_vector* and *sparse_matrix_times_matrix*, whose second arguments differ: a rank-1 array for the vector operand and a rank-2 array for the matrix case. The two operations could then both be written as y = h .p. x, where the rank of x determines which function is actually used to perform the computation.

It would also be useful to provide adjoint or transposed products of the form $y = x^T H$ and its matrix counterpart. We implement these as y = x .p. h and associate two further functions, *vector_times_sparse_matrix* and *matrix_times_sparse_matrix*, whose parameters are the reverse of those defined for the straightforward product. This ensures each associated function has a distinct argument list and allows us to implement the transposed product by exchanging the types of the operands.

Listing 4.9. *Defined operation between HB matrices and dense vectors/matrices.*

```
USE SparseOps
TYPE(dpHBSparseMatrix) :: H
INTEGER, PARAMETER :: n = 1000
REAL(dkind) :: w(n), x(n), y(n), z(n)
...
! Build H from list of triplets and define x(:), z(:).
! Compute  the matrix-vector product y = Hx + z
y = (H .p. x) + z ! Parentheses required to define precedence
w = (x .p. H) + z ! Compute w = transpose(x)*H +transpose(z)
! Clear storage representing H using overloaded assignment
H = 0
```

An example code segment using the *.p.* operator is shown in Listing 4.9. Readers interested in the mechanics of performing the products should study the four associated functions in the module *sparseOps*.

4.8 Documentation and Error Processing

A primary use of defined operations and overloaded assignment is to hide uninteresting complexity. If these operations are defined on derived or intrinsic data types, it places a burden on the programmer, who must understand and maintain the code. This means that source code comments must explain the computational procedure and relate this to the source text of the defined operation or overloaded assignment.

Within the module subprograms that implement lower-level steps of operators or assignments, we may detect error conditions or exceptional circumstances. These may be communicated to the user either via error flags or using an error or output routine like the tool, *messy*, which is described in more detail in Chapter 19.

When outputting any error message ensure that the reason for issuing the message is clearly explained and, if possible, provide advice to the user on how to correct or avoid the problem.

EXERCISE 4.2. *Sparse vectors x, y of unspecified size are given as lists of nonzero values $\{i, x_i, i \in N\}$, $\{i, y_i, i \in M\}$. The sets N and M are positive integers. There is no order implied for the integers in N and M and there may be repeats. Repeats are defined as equivalent to the single value $w_i = \sum x_k$ for all $k = i$, etc. Give an algorithm for computing $z = x + y$ and represent this as the list $\{i, z_i, i \in N \cup M\}$.*

EXERCISE 4.3. *Use the algorithm of the previous exercise to develop an algorithm for computing the sum of sparse matrices H and K using the HB representation. The matrices are assumed to have unspecified dimensions, and the row indices may occur in any order.*

EXERCISE 4.4. *Give an algorithm for inserting a single triplet $\{i, j, x_{i,j}\}$ into H, represented in HB format. If the entry for i, j is present in H, the resulting entry is to be updated with the sum of that value and $x_{i,j}$.*

Chapter 5

Object-Oriented Programming for Numerical Applications

Synopsis:

▶ *Objects, classes, and methods*

▶ *Inheritance and polymorphism*

▶ *Encapulation and data hiding*

▶ *Generalizing user-supplied functions*

▶ *Exercises*

5.1 Introduction

While Fortran 95 gave almost no assistance to the object-oriented (OO) programmer, the 2003 standard provides extensive support for this style of programming. In this chapter we look at the practical application of these facilities using a simple calendar date class along with an example of how to generalize user-supplied functions to application or numerical software. We provide a further, more complex, example of OO in Chapter 6, where we extend a Quicksort routine so that it may be used to sort arrays whose elements are user-defined types and the final ordering is specified by a user-defined comparison function.

We are not setting out to provide yet another comprehensive guide to OO programming but rather to provide some guidance as to how OO software may be constructed using Fortran 2003. There is an enormous choice of texts dealing with all aspects of OO, and a reader who has experience only with the procedural programming paradigm is encouraged to study one of these (for example, Barnes and Kölling [8]) before proceeding with the rest of this chapter.

We follow the definitions of the fundamental OO concepts given by Armstrong [6] and provide brief descriptions of how we may map these into Fortran constructs. Armstrong states the following definitions:

Object – an individual, identifiable item, either real or abstract, which contains data about itself and descriptions of its manipulation of the data.

Class – a description of the organization and actions shared by one or more similar objects.

Method – a way to access, set, or manipulate an object's information.

A class thus describes a particular object in terms of the data (attributes) needed to define its state along with the interface by which a programmer may interact with it. This interface is eventually implemented as a set of methods (executable procedures) that operate on the data stored within the objects.

In Fortran 2003 an object is represented within a class by an extensible user-defined type which specifies the associated attributes (as component declarations) and methods (type-bound procedures). These definitions, along with any actual method implementations, are packaged within a module.

As a simple example we build a class for representing and manipulating date information. We start with a definition of a date type containing the day, month, and year:

```
TYPE (date)
   INTEGER :: day, month, year
END TYPE date
```

As specified, variables of type *date* may be declared and initialized using assignment of the declared object, together with its components, in sequential order:

```
TYPE(date) :: today
today = date(14, 7, 1950)
```

However, we may use the new features of Fortran 2003 to associate particular procedures with this type (object) by adding a **CONTAINS** section to the type definition. Assuming we wish to add a routine to print out a date, we would change the type definition to

```
TYPE (date)
   INTEGER :: day, month, year
CONTAINS
   PROCEDURE :: printDate
END TYPE date
```

We then place the type definition into a module, which will be our date class, and the implementation of the *printDate* routine is placed in the body of the module:

```
MODULE classDate
! Type definition for date as shown above
...
CONTAINS
   SUBROUTINE printDate(ObjDate)
```

```
      CLASS(date), INTENT(IN) :: ObjDate
      WRITE(*,'(''Date: '',i2.2,''/'',i2.2,''/'',i4)') &
                     ObjDate%day, ObjDate%month, ObjDate%year
      WRITE(*,'(A)') &
      &   ' ''Carpe diem quam minimum credula postero'' -- Horace '
      END SUBROUTINE printDate
   END MODULE classDate
```

Note that we declare the parameter *ObjDate* to be of CLASS(date) rather than TYPE(date). We will say more about this later in the chapter.

To call the defined *printDate* method we use CALL today%printDate(), where the first argument of the call is the object to which the *printDate* method is being applied, i.e., this is equivalent to CALL printDate(today).

5.2   Inheritance and Polymorphism

Much of the power of OO programming comes from the following:

Inheritance – the mechanism that allows the data and behavior of one class to be included in or used as the basis for another class.

Polymorphism – the ability of different classes to respond to the same message and to implement the method appropriately.

Both of the above definitions are from [6].

In Fortran 2003, we form a subclass by extending an already defined type. For example, we might like to add time information to our date, but we don't want, nor do we need, to redefine the data and methods we already have for dealing with dates. We define a new class, *datetime*, by extending our existing date type:

```
   TYPE, EXTENDS(date) :: datetime
      INTEGER :: hour, minute, second
   CONTAINS
      PROCEDURE :: printTime
   END TYPE datetime
```

This means that a *datetime* object has the newly defined attributes (fields, components) *hour*, *minute*, and *second* as well as inheriting those defined for *date*, i.e., *day*, *month*, and *year*. We also define a new method *printTime* which will print the currently stored time. The *datetime* class also inherits the procedure *printDate*; i.e., we can print out the date part of a *datetime* object without writing any new code. This is an example of polymorphism at work; we apply a routine defined for use on a *date* object to a *datetime* object. However, the *printTime* procedure we supply within the *datetime* class cannot operate on a *date* object since it has no time information to print.

We could include the above type extension and the code for *printTime* in the *classDate* module, but it is structurally more sound to form a new class by extending the base type and including the extra code segments in the new module *classDatetime*.

5.3   Encapsulation

One way of trying to make our software safer and easier to maintain and change is to restrict the ways in which programmers can gain access to the internal data structures of objects. This has two advantages. First, it allows us to check that any data values being assigned are sensible. Second, by hiding the actual internal implementation details, we can change them without breaking code that relies on this level of detail.

As an example, we could allow a user to initialize a date by using a straight-forward derived type initialization of the form

```
ObjDate = date(14, 7, 1950)
```

Here we are forced to rely on the user providing legal data. To improve code robustness, we should restrict the setting of an object's attributes to a defined user interface (procedure call) which can check that the data is valid. This is called a *mutator* function.

```
FUNCTION setdate(ObjDate, day, month, year) RESULT(ok)
INTEGER, INTENT(IN) :: day, month, year
TYPE(date), INTENT(OUT) :: ObjDate
! Return true if date input data valid, false otherwise.
LOGICAL :: ok
! Check for valid data
  ...
! Set attributes for legal data
ObjDate%day = day; ObjDate%month = month;
ObjDate%year = year
ok = .TRUE.
END SUBROUTINE
```

In a similar fashion we can also define an *accessor* function that allows a user to obtain the current attribute settings of an object without knowledge of the internal data structure. This has the form

```
SUBROUTINE getdate(ObjDate, day, month, year)
INTEGER, INTENT(OUT) :: day, month, year
TYPE(date), INTENT(IN) :: ObjDate
day = ObjDate%day; month = ObjDate%month;
year = ObjDate%year
END SUBROUTINE
```

All that remains is to force the user to comply with our wish that they use the supplied procedure calls rather than directly assigning from the type components. We do this by making the components within the type definition **PRIVATE**. This means that they may not be altered directly by any code that is not contained in the same module. Consequently, the *accessor* and *mutator* functions must be packaged in this same module.

```
TYPE (date)
   PRIVATE
   INTEGER :: day, month, year
CONTAINS
   PROCEDURE :: printDate
```

```
   PROCEDURE :: getdate
   PROCEDURE :: setdate
END TYPE date
```

5.4   Using Classes for Passing Information to User-Written Routines

In many numerical application areas, for example, nonlinear least-squares, ordinary differential equations (ODEs), quadrature, etc., it is customary for users of software packages to define the problem they wish to solve by providing a function as a parameter in the call to the relevant solver. The form of this function is predefined and will, almost certainly, involve only parameters considered important to the package writer. For example, when solving a system of n ODEs of the form

$$\mathbf{y}' = \frac{d\mathbf{y}}{dt} = \mathbf{f}(t, \mathbf{x}),$$

a typical user-defined function would be of the form

```
   SUBROUTINE f(n, t, x, yp)
   INTEGER, INTENT(IN) :: n
   REAL(wp), INTEGER(IN) :: t, x(n)
   REAL(wp), INTENT(OUT) :: yp(n)
!
! Set yp = f(t, x) - this array provides the derivatives
!
   END SUBROUTINE f
```

In practice it is usual that such routines require problem-dependent parameters. If these parameters are constant for the complete execution, they could just be hard-wired into the function definition; otherwise, they need to be communicated to the function using **COMMON** blocks or module variables. However, they cannot be communicated via the user-supplied function's parameter list without changing the application source code or using an alternate way to gain access to the information. In addition, the information required may not be simply data; optional procedures might be utilized; for example, in differential equation solving code, an optional error vector norm might be included as a parameter. In Fortran 77, so-called **COMMON** variables were often used to pass data to the user's routines; this was accepted practice and worked well enough, but any changes in the structure of the data often required the editing and recompilation of several program units. This programming style also interferes with writing thread-safe numerical routines; this topic is covered in more detail in Chapter 15.

Using the OO facilities of the new Fortran standard, we may now write code that enables extra information to be passed to user-written routines in a clean and general manner. At the same time we may reduce the complexity of the user interface to the top level routine and provide suitable default values to user parameters. We will see more of this in Chapter 7, where we update the Quadpack [72] routine *qag* from Fortran 77 to use modern Fortran 2003 concepts and constructs. For now we will present a simple example in order to illustrate the new facilities. Consider a subroutine for solving a single nonlinear equation of the form $f(x) = 0$; we choose to use the implementation of a method by Brent taken from Forsythe, Malcolm, and Moler [29]. This has the following interface, where the user-provided function, *funct*, takes a simple **REAL(wp)** argument x and returns the function value at that point.

Listing 5.1. *Original interface to zeroin.*

```
!!  This code extract is part of the accompanying software
!!  that supports Chapter 5. It may be found in the file
!!  zeroinOrig.f
!!
      DOUBLE PRECISION FUNCTION zeroin(ax,bx,funct,tol)

C     .. Scalar Arguments ..
      DOUBLE PRECISION ax,bx,tol
C     ..
C     .. Function Arguments ..
      DOUBLE PRECISION funct
      EXTERNAL funct
```

Brent's algorithm requires the user to provide an interval, $[x_1, x_2]$, such that $f(x_1)$ and $f(x_2)$ have opposite signs, thus ensuring there is at least one root in the interval.

To improve the routine, we first replace the declaration of the routine, *funct*, by an interface block that allows the compiler to check both the number and type of all parameters as well as the type of the returned value in any user-provided definitions. We also replace **DOUBLE PRECISION** by **REAL(wp)** for improved portability and place the routine in a module.

We next use a derived type, *brentArgs*, to encapsulate the other parameters:

```
TYPE, PUBLIC :: brentArgs
   REAL(wp) :: ax
   REAL(wp) :: bx
   REAL(wp) :: tol
END TYPE brentArgs
```

From here the routine interface then becomes the following:

Listing 5.2. *Improved interface to zeroin.*

```
!!  This code extract is part of the accompanying software
!!  that supports Chapter 5. It may be found in the file
!!  brentTypes.f90
!!
      REAL(wp) FUNCTION zeroin(brentType,funct)

!     .. Scalar Arguments ..
      TYPE(brentargs) :: brentType
!     ..
!     .. Function Interface
      INTERFACE
         FUNCTION funct(x) RESULT(res)
! Use IMPORT to bring wp into local scope
```

```
            IMPORT wp
            REAL(wp), INTENT(IN) :: x
            REAL(wp) :: res
            END FUNCTION funct
        END INTERFACE
```

Better still, we take advantage of the definition of *brentArgs* to supply a default value for the *tol* component.

Listing 5.3. *Type definition for brentArgs.*

```
!! This code extract is part of the accompanying software
!! that supports Chapter 5. It may be found in the file
!! brentClass.f90
!!
    TYPE, PUBLIC :: brentargs
      REAL(wp) :: ax
      REAL(wp) :: bx
      REAL(wp) :: tol = SQRT(EPSILON(1.0E0_wp))
    END TYPE brentargs
```

A typical code segment for calling *zeroin* would now be the following:

Listing 5.4. *Improved interface to zeroin.*

```
!! This code extract is part of the accompanying software
!! that supports Chapter 5. It may be found in the file
!! testType.f90
!!
! Define the end points of the interval and use
! the default tolerance
    typeBrent%ax = 2.0E0_wp
    typeBrent%bx = 3.0E0_wp
    z = zeroin(typeBrent, f)
```

As things stand, we would appear to have gained very little apart from making the interface to the subroutine *zeroin* look a bit neater and being more specific about the form of the user-supplied function.

However, let us assume that we want to send additional information to the function in a general way. Fortran allows us to both extend derived types to add extra components—inheritance—and use actual arguments of the extended type in place of dummy arguments of the base type—polymorphism. These extended types may then be passed through to the user-supplied function; this requires that original calls of the form *funct(x)* inside *zeroin* be replaced by calls with the additional argument, *funct(x, extendArgs)*.

We can now extend the base type, *brentArgs*, to contain one or more extra components that we wish to pass through to our function routine.

Listing 5.5. *Extended base class.*

```
!! This code extract is part of the accompanying software
!! that supports Chapter 5. It may be found in the file
!! brentExtraArgsFinalize.f90
!!
    TYPE, EXTENDS(brentArgs) :: brentArgsExtra
```

```
        REAL(wp) :: param
        INTEGER  :: unitNumber = 13
        INTEGER  :: evaluations = 0

        CONTAINS
        FINAL :: close_evaluation_file
     END TYPE brentArgsExtra
```

By using the attribute EXTENDS(brentArgs), the new type *brentArgsExtra* contains all the components from the original *brentArgs* type plus, among others, a new *param* component. In order to pass variables of type *brentArgsExtra* to *zeroin* (and thence through to the user-defined routine, *funct*) we change the internal declaration of *brentType* from **TYPE** to **CLASS**. The type specification TYPE(brentArgs) declares its variables to be of the defined type *brentArgs*; using CLASS(brentArgs) allows actual parameters to be of type *brentArgs* or any type that extends *brentArgs*.

Our new interface to the *zeroin* routine then becomes the following.

Listing 5.6. *Routine interface with extended base class.*

```
!! This code extract is part of the accompanying software
!! that supports Chapter 5. It may be found in the file
!! brentClass.f90
!!
      FUNCTION ZEROIN(brentType,funct) RESULT(res)

!     .. Scalar Arguments ..
      CLASS(brentArgs) :: brentType
      REAL(wp) :: res
!     ..
!     .. Function Interface
      INTERFACE
        FUNCTION funct(x,extraArgs) RESULT(fres)
        IMPORT wp, brentArgs
        REAL(wp), INTENT(IN) :: x
        REAL(wp) :: fres
        CLASS(brentArgs) :: extraArgs
        END FUNCTION funct
      END INTERFACE
```

Now we use an extended *brentArgs* type to pass extra problem-dependent information to our function *funct*. Using our *brentArgsExtra* example above, we can vary the value of the component *param* to solve, for example, a family of equations. An example function would be the following.

Listing 5.7. *Example function for extended base class.*

```
!! This code extract is part of the accompanying software
!! that supports Chapter 5. It may be found in the file
!! brentExtraArgsFinalize.f90
!!
      FUNCTION extraF(x, extraArgs)
      REAL(wp), INTENT(IN) :: x
      REAL(wp) :: extraF
      CLASS(brentArgs) :: extraArgs
```

```
      SELECT TYPE (extraArgs)
        TYPE IS (brentArgsExtra)
          ASSOCIATE(param => extraArgs%param,&
                    unit => extraArgs%unitNumber,&
                    number => extraArgs%evaluations)
            extraF = x*(x*x-2.0d0)-param
            number = number+1
            WRITE(unit,'(2F15.10)') x, extraF
          END ASSOCIATE
      END SELECT

      END FUNCTION extraF
! This routine is called when extraArgs is deleted by
! a deallocate().
      SUBROUTINE close_evaluation_file(extraArgs)
        TYPE(brentArgsExtra) extraArgs
        ASSOCIATE(unit => extraArgs%unitNumber)
          WRITE(unit, '(''Number of function evaluations:'', I5)') &
              extraArgs%evaluations
          CLOSE(unit)
        END ASSOCIATE
      END SUBROUTINE close_evaluation_file
```

The **SELECT TYPE** statement is similar to the **SELECT** statement except that it allows execution to be diverted to a number of different code sections depending on the actual type provided for the named variable. Thus one function may be used to generate different return values depending on the actual type of the parameter provided. Also the user-supplied parameters required by *zeroin*—interval limits and the required tolerance—are components of the base class and may be accessed and used in the evaluation function, *extraF*. A complete example is provided by the main program *testClass*. This program use-associates the modules *brentClass* and *brentExtraArgs*, then makes a call to *zeroin* to solve the equation with the parameter *extraBrent%param*, which is now accessible to *extraF*.

Within the extended base class we also provide a unit number, *unitNumber*, that may be used, for example, to output the $(x, f(x))$ pairs requested by *zeroin*. In addition, the integer variable, *evaluations*, may be used to count the number of function evaluations required to obtain a solution. When the *brentExtraArgs* variable is deallocated, either explicitly or implicitly, a call to the type bound procedure with the tag **FINAL** is triggered (see Metcalf et al. [65, Section 16.8]). In our example this is the subroutine *close_evaluation_file* which has a single argument of type *brentClass*. The routine outputs the total number of function evaluations used and then closes the file. Any other tidying up code may also be included in this routine.

5.5   Summary

Using classes to communicate with user-supplied routines is obviously more complicated to consider than the "old" style of using **COMMON**; however, most of this complexity is hidden during its use. While it is far better if these concepts are designed into the user interface to the numerical routine when it is written, we have

also shown here (and in Chapter 7) that existing codes can be updated relatively
easily and to good effect. But there is new and important functionality in this
approach:

- Any declared data type or procedure pointer may be passed from the program
  unit calling the numerical routine to the user-written routine.

- Values of tolerances, and other problem information, are now available in the
  user-written evaluation routine; for example, the required tolerance for solving
  an equation using *zeroin* may be used to adjust the accuracy with which that
  function is computed and thus improve efficiency.

- Typical values of variables, objects, and procedure components can be given
  initial assignments when defining a derived type. When that type is extended,
  these values are accessible to the user evaluation routines. This generally
  simplifies the use of the numerical routine by encapsulating information.

- For threaded applications (see Chapter 15) a unique copy of the class object
  can be assigned for each thread. This is a cleaner solution to that obtained using **COMMON** variables when thread-private copies of data would be required.

Chapter 6

Recursion in Fortran

Synopsis:

- ▶ *Efficient sorting with Quicksort*

- ▶ *Recursion*

- ▶ *Function in-lining*

- ▶ *Type-bound procedures*

- ▶ *Generalized sorting using abstract data types and interfaces*

- ▶ *Efficiency considerations*

- ▶ *Exercises*

6.1 Introduction

Until Fortran 95, the language standard did not support recursion. Many programmers still believe that making any recursive calls will automatically make the resultant executable inefficient. It is, of course, possible to write inefficient recursive code just as it is possible to write inefficient sequential code. A difference is that inefficiency is often less obvious with recursive code. Properly used and understood, recursion can be a valuable technique in producing both efficient and easily understood software. This is particularly true when the mathematical algorithm is compactly or routinely stated using recursion. Further examples may be found in Chapter 7, which discusses the evaluation of multiple integrals using QUADPACK.

We focus our illustration of recursion by implementing the Quicksort algorithm, which was invented by Hoare [41] in the early 1960s and is well documented (see, for example, Knuth [53] and Sedgewick [85]). It is, almost invariably, presented using recursion. Implementing Quicksort in a nonrecursive way requires the programmer to simulate the effect of recursion by maintaining the underlying stacks and implementing their associated operations. This often leads to code that is difficult to read and, therefore, hard to understand and maintain.

For application library programmers there is also a second, more subtle, problem in that, prior to Fortran 2003, multiple implementations of a sorting routine would be needed, depending on the type of the data (real, integer, etc.), the form of the data (vector elements, derived type components, etc.), the required ordering (ascending, descending, etc.), and the result of the sorting (in-situ, ranked, etc.). This approach leads to severe maintenance problems as the number of versions grows to cover expanding user requirements. Indeed, the NAG Fortran 77 library [68] provides 11 primary routines for sorting integer, real, or character data presented in a number of different forms, and the *SLATEC* library [93], available from Netlib [23], includes seven routines for performing various sorting options. This abundance often dismays the programmer and leads to the unintended consequence of using an inefficient method, like Bubblesort, instead of a good one, like Quicksort. We show how to implement the Quicksort algorithm once in a way that allows users to provide additional, relatively simple, code to cover their own requirements. This results in one basic code that covers most sorting requirements.

In this chapter we attempt to convince the reader that Fortran recursion is an important and efficient programming technique. We will dispel some myths about the efficiency of the code produced by compilers and show how abstract data types and interfaces may be used to provide an extremely flexible version of a sorting algorithm.

6.2   Basic Quicksort

The Fortran code presented in Listing 6.1 is obtained directly from the pseudocode version of the *improved Quicksort* algorithm (see Sedgewick [85, p. 321]) with obvious code substituted in-situ for the functions *less, exch,* and *compexch.* This routine is contained within the subroutine *qsort* (Listing 6.2) which sorts a double precision, floating-point array to nondescending order. Note the use of the **RECURSIVE** keyword in the **SUBROUTINE** statement: any routine that may be called recursively needs to be flagged in this way.

Listing 6.1. *Recursive version of Quicksort.*

```
!! This code extract is part of the accompanying software
!! that supports Chapter 6. It may be found in the file
!! quicInline.f90
!!
    RECURSIVE SUBROUTINE quicksort(left, right)
    INTEGER, INTENT(IN) :: left, right

    INTEGER, PARAMETER :: switchsorts=10
    INTEGER :: i
    DOUBLE PRECISION :: t

    IF((right-left) > switchsorts) THEN
      t = a((right+left)/2)
      a((right+left)/2) = a(right-1)
```

```
      a(right-1) = t
      IF (a(right-1) < a(left)) THEN
        t=a(left)
        a(left) = a(right-1)
        a(right-1) = t
      END IF
      IF (a(left) < a(right)) THEN
        t=a(right)
        a(right) = a(left)
        a(left) = t
      END IF
      IF (a(right) < a(right-1)) THEN
        t=a(right-1)
        a(right-1) = a(right)
        a(right) = t
      END IF
      i = partition(left+1, right-1)
      CALL quicksort(left, i-1)
      CALL quicksort(i+1, right)
    END IF

  END SUBROUTINE quicksort
```

First, we need to ensure that our implementation works correctly and efficiently. Inspecting the code, we note that the "driver" routine *qsort* calls *quicksort*
followed by *insertion*. If the call to *Quicksort* has been correctly implemented, then
the insertion sort is called on an array of values which are very nearly ordered,
and hence this stage runs quickly. However, if the Quicksort routine is incorrectly
coded, then the insertion sort masks the error by ensuring that we still generate a
sorted array—albeit with times that increase as $O(N^2)$! Thus, when testing this
implementation, we not only need to check that we generate correctly sorted data
but also that the execution time reflects the expected efficiency.

Listing 6.2. *qsort "driver" routine.*

```
!! This code extract is part of the accompanying software
!! that supports Chapter 6. It may be found in the file
!! quicInline.f90
!!
  SUBROUTINE qsort(a, left, right)
  INTEGER , INTENT(IN) :: left, right
  REAL(wp), INTENT(INOUT) :: a(left:right)
  REAL(wp) :: saved_val

  CALL quicksort(left, right)
  CALL insertion

  CONTAINS

  ...
```

For the implemented Quicksort the average number of comparisons—and
possibly associated operations like element exchanges—is bounded by $2N \log(N)$
when the elements are random (see Sedgewick [85, p. 311]). Thus if we increase
the number of elements by a factor α, we would expect the run time to increase by

Table 6.1. *Timing ratios for correct and incorrect versions of Quicksort.*

Number of elements	Timing ratio for correct version	Ratio (6.1)	Timing ratio for erroneous version
312500	—	5.73	—
1562500	5.00	5.64	18.29
7812500	1.87	5.56	17.61
39062500	5.55	5.51	
195312500	5.46	5.46	
976562500	5.78	5.42	

approximately

$$\alpha \left(1 + \frac{\log(\alpha)}{\log(N)} \right). \tag{6.1}$$

If there is an undetected coding error in the Quicksort implementation, then the run time of the insertion sort would be expected to increase as N^2; i.e., the equivalent ratio to (6.1) would be approximately α^2.

Table 6.1 shows two runs of Quicksort; one "correct" and the other with a purposeful mistake which ensures that the Quicksort routine terminates but fails to implement the algorithm correctly. The ratio of differences in expected execution times illuminates the erroneous version. We expect the ratio in the last column to be close to $\alpha^2 = 25$; only three timings were obtained in this column as the execution times became prohibitively high for larger data sets.

The code presented by Sedgewick attempts to be as flexible as possible by separating out the basic operations on the data to be sorted. These include comparison between values, exchange of elements, and saving and restoring a value—from and to—an element. By organizing the algorithm in this way, it is straightforward to produce versions of Quicksort that, for a given data type, allow different modes of sorting, for example, in-situ ascending order, in-situ descending order, ordered by index, etc.

Listing 6.3 shows a version of the *quicksort* routine where all the basic operations required by the sort procedure, along with those that control the order of sorting, are implemented as a set of simple functions. An implementation of these functions for generating an in-situ ascending order sort on a real array is given in Listing 6.4.

Listing 6.3. *Recursive version of Quicksort using function call.*

```
!! This code extract is part of the accompanying software
!! that supports Chapter 6. It may be found in the file
!! quicksort.f90
!!

   RECURSIVE SUBROUTINE quicksort(left, right)
   INTEGER, INTENT(IN) :: left, right

   INTEGER, PARAMETER :: switchsorts=10
```

```
    INTEGER :: i

    IF((right-left) > switchsorts) THEN
      CALL exchange((right+left)/2, (right-1))
      CALL compex(left, right-1)
      CALL compex(right, left)
      CALL compex(right-1, right)
      i = partition(left+1, right-1)
      CALL quicksort(left, i-1)
      CALL quicksort(i+1, right)
    END IF

    END SUBROUTINE quicksort
```

Listing 6.4. *Basic functions for in-situ ascending order sort on a real array.*

```
!! This code extract is part of the accompanying software
!! that supports Chapter 6. It may be found in the file
!! qsfuns.f90
!!
    SUBROUTINE exchange(i,j)
! Exchange the contents of the ith and jth elements
    INTEGER, INTENT(IN) :: i,j
    REAL(wp) :: t
    t = a(i)
    a(i) = a(j)
    a(j) = t
    END SUBROUTINE exchange

    LOGICAL FUNCTION compare(i,j)
! Compare the contents of the ith and jth elements
! This determines the final sorting order.
! Code for ascending order.
    INTEGER, INTENT(IN) :: i,j
    compare = a(i) < a(j)
    END FUNCTION compare

    SUBROUTINE compex(i,j)
    INTEGER, INTENT(IN) :: i,j
    IF(compare(j,i)) CALL exchange(i,j)
    END SUBROUTINE compex

    SUBROUTINE moveValue(i,j)
! Overwrite the contents of the jth element
! with the contents of the ith element
    INTEGER, INTENT(IN) :: i,j
    a(i) = a(j)
    END SUBROUTINE moveValue

! The next three subprograms are used to store,
! compare against and restore a particular element.
    LOGICAL FUNCTION compareValue(j)
    INTEGER, INTENT(IN) :: j
    compareValue = savedVal < a(j)
    END FUNCTION compareValue
```

Table 6.2. *Compiler generated in-lining and actual code in-lining.*

Number of	Optimized code		Unoptimized code	
elements	In-line	Functions	In-line	Functions
312500	0.02	0.02	0.06	0.08
1562500	0.08	0.05	0.10	0.12
7812500	0.19	0.19	0.53	0.64
39062500	1.06	1.07	3.01	3.66
195312500	5.78	5.80	16.34	19.90

```
SUBROUTINE saveValue(i)
INTEGER , INTENT(IN) :: i
savedVal = a(i)
END SUBROUTINE saveValue

SUBROUTINE restoreValue(i)
INTEGER , INTENT(IN) :: i
a(i) = savedVal
END SUBROUTINE restoreValue
```

Many programmers would insist that providing all the low-level operations as function calls would have a severe impact on run-time efficiency. But most modern Fortran compilers provide a means of in-lining user-defined subprograms. This means that much of the cost of memory address setting, placing data onto internal stacks, and branching is avoided. The downside is that, as noted in Chapter 18, there is no standard way of requesting that the compiler in-line specific functions.

Table 6.2 gives a performance comparison using the code presented in Listing 6.3. The first two columns compare run-times between in-lining provided by the compiler (in this case *gfortran* with optimization level −O3) and a version of the code with the contents of the functions hardwired into the code. Columns 3 and 4 give a similar comparison using the lowest level of optimization, where no in-lining is provided by the compiler. These timings clearly show how effective compilers can be with this optimization as well as giving an indication of the overhead involved when this optimization is not performed. If the compiler does perform such optimization, this approach of moving the basic operations into small functions allows the programmer to produce code that is easy to extend and modify.

For example, if we wish to alter the sorting order to descending order, we just need to replace the "less than" operator in the functions *compare* and *compareSaved* with "greater than." Compare this with the number of changes required to reverse the order of sorting for the code presented in Listing 6.1.

As a second illustration we extend the code so that, rather than sorting the data in-situ, the sort routine returns a permutation vector, *index(:)*, such that the required ordering is: *[a(index(left)), a(index(left+1)), ... ,a(index(right))]*.

To implement this, we extend the parameter list of *qsort* to include an integer array, *index(left:right)*, which will be initialized so that $index(j) = j$, for $j = left, \ldots , right$. For an ascending order sort we would then use the set of basic operations given in Table 6.3.

Table **6.3.** *Basic operations for sorting in ascending order.*

---

exchange(i,j): `it = index(i); index(i) = index(j); index(j) = it`

compare(i,j): `a(index(i)) < a(index(j))`

compareValue(i): `savedVal < a(index(i))`

saveValue(i): `savedIndex = index(i); savedVal = a(savedIndex)`

restoreValue(i): `index(i) = savedIndex`

moveValue(i,j): `index(i) = index(j)`

The changes required affect only the interface to *qsort* and the set of functions implementing the basic operations. Once again, localized changes like these are likely to be far less error prone than attempting to alter the in-line code in Listing 6.1.

EXERCISE 6.1. *Implement the permutation sort in-line by using the code in Listing 6.1 as a starting point. How many lines of code did you have to change?*

Compare the execution time of your in-line version with the code using the set of functions as described above and compiler generated in-lining. Is the overhead different to that observed for in-situ sorting?

6.3 Generalizing Using Type-Bound Procedures

The main problem with the approach presented in the previous section is that we need to alter the interface of the *qsort* routine and the associated basic operation functions every time we wish to change the way we want our data sorted. Effectively, we still generate many versions of the sort routine.

Our approach to achieve maximum flexibility is to encapsulate all the data and procedures we require in a derived type or class and associate with this the functions to perform our chosen sort. Starting with in-situ sorting of a real array, we define a base type of the following form.

Listing **6.5.** *Type definition for sortbase.*

```
!! This code extract is part of the accompanying software
!! that supports Chapter 6. It may be found in the file
!! sortdef.f90
!!
  TYPE sortbase
    REAL(wp), ALLOCATABLE :: items(:)
    REAL(wp) :: saved_val
    INTEGER :: left, right
  CONTAINS
    PROCEDURE :: exchange
    PROCEDURE :: compare
    PROCEDURE :: compareValue
    PROCEDURE :: saveValue
```

```
      PROCEDURE :: restoreValue
      PROCEDURE :: moveValue
  END TYPE
```

and alter the sorting routine to call the type-bound procedures. By default each
procedure component has the **PASS** attribute, which means that the invoking object
is associated with the first actual argument in all procedure component references.
For example,

```
      CALL sortdata%saveValue(i)
```

invokes the *saveValue* procedure with two actual arguments: *(sortdata, i)*. This
"hidden" argument is termed a *passed-object dummy argument*.

    If no passed-object dummy argument is required, then the **NOPASS** attribute
should be specified; to associate it with a specific dummy argument, not necessarily
the first, the attribute **PASS(arg-name)** should be used.

    Thus given the following three declarations of a procedure component:

1. PROCEDURE :: exchange

2. PROCEDURE, NOPASS :: exchange

3. PROCEDURE, PASS(sortdata) :: exchange

A reference of the form CALL sortdata%exchange(i,j) would require respective subroutine definitions of the following forms, where *sortdata* may be in any position in the
last example:

1. SUBROUTINE exchange(sortdata, i, j)

2. SUBROUTINE exchange(i, j)

3. SUBROUTINE exchange(i, j, sortdata)

    In addition, use of the **PASS** attribute (either implicitly or explicitly) means
that the associated type is extendable and the passed-object argument must be
polymorphic. This means it must be declared using the **CLASS** type specification
rather than **TYPE**. In Listing 6.6 we illustrate the code changes this causes in the
routine *insertion*.

Listing 6.6. *QuickSort using type-bound procedures.*

```
!! This code extract is part of the accompanying software
!! that supports Chapter 6. It may be found in the file
!! qstypeSep.f90
!!
   SUBROUTINE insertion
! Sorts the elements items(left:right), using an insertion sort
   INTEGER :: i, j

   ASSOCIATE (left=>sortdata%left, right=>sortdata%right)
   DO i = left+1, right
     CALL compex(left, i)
   END DO
```

```
      DO i = left+2, right
        j = i
        CALL sortdata%saveValue(i)
        DO WHILE(sortdata%compareValue(j-1))
          CALL sortdata%moveValue(j, j-1)
          j = j-1
        END DO

        CALL sortdata%restoreValue(j)
      END DO
    END ASSOCIATE

    END SUBROUTINE insertion
```

The actual procedures performed are the same computational tasks as those given in Listing 6.3 but are slightly different in structure. We illustrate the changes required to *compareValue*.

Listing 6.7. *compareVal routine.*

```
!! This code extract is part of the accompanying software
!! that supports Chapter 6. It may be found in the file
!! sortdef.f90
!!
  FUNCTION compareValue(sortdata,j)
  CLASS(sortbase), INTENT(INOUT) :: sortdata
  INTEGER, INTENT(IN) :: j
  LOGICAL :: compareValue

  ASSOCIATE(a=>sortdata%items, saved_val=>sortdata%saved_val)
    compareValue = saved_val < a(j)
  END ASSOCIATE

  END FUNCTION compareValue
```

It is now possible to supply a default set of procedures and allow the user to override these by extending *sortbase*. We illustrate this by changing the order of sorting from ascending to descending by altering the two routines *compare* and *compareValue*. The extended type and the replacement routines are encapsulated in the module *usersort* which is given in Listing 6.8.

Listing 6.8. *Example of extending sortbase to change order of sorted items.*

```
!! This code extract is part of the accompanying software
!! that supports Chapter 6. It may be found in the file
!! usersort.f90
!!
MODULE usersort

  USE sortdef, ONLY: sortbase

  TYPE, EXTENDS(sortbase) :: sortbaseup
  CONTAINS
    PROCEDURE :: compare => mycompare
    PROCEDURE :: compareValue => mycompareValue
  END TYPE
```

```
CONTAINS
  FUNCTION mycompare(sortdata,i,j)
    CLASS(sortbaseup), INTENT(INOUT) :: sortdata
    LOGICAL :: mycompare
    INTEGER, INTENT(IN) :: i,j
! Descending in-situ sorting
    ASSOCIATE(a=>sortdata%items)
      mycompare = a(i) < a(j)
    END ASSOCIATE

  END FUNCTION mycompare

  FUNCTION mycompareValue(sortdata,j)
    CLASS(sortbaseup), INTENT(INOUT) :: sortdata
    LOGICAL :: mycompareValue
    INTEGER, INTENT(IN) :: j
! Descending in-situ sorting
    ASSOCIATE(a=>sortdata%items, saved_val=>sortdata%saved_val)
      mycompareValue = saved_val < a(j)
    END ASSOCIATE

  END FUNCTION mycompareValue

END MODULE usersort
```

6.4   Using Abstract Data Types and Interfaces

The code is still not as general purpose as we could wish. It would be better if we could implement one version of the Quicksort algorithm and use this to sort what we like, how we like. As things stand, we are restricted by the definition of *sortbase* to sorting an array of double precision values. If we wish to sort an array of integers, we would need to redefine the *sortdata* data type, generate a new set of worker functions, and recompile the module *sorting*. There is no simple solution if we wish to sort both integer and double precision array data using a single implementation of a sorting algorithm. We would need two definitions of *sortbase* (one having **REAL(wp)** and one having **INTEGER** declarations) with different names, say, *sortdp* and *sortint* along with two different *sorting* modules, one using *sortdp* and the other *sortint*. This repetition of code is obviously not a good idea as far as maintenance is concerned.

What we want to do is abstract out any dependence of the sorting module on the type of data being sorted. The routine *qsort* actually only needs to know the result of comparing values and how to move data items around; it does not need to know how this is done or on what data it is operating. We have encapsulated these basic operations within the six routines defined in Listing 6.4.

Fortran 2003 gives us the tools to do exactly this using abstract data types. The routine *qsort* is implemented once in terms of the abstract data type *abstractSortbase* using a number of procedures with predefined interfaces that define each subprogram type and its parameter list. We then produce a module defining a data type that extends *abstractSortbase* to include the particular data items to be sorted and that gives explicit definitions of each of the abstract procedures which define the way individual items are to be compared and manipulated. Data may then be sorted by calling *qsort* and passing it a variable of the extended type containing the values to be sorted.

Listing 6.9 shows the definition of the abstract data type, *abstractSortbase*, that declares two integers for defining the range of elements to be sorted, and gives the six procedures that need to be implemented for each extended data type defined. The listing also shows the abstract interface associated with each of these procedures. The use of the keyword **DEFERRED** in the procedure definitions informs the compiler that actual procedures will be defined explicitly by the user somewhere else in the code.

Listing 6.9. *Abstract data type and abstract interface.*

```
!! This code extract is part of the accompanying software
!! that supports Chapter 6. It may be found in the file
!! sortElements.f90
!!
      MODULE sortElements

      TYPE, ABSTRACT ::   abstractsortbase
        INTEGER :: left, right
        CONTAINS
          PROCEDURE(exchangeElements), DEFERRED :: exchange
          PROCEDURE(compareElements), DEFERRED :: compare
          PROCEDURE(compareElementValue), DEFERRED :: compareValue
          PROCEDURE(saveElementValue), DEFERRED :: saveValue
          PROCEDURE(restoreElementValue), DEFERRED :: restoreValue
          PROCEDURE(moveElementValue), DEFERRED :: moveValue
      END TYPE abstractsortbase

      ABSTRACT INTERFACE
        SUBROUTINE exchangeElements(elem, i, j)
          IMPORT :: abstractsortbase
          CLASS(abstractsortbase), INTENT(INOUT) :: elem
          INTEGER, INTENT(IN) :: i, j
        END SUBROUTINE
        LOGICAL FUNCTION compareElements(elem, i, j)
          IMPORT :: abstractsortbase
          CLASS(abstractsortbase), INTENT(IN) :: elem
          INTEGER, INTENT(IN) :: i, j
        END FUNCTION
        LOGICAL FUNCTION compareElementValue(elem,j)
          IMPORT :: abstractsortbase
          CLASS(abstractsortbase), INTENT(IN) :: elem
          INTEGER, INTENT(IN) :: j
        END FUNCTION
        SUBROUTINE saveElementValue(elem,j)
          IMPORT :: abstractsortbase
          CLASS(abstractsortbase), INTENT(IN) :: elem
          INTEGER, INTENT(IN) :: j
        END SUBROUTINE
        SUBROUTINE restoreElementValue(elem,i)
          IMPORT :: abstractsortbase
          CLASS(abstractsortbase), INTENT(INOUT) :: elem
```

```
          INTEGER, INTENT(IN) :: i
        END SUBROUTINE
        SUBROUTINE moveElementValue(elem, i, j)
          IMPORT :: abstractsortbase
          CLASS(abstractsortbase), INTENT(INOUT) :: elem
          INTEGER, INTENT(IN) :: i, j
        END SUBROUTINE
      END INTERFACE

    CONTAINS
...
```

The *qsort* routine is then exactly as the code generated in Section 6.3 but with all occurrences of *sortbase* replaced by *abstractSortbase*. To use this implementation to sort an array of double precision values, we need to define a type, *dpdata*, that extends *abstractSortbase*, and explicitly link the abstract procedure names to actual procedures. Listing 6.10 shows the definition of *dpdata* and gives just the *exchangeDP* routine as an example.

Listing 6.10. *Specific implementation.*

```
!! This code extract is part of the accompanying software
!! that supports Chapter 6. It may be found in the file
!! concrete.f90
!!
    MODULE concrete
      USE set_precision, ONLY : wp
      USE sortElements, ONLY: abstractSortbase

      TYPE, EXTENDS(abstractSortbase) :: dpdata
        REAL(wp), ALLOCATABLE :: items(:)
      CONTAINS
        PROCEDURE :: exchange => exchangeDP
        PROCEDURE :: compare => compareDP
        PROCEDURE :: compareValue => compareValueDP
        PROCEDURE :: saveValue => saveValueDP
        PROCEDURE :: restoreValue => restoreValueDP
        PROCEDURE :: moveValue => moveValueDP
      END TYPE dpdata

      REAL(wp) :: savedValue

    CONTAINS
      SUBROUTINE exchangeDP(elem, i, j)
      CLASS(dpdata), INTENT(INOUT) :: elem
      INTEGER, INTENT(IN) :: i, j
      REAL(wp) :: temp
        ASSOCIATE(vals=>elem%items)
        temp = vals(i)
        vals(i) = vals(j)
        vals(j) = temp
        END ASSOCIATE
      END SUBROUTINE exchangeDP
...
```

Finally, Listing 6.11 shows a simple driver program for testing the new implementation.

Listing 6.11. *Sample driver program.*

```
!! This code extract is part of the accompanying software
!! that supports Chapter 6. It may be found in the file
!! concreteDriver.f90
!!
   PROGRAM driver
   USE set_precision, ONLY: wp
   USE concrete, ONLY : dpdata
   USE sortElements, ONLY : qsort
   TYPE(dpdata) :: datavals
   INTEGER :: n
   n = 10
   datavals%left = 1
   datavals%right = n
   ALLOCATE (datavals%items(n))
   datavals%items(1:n) = [5.0e0_wp, 4.0e0_wp, 3.0e0_wp, 2.0e0_wp, &
                          1.0e0_wp, 10.0e0_wp, 9.0e0_wp, 8.0e0_wp, &
                          7.0e0_wp, 6.0e0_wp]
   WRITE(*,'(''Before sorting: '')')
   WRITE(*,'(5e16.8)')datavals%items(1:n)
   WRITE(*,'(''------------------------------------'')')
   CALL qsort(datavals)
   WRITE(*,'(''After sorting: '')')
   WRITE(*,'(5e16.8)')datavals%items(1:n)
   END
```

EXERCISE 6.2. *Consider the type definition*

```
   TYPE personal
      CHARACTER (LEN=32) :: surname
      INTEGER :: age
      REAL :: salary
      CHARACTER :: sex
   END TYPE personal
```

Implement a set of procedures for use with the abstract class version of Quicksort that will generate an index set of the females in an array of type personal ordered on salary. Print out a list of the sorted names and their respective salaries.

Hint: Use an integer array to store the indices of the elements that contain female details and use this to drive the sorting. You can use a pointer to the personal array in your class extension to abstractSortbase rather than copying the array.

6.5 Efficiency Considerations

By using abstract classes and interfaces we have seen how we may improve the generality and flexibility of our code. We need to produce just one implementation of the Quicksort algorithm, and a specific form of sorting may then be generated by providing a set of simple problem specific subprograms. Extending the class of sorting problems that we may solve using our routine is thus made efficient both in terms of coding and maintenance.

However, we need to consider the effect that these approaches have on the runtime efficiency of the resultant executables. Table 6.4 shows timings for the four

Table 6.4. *Timings for different versions of Quicksort.*

Number of elements	In-line code	Simple procedures	Type-bound procedures	Abstract classes
312500	0.01	0.01	0.02	0.01
1562500	0.04	0.04	0.09	0.08
7812500	0.22	0.21	0.46	0.45
39062500	1.22	1.18	2.70	2.51
195312500	6.77	6.58	13.85	14.11
976562500	39.45	35.82	75.78	74.54

main versions of the Quicksort code we have considered in this section: all code in-line (Listing 6.1), using simple function calls (Listing 6.3), using type-bound procedures (Section 6.3), and using abstract classes and interfaces (Section 6.4).

Interestingly it is the move from simple procedures to type-bound procedures that causes the increase in execution times. The final transformation to use abstract classes and interfaces does not add to the timings significantly. Within the accuracy of the timers, they are effectively identical.

Chapter 7

Case Study: Toward A Modern QUADPACK Routine

Synopsis:

    Quadrature solutions using:

- ▶ *Conversion of source form and tidying*
- ▶ *Type extension with inheritance*
- ▶ *Abstract interfaces*
- ▶ *Class(...) objects*
- ▶ *Type IS selection*
- ▶ *Recursion for multiple integrals*
- ▶ *Procedure pointers*
- ▶ *Vectorization and vector integrals*
- ▶ *Associate and generic naming*
- ▶ *Replacing default error norm*
- ▶ *Exercises*

7.1   Introduction

This chapter illustrates new features of Fortran in the context of modifying the routine *qag* from the Fortran 77, numerical quadrature package QUADPACK (see Piessens et al. [72]). Although old, this package is still in wide use and its conversion to a modern style is the primary reason for this chapter. When the package was originally written, the Fortran 77 standard [46] severely restricted its applicability.

Hence, we begin by asking what desirable software capabilities are currently lacking in qag and how these may be provided using facilities from the newer standards.

The ideas illustrated in Chapter 5, and here, for passing data and functions to user-defined routines have an essential place in designing useful numerical software implemented in Fortran. Several newer elements of the Fortran standards for '90, '95, and 2003 are used as an ensemble in our development that follows. We continue to use the algorithms of QUADPACK, but now we provide access to user data and functions which is useful, for example, in supporting different execution threads. A side effect of our design is that we can now support numerical quadrature for the computation of repeated or multiple integrals, each with variable limits, over a small number of dimensions:

$$I_1 = \int_a^b f(x)\,dx,$$

$$I_2 = \int_a^b \int_{g_1(x)}^{g_2(x)} f(x,y)\,dy\,dx,$$

$$I_3 = \int_a^b \int_{g_1(x)}^{g_2(x)} \int_{h_1(x,y)}^{h_2(x,y)} f(x,y,z)\,dz\,dy\,dx$$

(7.1)

$$\dots$$

We also add functionality for the integration of vector functions, where the function $f(x)$ above can have $m > 0$ vector components $f(x) \equiv [f_1(x), \ldots, f_m(x)]$. We often find, in practice, that we need to evaluate a sequence of vectors whose components are related to their neighbors through recursive formulae or other relationships. This fact may then be used to achieve greater efficiency than the alternative, i.e., integrating each component separately.

As a bonus, this observation allows us to evaluate complex line integrals $\int_C f(z)dz$ over a suitable path C. The complex integrand function, $f(z)$, does not have to be analytic, but the path must define the branch of $f(z)$ returned by the user's evaluation routine. For a single complex line integral we have $m = 2$, and the components of the vector function are the real and imaginary parts of the integrand along the path. Typically it is most natural to compute the integrand function $u(t)+iv(t) = f(z(t))dz(t)/dt$, where the parameter t describes the path, C, and the limits of integration define the direction. The components $u(t)$ and $v(t)$ are implicitly available upon completion of the evaluation $f(z(t))dz(t)/dt$, so it is not necessary to separate the components algebraically as a preliminary step.

The original Fortran 77 QUADPACK codes were designed to approximate single integrals of the form I_1 above, and there are a number of shortcomings with the user interface which are particularly noticeable when the routines are called as components in practical applications. The original version of the subroutine qag evaluates the integrand function, $f(x)$, using a user-defined function that is supplied as an external function argument. This function has an implied interface of the form

```
INTERFACE
   FUNCTION fint(xval) RESULT(yval)
   REAL, INTENT(IN) ::  xval
```

```
    REAL :: yval
    END FUNCTION fint
END INTERFACE
```

The following restrictions exist with the original code:

- *The user routine for the function fint can have only a single argument, xval.*

For most applications the evaluation of the integrand function requires extra parameters or data. Using the Fortran 77 routine, *qag*, this data is typically made accessible to the user-supplied function, *fint*, by using either **COMMON** storage, or **MODULE** data and **USE**-association. One side effect of these methods is that they are often a barrier to parallel computation.

- *The software cannot be applied to multiple integrals of the form $I_2, I_3, \ldots$ with nonconstant limit functions.*

Recursive calls to QUADPACK subroutines from within *fint* could be used to evaluate the inner integral of I_2, say. However, either there must be run-time support for recursion, or a renamed version of the QUADPACK routine must be called for the inner integrals. The functional form of the inner integral limit functions (for example, g_1 and g_2) cannot be passed directly through the QUADPACK routines to the original *fint*. While this could be accomplished with module procedures and **USE**-association, such an approach would generally require fixing the procedure names for the limit functions in the evaluation routine *fint*. This approach becomes increasingly contorted as the dimension of the problem increases.

- *Each request for integrand values is made using a single xval value with each call to fint, which is often inefficient.*

In fact, the *qag* routine requests blocks of function values (where the size of the block is one of the values $15, 21, 31, 41, 51$, or 61) by repeatedly calling *fint*. We can take advantage of the fact that the *xval* values within each block are independent in order to "vectorize" these calculations and, potentially, evaluate them in parallel.

To deal with these shortcomings and modernize the source code, we used the following Fortran 2003 language features:

- *Cleaner syntax and better packaging:* conversion to free source form; replacement of data statements; removal of statement labels; packaging of derived types, quadrature formulas, and all integration subprograms within a module; use of a global *KIND* parameter in the module to allow easy conversion between supported precisions;

- *Type extension:* allows the passing of data required to evaluate both the integrand function and limits for repeated integration;

- *Abstract interfaces:* remove the need to repeat equivalent interface specifications;

- *CLASS(...) objects:* allow the passing of application-specific data to the user-defined integrand function;

- *Type IS selection:* provides access to the appropriate data of the extended type;

- *Recursion:* allows for repeated integration;

- *Procedure pointers:* allow the passing of user functions as limits for inner integrals;

- *Associate:* enhances the readability of source code;

- *Vectorization:* allows for an array evaluation of the integrand function;

- *Generic names:* provide a single routine name for both scalar and vector integration.

In addition, we extend the user interface to allow for the following:

- *Vector of integrals:* integration of vector functions;

- *Error estimator replacement:* replacement of the l_∞ default norm for vector integration by a user-defined function, say, one that implements an l_2 norm.

7.2   Converting Source Form

The *qag* suite of codes was first converted to free source form where

- **DATA** statements were replaced by initializations;

- a declaration of **IMPLICIT NONE** was used to enforce explicit typing of all program variables;

- the **INTENT** attribute was provided for all dummy subprogram arguments;

- statement labels were eliminated by using **END DO** to terminate all **DO**-loops and **SELECT CASE()** constructs along with **CYCLE** and **EXIT** statements to break out of loops.

7.3   Transformed Interface

We focus here on how the new interface will appear to the programmer. While there are many choices that can be made affecting the final form, our goal is to have an easily understood calling sequence which provides a mechanism for user data and variable limit functions to be passed into the integrand evaluation routine.

The original implicit interface for the routine *qag* was

```
INTERFACE
  SUBROUTINE qag(fint, a, b, epsabs, epsrel, &
                 key, approx, abserr, neval, ier)
    INTERFACE
      FUNCTION fint(xval) RESULT(yval)
      REAL, INTENT(IN) ::  xval
      REAL ::  yval
      END FUNCTION
    END INTERFACE fint

    REAL, INTENT(IN) :: a, b, epsabs, epsrel
    REAL, INTENT(OUT) :: approx, abserr
    INTEGER, INTENT(IN) :: key
    INTEGER, INTENT(OUT) :: neval, ier
  END SUBROUTINE
END INTERFACE
```

We first define a derived type, *quadpackbase*, that includes several of the original arguments to *qag* with the intention that the user's application code will extend this type to include his or her own data. In order to assist the user as much as possible we initialize a number of the components to provide reasonable default values.

The base class and its initialized components are shown in Listing 7.1.

Listing 7.1. *Base class for quadpackbase.*

```
!! This code extract is part of the accompanying software
!! that supports Chapter 7. It may be found in the file
!! quadpack2003.f90
!!
! A fuller description of all the components is included in the
! comments immediately preceding this type definition.
      TYPE, PUBLIC :: quadpackbase
    ! Define Gauss rule to be used on each subinterval
        INTEGER :: key = 6
    ! Maximum number of subdivisions allowed
        INTEGER :: limit = 50
    ! Absolute and relative error tolerances required
        REAL (wp) :: epsabs = 0.0E0_wp
        REAL (wp) :: epsrel = sqrt(epsilon(1.0E0_wp))
    ! Total number of function evaluations and subintervals used
        INTEGER :: nfunction_evaluations
        INTEGER :: nvector_evaluations
    ! Estimate of absolute error in result
        REAL (wp) :: abserr
    ! Error status flag
        INTEGER :: ier
    ! Number of components in vector integration
        INTEGER :: ncomponents
    ! Pointer to user-supplied function for norm calculations
        PROCEDURE(errnorm), POINTER, NOPASS :: enorm=>NULL()
      END TYPE quadpackbase
```

The arguments of the original *qag* code, *epsabs*, *epsrel*, *abserr*, *key*, and *ier*, are now components of the derived type *quadpackbase*. An additional parameter *limit* is included in the derived type that gives the maximum allowable number of subdivisions of the integration interval $[a, b]$. In the Fortran 77 version of *qag* this value was fixed at 500, whereas this default value may now be changed by the user. By default, we use the most accurate quadrature method by initializing *quadpack%key* to 6, although this will not be the optimal choice for all quadrature problems.

Users are often uncertain of the tolerances to use for absolute and relative error requests, so we provide default values that will usually yield acceptable results, although there is no guarantee that these will be appropriate tolerances for every application. The additional output arguments *nfunction_evaluations* and *nvector_evaluations* provide the number of function and vector evaluations which, if required, are totaled in the user-provided function. Note that in addition to user data or parameters, the requested error tolerances are now passed to the evaluation function, where they may be used to achieve an appropriate accuracy in the computation of the integrand function.

We generate an abstract procedure interface for the user function, *fint*, depending on whether it defines a scalar or a vector integrand function. The interface for an alternate error norm is also given for use with vector integration.

Listing 7.2. *Abstract interface for user functions.*

```
!! This code extract is part of the accompanying software
!! that supports Chapter 7. It may be found in the file
!! quadpack2003.f90
!!
    ABSTRACT INTERFACE
      RECURSIVE FUNCTION fs(xval,extend) RESULT (yval)
        IMPORT wp, quadpackbase
        REAL (wp), INTENT (IN) :: xval(:)
        CLASS (quadpackbase), INTENT (INOUT) :: extend
        REAL (wp) :: yval(size(xval))
      END FUNCTION fs

      RECURSIVE FUNCTION fv(xval,extend) RESULT (yval)
        IMPORT wp, quadpackbase
        REAL (wp), INTENT (IN) :: xval(:)
        CLASS (quadpackbase), INTENT (INOUT) :: extend
        REAL (wp) :: yval(size(xval),extend%ncomponents)
      END FUNCTION fv

      FUNCTION errnorm(e,extend) RESULT (norm)
        IMPORT wp, quadpackbase
        REAL (wp), INTENT (IN) :: e(:)
        CLASS (quadpackbase), INTENT (INOUT) :: extend
        REAL (wp) :: norm
      END FUNCTION errnorm
    END INTERFACE
```

The source code for the derived type *quadpackbase* and the abstract interface for the user functions *fs*, *fv*, and *errnorm* are normally not available and, therefore, not subject to any user modification. A user will typically write a secondary module that extends *quadpackbase* to include specific application data and this module will include an evaluation function. It will use an interface *fs* or *fv*, inherit application data, and use the variables *xval(:)* from the integration interval to compute the output array of function values, *yval(:)*, or, in the vector case, a rank-2 array *yval(:,:)*. This evaluation can take any form that is convenient, including the use of parallel computing. In the next sections, examples are given that illustrate these cases.

The source code for the new *qag* routine has replaced an inner sequence of calls of the form *fint(xval)* by a single call to *fint(xval,extend)*, where the first argument *xval* is now an assumed-shape array of rank 1. The extended derived type is provided as an additional argument to the evaluation routine. The following is our modified interface for the new *qag2003s*:

```
INTERFACE
   RECURSIVE SUBROUTINE qag2003s(fint, extype, a, b, approx)
      PROCEDURE(fs) :: fint
      CLASS(quadpackbase), INTENT(INOUT) :: extype
      REAL(wp), INTENT(IN)  :: a,b
      REAL(wp), INTENT(OUT) :: approx
   END SUBROUTINE qag2003s
END INTERFACE
```

For integrating vector functions there is a separate interface:

```
INTERFACE
   RECURSIVE SUBROUTINE qag2003v(fint, extype, a, b, approx)
      PROCEDURE(fv) :: fint
      CLASS(quadpackbase), INTENT(INOUT) :: extype
      REAL(wp), INTENT(IN)  :: a,b
      REAL(wp), INTENT(OUT) :: approx(:)
   END SUBROUTINE qag2003v
END INTERFACE
```

A user should call the quadrature routine via the generic routine name *qag2003* which will select either of the relevant routines *qag2003s* or *qag2003v* depending on the type and rank of the final argument *approx*. For the case of a vector of integrals, the number of vector components, m, is determined by the size of this array and this value is stored in the component *quadpackbase%nocomponents*, which is used in the abstract interface for *fv*.

7.4 A One-Dimensional Integration with User Data

Consider the computation of the following scalar integral:

$$I_\omega = \int_0^\pi \cos(\omega \sin(x)) \, dx.$$

The value of this integral $I_\omega = \pi J_0(\omega)$ is given in Abramowitz and Stegun [see 1, Equation (9.1.8)]. For numerical quadrature, the user-defined function requires access to the value of ω, which may be achieved by extending the *quadpackbase* derived type to include the desired value.

Listing 7.3. *Single integrand type definition.*

```
!! This code extract is part of the accompanying software
!! that supports Chapter 7. It may be found in the file
!! testModEx1fs.f90
```

```
!!
! The type extension declaration: my_quad_data goes here.
     TYPE, EXTENDS (quadpackbase) :: my_quad_data
! The integrated function is cos(omega * sin(x)),
! and the interval of integration is [0, PI].
        REAL (wp) :: omega
     END TYPE my_quad_data
```

The user-defined function has a **CLASS** argument of type *quadpackbase* passed as a second argument. From this argument the code selects the user-extended type, *my_quad_data*, and evaluates the function using the supplied value of ω. The **ASSOCIATE** feature is used to emphasize the mathematical definition of the integrand function $f(x) = \cos(\omega \sin(x))$, although we could just as well have written the function value as y=COS(extend%omega*SIN(x)). The independent variable $x(:)$ is an assumed-shape array of values whose size depends on the degree of Gauss–Kronrod rule used. Our default choice, *key* set to 6, means *SIZE(x)* is 61 and the output array, $y(:)$, of the same size. Here we use the fact that the Fortran elementary functions *COS* and *SIN* may be called with either scalars or arrays as arguments.

Listing 7.4. *Single integrand function.*

```
!! This code extract is part of the accompanying software
!! that supports Chapter 7. It may be found in the file
!! testModEx1fs.f90
!!
! This is a single integrand function evaluation code.
! It selects the type that contains the value OMEGA.
     FUNCTION my_f(xval,extend) RESULT (yval)
        IMPLICIT NONE
        REAL (wp), INTENT (IN) :: xval(:)

        CLASS (quadpackbase), INTENT (INOUT) :: extend
        REAL (wp) :: yval(SIZE(xval))

        SELECT TYPE (extend)
! Any other data types than the extended one are ignored:
        TYPE IS (my_quad_data)
           ASSOCIATE(omega => extend%omega)
              yval = COS(omega*SIN(xval))
! Can also maintain totals of evaluations here using
! components of EXTEND.
           END ASSOCIATE
        END SELECT

     END FUNCTION my_f
```

A user-defined module combines the type extension declaration and any other user-required functions.

```
     MODULE my_quadrature_module1
     USE set_precision, ONLY : wp
     USE quadpack2003, ONLY : qag2003
     USE set_quadpack_data, ONLY : quadpackbase
     IMPLICIT NONE
```

```
REAL(wp), PARAMETER :: zero = 0.0_wp, one = 1.0_wp
! The above type extension declaration for my_quad_data
! goes here.
! ...
! Followed by:
CONTAINS
! The above integrand function my_f goes here.
! ...
END MODULE my_quadrature_module1
```

A user-defined main program accesses the module *my_quadrature_module1* via use-association. This program declares an extended type, defines the value of its extended component, ω, and calls our Fortran 2003 version of *qag*, now named *qag2003*. Below we use the identity $\pi = 4tan^{-1}(1)$ to define the numerical upper limit of the integral.

Listing 7.5. *Single integral module definition.*

```
!! This code extract is part of the accompanying software
!! that supports Chapter 7. It may be found in the file
!! testEx1fs.f90
!!
   PROGRAM testEx1fs
      USE set_precision, ONLY : wp
      USE quadpack2003, ONLY : qag2003
      USE testModEx1fs, ONLY : my_f, my_quad_data

      IMPLICIT NONE
      REAL (wp), PARAMETER :: zero = 0.0E0_wp, one = 1.0E0_wp, &
        pi = 4.0E0_wp*ATAN(one)
      TYPE (my_quad_data) :: my_data
      REAL (wp) :: intapprox

      my_data%omega = 100.0E0_wp
      CALL qag2003(my_f,my_data,zero,pi,intapprox)
      WRITE (*,'(A,F9.6)') ' Integral (PI*J_0(100)) is  = ', intapprox

! Expected result with WP=kind(1.D0):
! Integral (PI*J_0(100)) is  =  0.062787

   END PROGRAM testEx1fs
```

Next we illustrate how to compute several integrals for different values of ω, say, $\omega_i = 0, 1, 2, \ldots, 100$. First, we need to define two arrays of size 101 for storing the extended data type and the results. Since each quadrature problem is independent of the others, we may be able to improve the execution speed by computing the integrals in parallel. We illustrate one way of achieving this by using OpenMP [18] (see Chapter 15 for a more detailed discussion).

OpenMP parallel directives are placed around the limits of a Fortran DO-loop that computes the integrals. It is important to note that each evaluation of the integrand has access to the appropriate value of ω_i passed as a component within each copy of the derived type *my_quad_data*. There is no need for other OpenMP declarations regarding private access to the data. The number of threads used in this case will depend on the Fortran compiler recognizing the OpenMP directives and other system-dependent settings. We also note that the order of completion is undefined for the threads implied within the loop, and thus we write the results only after all threads have completed.

Alternate approaches for exploiting the inherent parallelism of the computation are possible. For example, one could use *coarrays*, as outlined in Chapter 14. The loop organization would then use the number of executing images, $k=num\_images()$, functioning as a group. The range of the loop would be broken into k chunks of size l where, in this example, $l = \lceil 101/k \rceil$. Each computation could then also use OpenMP on a loop of size not exceeding l. This approach uses two levels of parallel computation—a number of images, with each executing a number of threads.

Listing 7.6. *Drivers for a batch of integrals.*

```fortran
!! This code extract is part of the accompanying software
!! that supports Chapter 7. It may be found in the file
!! testEx1fv.f90
!!
    PROGRAM testEx1fv
      USE set_precision, ONLY : wp
      USE quadpack2003, ONLY : qag2003
      USE testModEx1fs, ONLY : my_f, my_quad_data

      IMPLICIT NONE
      REAL (wp), PARAMETER :: zero = 0.0E0_wp, one = 1.0E0_wp, &
        pi = 4.0E0_wp*ATAN(one)
      INTEGER, PARAMETER :: nvalues = 100
      INTEGER :: i
      TYPE (my_quad_data) :: my_data(0:nvalues)
      REAL (wp) :: intapprox(0:nvalues)

      my_data(:)%omega = (/ (REAL(i,wp),i=0,nvalues) /)
!$OMP PARALLEL DO
      DO i = 0, nvalues
        CALL qag2003(my_f,my_data(i),zero,pi,intapprox(i))
      END DO
!$OMP END PARALLEL DO
      DO i = 0, nvalues
        WRITE (*,'(A,F9.6,A,I4)') 'Integral (PI*J_0(i)) is  = ', &
          intapprox(i), ', with i = ', i
      END DO
    END PROGRAM testEx1fv
```

EXERCISE 7.1. *Modify the user function for computing I_ω so that it totals the number of calls to the cos() and sin() functions; save this total in the component extend%nfunction_evaluations.*

EXERCISE 7.2.   *Within the integrand evaluation function for I_ω, record the abscissas and function values for later use by accumulating them in an unordered list. Extend the base type so this list is a component of the extended type.*

EXERCISE 7.3. *Write a module and main program that computes the arc length of the integrand function that defines I_ω.*

7.5 Two-Dimensional Integration Using Extended Types and Recursion

We now consider the computation of integrals of the form

$$I_2 = \int_a^b \int_{g_1(x)}^{g_2(x)} f(x, y) \, dy \, dx \qquad (7.2)$$

using recursive calls to *qag2003*.

We can rewrite (7.2) as $I_2 = \int_a^b h(x) \, dx$ where $h(x) = \int_{g_1(x)}^{g_2(x)} f(x, y) \, dy$, which is itself a quadrature problem that we can evaluate via a recursive call to *qag2003*. The user-defined function to evaluate $h(x)$ needs access both to the function for evaluating $f(x, y)$ and to the limit functions $g_1(x)$ and $g_2(x)$.

We can also evaluate more general repeated integrals, for example,

$$h(x) = \kappa \left(\int_{g_1(x)}^{g_2(x)} f(x, y) \, dy \right), \qquad (7.3)$$

where $\kappa(t) = \exp(t)$. This functionality is not used in our example here.

The use of recursion requires all routines in the call chain to *qag2003* to be specifically declared as recursive by prefixing the keyword **RECURSIVE** to the initial **SUBROUTINE** and **FUNCTION** statements. Prefixes are used in the subroutines contained within the module *set_quadpack_data*.

As an illustration, consider the scalar integrand function

$$\phi(\alpha, \beta) = \int_{-1}^{1} \int_{-g(x)}^{g(x)} (1 + \alpha x^2 + \beta y^2)^{-1/2} \, dy \, dx, \ \alpha, \beta > 0, \text{ and } g(x) = 1 - x^2. \ (7.4)$$

Here we extend the base data type *quadpackbase* to include the desired values of α, β, and a procedure pointer for the limit function $g(x) = 1 - x^2$. For the inner quadrature, invoked recursively, we require additional components f, *inner_integral_number*, and y_i to denote the function evaluation required, together with the fixed abscissa value of y used in evaluating the integrand. We also include a procedure pointer f to the evaluation function itself. The key word **NOPASS** is a necessary attribute in this declaration, as otherwise the extended type itself would be the default first argument to the function.

Listing 7.7. *Extended type for two-dimensional integrals.*

```
!! This code extract is part of the accompanying software
!! that supports Chapter 7. It may be found in the file
!! testModEx2.f90
!!
      TYPE, EXTENDS (quadpackbase) :: my_2dquad_data
         REAL (wp) :: alpha, beta
         PROCEDURE(limit), POINTER, NOPASS :: g
         PROCEDURE(fs), POINTER, NOPASS :: f
! Used for recursion:
         INTEGER :: inner_integral_number = -1
         REAL (wp) :: y_i
      END TYPE my_2dquad_data
```

The extended type, *my_2dquad_data*, also declares a procedure pointer, *g*, whose interface is defined via the abstract interface for the procedure *limit* given in Listing 7.8.

Listing 7.8. *Abstract function for defining integration limits.*

```
!! This code extract is part of the accompanying software
!! that supports Chapter 7. It may be found in the file
!! testModEx2.f90
!!
! This is the interface for the upper limit function.
      ABSTRACT INTERFACE
      FUNCTION limit(xval) RESULT (g)
        IMPORT wp
        REAL (wp), INTENT (IN) :: xval
        REAL (wp) :: g
      END FUNCTION limit
      END INTERFACE
```

The recursive user-defined function itself has two internal cases. The first, CASE (0), requests an array-valued evaluation of the integrand function, $f(x, y)$, given an array of quadrature abscissa points x and a single abscissa point, y, from the outer integration. The second, CASE (1), requests an evaluation of each inner quadrature using a recursive call to *qag2003*. The Fortran function argument to the inner use of *qag2003* is defined in the extended type itself.

Note that we also show the use of OpenMP for evaluations of the inner integrand; while generally this may not be necessary, it could be useful in reducing execution times for computationally expensive integrand functions.

In the case of (7.3) we would follow the computation of the inner integrals by a further evaluation of the vector of values using $\kappa(t)$; for example, if $\kappa(t) = \exp(t)$, we would insert the array evaluation yval = EXP(yval) after the line *!OMP END PARALLEL DO*. Procedure pointers to other functions for $\kappa(t)$ could also be imported as extensions to the derived type *quadpackbase*.

Listing 7.9. *Function definitions for two-dimensional integrals.*

```
!! This code extract is part of the accompanying software
!! that supports Chapter 7. It may be found in the file
!! testModEx2.f90
!!
! This limit function defines integration over the curved region
!       [-g(x),g(x)=1-x**2], -1 <= x <= 1.
      FUNCTION my_limit(xval) RESULT (gval)
        REAL (wp), INTENT (IN) :: xval
        REAL (wp) gval

        gval = one - xval**2
      END FUNCTION my_limit

      RECURSIVE FUNCTION my_2df(xval,extend) RESULT (yval)
        REAL (wp), INTENT (IN) :: xval(:)
        REAL (wp) :: yval(SIZE(xval))
        REAL (wp), ALLOCATABLE :: p(:)
        REAL (wp), EXTERNAL, POINTER :: gval
```

```
          INTEGER :: i
          CLASS (quadpackbase), INTENT (INOUT) :: extend
          TYPE (my_2dquad_data), ALLOCATABLE :: extend_inner(:)
          PROCEDURE(fs), POINTER :: ff

          INTEGER, PARAMETER :: inner = 1, outer = 2

          SELECT TYPE(EXTEND)
          TYPE IS (my_2dquad_data)
          ASSOCIATE(alpha => extend%alpha,&
                    beta  => extend%beta,&
                    yy    => extend%y_i,&
                    iin   => extend%inner_integral_number)

            SELECT CASE (iin)
            CASE (inner)
! This is the evaluation of the inner integrand, a
! vector at each call.  Note the fixed value y_i
! in each evaluation that also uses the array xval(:).
              yval = one/SQRT(one+alpha*xval**2+beta*yy**2)

            CASE (outer)
              gval => extend%g
              ALLOCATE (extend_inner(SIZE(xval)),p(SIZE(xval)))
! Next line insures that all integrands get values
! of alpha, beta in their copy of the extended type.
              extend_inner(:)%alpha = alpha
              extend_inner(:)%beta = beta
! Set current value of one variable and then force further calls
! to evaluate the integrand as a vector function.

              extend_inner(:)%y_i = xval(:)
              DO i = 1, SIZE(xval)
                p(i) = gval(xval(i))
              END DO
              ff => extend%f
!OMP PARALLEL DO
              DO i = 1, SIZE(xval)
! This flag makes the recursive call execute CASE(0) for each inner
! integral.  This evaluates the integrand for the inner integral.
                extend_inner(i)%inner_integral_number = inner
! This evaluates the integrand for the outer integral.  It is
! necessary to assign the pointer extend%fptr to the integrand
! function itself.  Otherwise a missing routine will be reported at
! link time.
                CALL qag2003(ff,extend_inner(i),-p(i),p(i),yval(i))
              END DO
!OMP END PARALLEL DO
            END SELECT ! Case
          END ASSOCIATE
          END SELECT ! Type
        END FUNCTION my_2df
```

The user-defined module now includes both the type extension declaration and user functions:

```
MODULE my_quadrature_module2
 USE set_quadpack_data, ONLY : quadpackbase, wp, fs, qag2003
```

```
IMPLICIT NONE
! The type extension declaration: my_2dquad_data goes here.
! ...

! Followed by:
! Abstract interface for the inner integrand function limit,
! limit(xval) goes here.

! Followed by:
CONTAINS
! The integrand function my_2df and the integrand
! LIMIT function go here.
! ...
END MODULE my_quadrature_module2
```

Listing 7.10 gives the main program for approximating the integral (7.2) for $\alpha = \beta = 1$. We declare an extended type, *my_data*, and define, as extended components, the required values of α and β, the inner limit function defined by $g(x)$, and the invoked function itself.

Listing 7.10. *Driver for two-dimensional integrals.*

```
!! This code extract is part of the accompanying software
!! that supports Chapter 7. It may be found in the file
!! testEx2.f90
!!
PROGRAM testEx2
  USE set_precision, ONLY : wp
  USE quadpack2003, ONLY : qag2003
  USE testModEx2, ONLY : my_2df, my_2dquad_data, my_limit

  IMPLICIT NONE
  INTEGER, PARAMETER :: outer = 2
  REAL (wp), PARAMETER :: one = 1.0E0_wp
  TYPE (my_2dquad_data) :: my_data
  REAL (wp) :: intapprox, lowLimit=-one, upLimit=one

  ASSOCIATE(alpha => my_data%alpha,&
            beta => my_data%beta)
! The inner integrals specify absolute error requests
  my_data%epsabs = EPSILON(one)
! Define the problem dependent parameter values
  alpha = one
  beta = one
! Point to the inner integral limit function
  my_data%g => my_limit
! Point to the recursive integrand function
  my_data%f => my_2df
! Initialize the integral type to outer -- recursion
! will take care of the rest
  my_data%inner_integral_number = outer

  CALL qag2003(my_2df, my_data, lowLimit, upLimit, intapprox)

  WRITE (*,'(''ALPHA, BETA, MY_PHI(ALPHA,BETA) = '', 3F9.6)') &
    alpha, beta, intapprox
END ASSOCIATE
```

```
! Expected Result:
! ALPHA, BETA, MY_PHI(ALPHA,BETA) =  1.000000 1.000000 2.257974

END PROGRAM testEx2
```

EXERCISE 7.4. *Change the module my_quadrature_module2 to evaluate (7.4) with* $g(x) = 1$. *Verify numerically that for* $\alpha = \beta = 1$ *the result is* $4\ln(2 + \sqrt{3}) - (2/3)\pi$.

EXERCISE 7.5. *Change the abstract interface for the inner limit function* $g(x)$ *so that the class quadpackbase is passed to it as an argument. (This also requires a change when evaluating the inner limit function in my_2df.) Keep a total of the number of evaluations of* $g(x)$ *as a new component of the extended type.*

EXERCISE 7.6. *Three points,* p_1, p_2, p_3 *define a triangle,* T, *in two dimensions. Develop an algorithm for quadrature over the triangle where* $p_1 = (0,0)$, $p_2 = (x,0)$, $x > 0$, *and* $p_3 = (q, y)$, $0 \leq y \leq x$, $q^2 + y^2 \leq x^2$ *by transforming the quadrature of an arbitrary integral* $\int_T f(s,t) ds\, dt$ *to this special case. This will require a translation, a plane rotation, and perhaps a reflection. Show that the special case can be evaluated with one two-dimensional integration.*

EXERCISE 7.7. *Extend the use of qag2003 for integrating a three-dimensional scalar function,* I_3 *defined in (7.1). This requires changing the module my_quadrature_module2 so that limit functions* g_1, g_2, h_1, *and* h_2 *are passed as components of a new extended type. Can this evaluation procedure be generalized to integrate over any number of dimensions?*

EXERCISE 7.8. *Apply the last exercise to compute*

$$V = \int_{-2}^{2} \int_{x^2/2}^{2} \int_{0}^{y/2+1} (x^2 + z)\, dz\, dy\, dx.$$

The exact value $= 1504/105$.

7.6 A Complex Line Integral

We illustrate the use of *qag2003* for vector function integration by considering the evaluation of the complex integral $U + iV = \int_C z^{-\alpha} dz$, where the curve C is the upper half of the unit circle, and α is a complex parameter.

On the upper unit circle C the complex integrand is $iz^{-\alpha}\exp(it) = izz^{-\alpha}$ for $0 \leq t \leq \pi$. The real array argument, $t(:)$, of abscissa points passed to the user-defined routine is used to evaluate the array of complex values $z(t) = \cos(t) + i\sin(t)$. Then the temporary complex quantity $w \equiv izz^{-\alpha}$ yields the vector integrand components $[\Re(w), \Im(w)]$. Note that there is no need to separate the real and imaginary parts of w algebraically as a preliminary step. We can conveniently evaluate the complex integrand by returning the numerical values of real and imaginary parts as the vector integrand components.

The user evaluation function requires the complex value of α, so we extend the *quadpackbase* derived type to include it as shown in Listing 7.11.

Listing 7.11. *Type definition for complex line integral.*

```
!! This code extract is part of the accompanying software
!! that supports Chapter 7. It may be found in the file
!! testModEx3.f90
!!
      TYPE, EXTENDS (quadpackbase) :: my_complex_data
! The integrated function is z**-alpha and the interval of
! integration is normally [0, PI] on the upper unit circle.

      COMPLEX (wp) :: alpha
      END TYPE my_complex_data
```

The routine for evaluating the vector function, *my_complex*, uses the abstract interface associated with *PROCEDURE(fv)*. The integration routine *qag2003* takes the size of the actual array argument, *approx*, as defining the number of vector components, and this size information is stored in the component *ncomponents* of the base type. This can then be used to dimension other arrays as necessary; for example, y, in the function *my_complex* in Listing 7.12.

Listing 7.12. *Function definition for complex line integral.*

```
!! This code extract is part of the accompanying software
!! that supports Chapter 7. It may be found in the file
!! testModEx3.f90
!!
      FUNCTION my_complex(t,extend) RESULT (y)
      IMPLICIT NONE
      REAL (wp), INTENT (IN) :: t(:)

      CLASS (quadpackbase), INTENT (INOUT) :: extend
      REAL (wp) :: y(SIZE(t),extend%ncomponents)
      COMPLEX (wp) z(SIZE(t)), w(SIZE(t))
      SELECT TYPE (EXTEND)
        TYPE IS (my_complex_data)
          ASSOCIATE(alpha => extend%alpha)
! Evaluation of z**-alpha, integrating around the upper
! half of the unit circle. The value of alpha is complex

! This is the z value on the unit circle, exp(i*t)
          z(:) = CMPLX(COS(t),SIN(t),wp)
! This is z**-alpha, intent is a principal branch
          w = z**(-alpha)
! This defines the differential, dz(t) = i*exp(i*t)dt,
! i=sqrt(-1), i.e. = CMPLX(zero,one,wp)
          w = CMPLX(zero,one,wp)*z*w
! Return integrand result as a vector quantity:
! real then imaginary parts
          y(:,1) = REAL(w,wp)
          y(:,2) = AIMAG(w)
        END ASSOCIATE
      END SELECT
      END FUNCTION my_complex
```

The type extension and evaluation code for this computation are packaged in a user-defined module which once again combines the type extension declaration and user function:

```
MODULE my_quadrature_module3
USE set_quadpack_data , ONLY : quadpackbase , wp , fv , qag2003
IMPLICIT NONE
! The Type Extension declaration: my_complex_data goes here.
!...
! Followed by:
CONTAINS
    FUNCTION my_complex (t, extend) RESULT (y)
!...
    END FUNCTION
END MODULE
```

The main program use-associates this module and calls *qag*2003. Note that the type and kind of the output, *c(:)*, forces a call to the vector integration code *qag*2003*v*. This, in turn, results in a call to the user evaluation routine *my_complex(...)* for evaluating the $m = 2$ integrand components.

Listing 7.13. *Driver program for complex line integral.*

```
!! This code extract is part of the accompanying software
!! that supports Chapter 7. It may be found in the file
!! testEx3.f90
!!
    PROGRAM testEx3
    USE set_precision , ONLY : wp
    USE quadpack2003 , ONLY : qag2003
    USE testModEx3 , ONLY : my_complex , my_complex_data

    IMPLICIT NONE
    REAL (wp), PARAMETER :: zero = 0.0E0_wp, one = 1.0E0_wp, &
      half = 0.5E0_wp, pi = 4.0E0_wp*ATAN(one)
    TYPE (my_complex_data) my_data
    REAL (wp) :: c(2) ! Result is a complex value.
    ASSOCIATE (alpha  => my_data%alpha , &
               abserr => my_data%abserr , &
               ier    => my_data%ier)

    alpha = CMPLX(half , zero , wp)

    CALL qag2003 (my_complex , my_data , zero , pi , c)

    WRITE (*,'(/A, 2F10.6)') ' Complex Value of ALPHA = ', alpha
    WRITE (*,'(A/20x,1pG12.4,A, 1pG12.4)') &
      ' Upper Unit Circle Integral of 1/z**ALPHA is  = ', c(1),&
      ' + I *', c(2)
    WRITE (*,*) ' IER from line integration = ', ier
    WRITE (*,'(A,1pG12.4)') &
      ' Line integral max. error estimate = ', abserr
    END ASSOCIATE

! Expected results:
! Complex Value of ALPHA =    0.500000  0.000000
```

```
! Upper Unit Circle Integral of 1/z**ALPHA is  =
!                      -2.000        + I *   2.000
!  IER from line integration =           0
! Line integral max. error estimate =   2.2204E-14

    END PROGRAM testEx3
```

7.6.1   Exercises

EXERCISE 7.9. *Change my_quadrature_module3 to compute $\int_C \bar{z}^{-\alpha} dz$, where $\bar{z}$ is the complex conjugate of z and the curve C is the upper half of the unit circle. Use $\alpha = 1/2$ as in the sample code.*

EXERCISE 7.10. *With $\alpha = 1 - i$, use the sample code and verify to working precision that the integral has the value $i(1 - e^{-\pi})$. What is the numerical value of $\int_C z^{-\bar{\alpha}} dz$?*

EXERCISE 7.11. *With $\alpha = 1$, use the sample code to verify numerically that the integral once around the unit circle has the value $2\pi i$.*

EXERCISE 7.12. *In my_quadrature_module3 define the root-mean-square error norm function $l_{RMS}(e) = ((\sum_{j=1}^{m} e_j^2)/m)^{1/2}$. Use this in place of the l_∞ error norm. Which norm requires the least number of integrand evaluations?*

Chapter 8

Case Study: Documenting the Quadrature Routine qag2003

Synopsis:

> *Quadrature software usage:*
>
> ▶ *Document accessible PUBLIC symbols*
>
> ▶ *Document base CLASS derived type*
>
> ▶ *Document routine arguments*
>
> ▶ *Provide discussion of use of public routines and basic examples*
>
> ▶ *Document internal working parameters*
>
> ▶ *Exercises*

8.1 Introduction

This chapter illustrates how to produce documentation for user-callable routines by using, as an example, the recursive, numerical quadrature routine *qag*2003 described in detail in Chapter 7. While there is no formula for documenting such material, certain good practices can be identified and these should be followed. For example, good writing principles should obviously be applied to the text, and information pertaining to the safe use of the software should be covered. Numerical software is often modified during its lifetime as bugs are fixed or as additional features are implemented. In many cases the person tasked to perform these code modifications is not the original author. Thus, to assist in the maintenance process we need to fully document the code internally using comments. Since this type of software is often provided as part of a precompiled library, we need to assume that the source code for the module *quadpack*2003 (containing the generic routine *qag*2003) will not be available. It is, therefore, essential to cover the critical usage issues with separate written documentation and to provide working examples to assist as an adjunct to the text.

The recursive subroutine *qag*2003 is a reorganized version of the routine *qag* (described in QUADPACK [72]) which numerically approximates integrals of the form $\int_a^b f(x)\,dx$ using Gauss–Kronrod formulas. We have added extra functionality for integrating vector functions where the integrand, $f(x)$ above, can be a vector; i.e., $f(x) \equiv [f_1(x), \ldots, f_m(x)]$, $m > 0$. While we have not changed the underlying algorithms, we have changed the interface to the routine to allow additional options, for example, using an alternative error norm when integrating a vector of integrals.

8.2   The PUBLIC Symbols and Base Class

The module *quadpack*2003 has all the required routines packaged within a **CONTAINS** block. Unless otherwise stated, all module symbols are **PRIVATE** and hence not accessible by use-association from another compilation unit. These routines are as follows:

- **PUBLIC** subroutine *qag*2003*s*: Integrates scalar functions, $f(x)$.

- Subroutines *qage*2003*s* and *qkgens*: Called by *qag*2003*s*.

- Subroutine *qsort_*2003: Called by *qkgens*.

- **PUBLIC** subroutine *qag*2003*v*: Integrates vector functions, $f(x)$.

- Subroutines *qage*2003*v* and *qkgenv*: Called by *qag*2003*v*.

- Subroutine *qsort_*2003: Called by *qkgenv*.

- Function *norm*: Called by *qkgenv*.

The generic **PUBLIC** name for the integration routines *qag*2003*s* and *qag*2003*v* is *qag*2003. The argument kind and type for the approximation determines which one is called.

A number of the arguments to the original QUADPACK routine *qag* are now included in a derived type parameter of base class *quadpackbase* and have been preassigned values which are considered to be reasonable defaults for well-behaved integrand functions. The base class and its components introduced in Chapter 7 are repeated here for convenience.

Listing 8.1. *Base class for quadpackbase.*

```
!! This code extract is part of the accompanying software
!! that supports Chapter 7. It may be found in the file
!! quadpack2003.f90
!!
! A fuller description of all the components is included in the
! comments immediately preceding this type definition.
    TYPE, PUBLIC :: quadpackbase
```

```
! Define Gauss rule to be used on each subinterval
      INTEGER :: key = 6
! Maximum number of subdivisions allowed
      INTEGER :: limit = 50
! Absolute and relative error tolerances required
      REAL (wp) :: epsabs = 0.0E0_wp
      REAL (wp) :: epsrel = sqrt(epsilon(1.0E0_wp))
! Total number of function evaluations and subintervals used
      INTEGER :: nfunction_evaluations
      INTEGER :: nvector_evaluations
! Estimate of absolute error in result
      REAL (wp) :: abserr
! Error status flag
      INTEGER :: ier
! Number of components in vector integration
      INTEGER :: ncomponents
! Pointer to user-supplied function for norm calculations
      PROCEDURE(errnorm), POINTER, NOPASS :: enorm=>NULL()
   END TYPE quadpackbase
```

There is an abstract procedure interface for the user function, F, depending on whether it defines a scalar or a vector integrand function. In addition, the interface for an alternate error norm is defined for use with vector integration.

Listing 8.2. *Abstract interface for user functions.*

```
!! This code extract is part of the accompanying software
!! that supports Chapter 7. It may be found in the file
!! quadpack2003.f90
!!
   ABSTRACT INTERFACE
     RECURSIVE FUNCTION fs(xval,extend) RESULT (yval)
       IMPORT wp, quadpackbase
       REAL (wp), INTENT (IN) :: xval(:)
       CLASS (quadpackbase), INTENT (INOUT) :: extend
       REAL (wp) :: yval(size(xval))
     END FUNCTION fs

     RECURSIVE FUNCTION fv(xval,extend) RESULT (yval)
       IMPORT wp, quadpackbase
       REAL (wp), INTENT (IN) :: xval(:)
       CLASS (quadpackbase), INTENT (INOUT) :: extend
       REAL (wp) :: yval(size(xval),extend%ncomponents)
     END FUNCTION fv

     FUNCTION errnorm(e,extend) RESULT (norm)
       IMPORT wp, quadpackbase
       REAL (wp), INTENT (IN) :: e(:)
       CLASS (quadpackbase), INTENT (INOUT) :: extend
       REAL (wp) :: norm
     END FUNCTION errnorm
   END INTERFACE
```

We recommend writing a secondary module that use-associates from the primary module *quadpack*2003 and, optionally, extends the base class *quadpackbase* to include application data. However, such an extension is not necessary, as a derived type declaration using just the base class is permitted. Indeed, this is natural if evaluation of the function, $f(x)$, does not require additional user data or procedures to be passed through the calling sequence.

This secondary module should normally include the evaluation function, *userF*, which needs to be written to conform to the appropriate interface *fs* or *fv* depending on the type of integrand. This user function inherits, and possibly uses, application data from within the extended type, along with the input abscissa points $x(:)$ sampled from the integration interval, to compute the output array of function values, $y(:)$. In the vector case, this will be a rank-2 array $y(:,:)$, where the first subscript matches the abscissa points, $x(:)$, and the second matches the index of the vector component function.

8.3   The Arguments for qag2003

The routine *qag2003* attempts to approximate integrals of the form *approx* $\approx \int_a^b f(x)\,dx$ using adaptive Gauss–Kronrod quadrature rules. An example of a call to this recursive subprogram is

```
CALL qag2003(userF, extend, alim, blim, approx)
```

where the parameters are defined as follows:

userF [Procedure]

The user-supplied evaluation function to compute the integrand, $f(x)$.

The provided function must match the interface for either *fs* or *fv* depending on whether *approx* is a rank-1 array or a scalar.

Any legal Fortran name may be used for this function; i.e., it does not have to be named *userF*.

extend [CLASS(quadpackbase), INTENT(INOUT)]

This is an extended or base class derived type which generally contains user input and output data required by the evaluation function *userF*.

On input this also defines a number of parameters that are used to control the integration procedure, for example, the relative and absolute tolerances requested, *epsrel* and *epsabs*.

These values are best considered as "tuning" parameters that determine the sampling density of the integrand. Default values are provided for all parameters, but these may need to be overridden for certain problems. A description of each component is given in the type definition of *quadpackbase*.

The integer component *key* should be in the range $[1, 6]$; input values less than 1 or greater than 6 are reset to 1 and 6, respectively.

This value determines the sampling density of the integrated subintervals and the number of evaluations per call to the integrand function. For a given value of *key*, the number of Gauss–Kronrod points shown in Table 8.1 is the value of *SIZE(x)* that appears in the interface for *fs* or *fv*.

Table 8.1. *Number of Gauss–Kronrod abscissa points associated with key values.*

Key	1	2	3	4	5	6
No. of Gauss points	7	10	15	20	25	30
No. of Gauss–Kronrod points	15	21	31	41	51	61

Additional user data or procedures may be defined as required by extending this base type.

alim, blim [REAL(wp), INTENT(IN)]

These values define the limits of the integration, a, b; either $a < b$ or $a > b$ is permitted.

approx [REAL(wp), INTENT(OUT)]

This parameter is used to return the approximation to the integral.

If *approx* is a scalar, then the routine *qag2003s* is called and the user-defined function *userF* must match the interface for *fs*.

If *approx(:)* is a rank-1 array, then the routine *qag2003v* is called and the user-defined function *userF* must then match the interface for *fv*. The number of components in the vector integrand, $m = SIZE(approx)$, is written by *qag2003v* to the component *extend%ncomponents*.

Using an alternative error norm is allowed only when *approx* is a rank-1 array; use of an alternate norm for scalar integrals may be achieved by calling *qag2003* with *approx* a rank-1 array of length one.

The default error estimator uses the l_∞ norm of differences in the higher order Gauss–Kronrod formulae applied to $f(x)$ on subintervals of $[a, b]$. Certain applications may use different error norms that might depend on the location within the integration subinterval, or on other smoothing properties. Such smoothing requires knowledge of the set of abscissa points used in the last evaluation, which could be recorded by extending the base class *quadpackbase*. This data would then be available to the user-defined *errnorm* function.

Analyzing Output

A number of components of the base class *quadpackbase* are set on output, and these may be useful in evaluating the quality of the returned approximation to the integral, *approx*.

abserr [REAL(wp), INTENT(OUT)]

This contains an estimate of the error in the approximation. For a vector integration, *abserr* is the maximum value of the estimated error using the operative norm function over all components of $f(x)$.

It is important to remember that this is only an estimate and may be very different from the value requested by the user input values for *epsabs* and *epsrel*. The returned value can be misleading if the integrand behaves poorly or the function is not sampled sufficiently.

This estimate is for a one-dimensional quadrature only; for multiple integrals all the generated estimates need to be propagated through the computation and combined to obtain an appropriate estimate.

ier [INTEGER, INTENT(OUT)]

This is a returned status flag

= **0** Normal and reliable termination of the routine; the indicated accuracy has usually been obtained.

= **1** The maximum number of subdivisions allowed within the integration limits has been reached. More subdivisions may be allowed by increasing the input value of the component *limit* although there is no guarantee that this will result in normal termination. If this condition occurs we suggest first reading Krogh's essay [55] for ways to analyze the integrand function.

= **2** The occurrence of roundoff error has been detected and this is preventing the requested tolerances from being achieved.

= **3** Extremely bad integrand behavior occurs at some points within the integration interval.

= **6** The input is invalid, either *epsabs* < 0 or *epsrel* < 0.

8.4   Example: Three Ways to Package the User Function

For a normally distributed random variable with mean μ and variance σ^2 the cumulative probability for the interval $[\mu - 1, \mu + 1]$ is given by the integral

$$I_{cp} = \frac{1}{\sqrt{2\pi\sigma^2}} \int_{\mu-1}^{\mu+1} \exp\left(\frac{-(x-\mu)^2}{2\sigma^2}\right) dx.$$

We illustrate the use of *qag*2003 by computing an approximation to I_{cp} where the values μ and σ are passed to the evaluation routines using type extension.

Here we describe three ways to write and package the function required by *qag*2003. Each method use-associates a secondary module, *normalPdf*, that defines the type extension. We may then write the following function:

1. *fmodule*, contained as a secondary module routine; use-associate this module in the program unit that calls *qag*2003.

2. *fexternal*, a separate program unit; designate this procedure name using the abstract interface, *fs*. This function is then linked with the program unit calling *qag*2003.

3. *fcontained*, an internal procedure contained within the program unit that calls *qag*2003. This was illegal in Fortran 2003 but the restriction was lifted in the 2008 standard.

Our preference is to use method 1. However, if for some reason a secondary module is not possible, then method 2 or 3 must be used.

8.4.1 Defining the User Function

Listing 8.3 shows a main program that makes three calls to *qag*2003 illustrating the use of all three packaging methods. It also provides the details of the internal procedure, *fcontained*, which is contained within the main program; we repeat that prior to the 2008 standard such procedures could not be used as actual arguments to dummy procedure parameters.

The module *normalPdf* (Listing 8.4) performs two tasks. First, it provides the definition of the type *extype*, an extension of *quadpackbase* to include the parameters μ and σ that are required in the evaluation of the integrand. This extended type is used both to declare the type of the variable *extend*, which is passed to *qag*2003, and as a selector in the function *fcontained*. Second, it defines the user function, *fmodule*.

Listing 8.3. *Main program and contained internal function.*

```
!! This code extract is part of the accompanying software
!! that supports Chapter 8. It may be found in the file
!! documentExample.f90
!!
    PROGRAM documentExample
      USE set_precision, ONLY : wp
      USE normalPdf, ONLY : extype, fmodule
      USE quadpack2003, ONLY : quadpackbase, qag2003, wp, fs
! Define a variable of the extended type:
      TYPE (extype) :: extend
      REAL (wp), PARAMETER :: one = 1.0E0_wp, two = 2.0E0_wp

! These are the values of mu, sigma used:
      REAL (wp) :: mu1 = one, sigma1 = two
      REAL (wp) approx1, approx2, approx3

! Since FEXTERNAL is not a module routine,
! nor a contained routine,
! it is necessary to specify its abstract interface.
      PROCEDURE(fs) :: fexternal
! This improves readability, by simplifying the
! symbols associated with derived types.

      ASSOCIATE (mu => extend%mu, sigma => extend%sigma)
! Evaluate the integral with three methods of
! defining the routine that gives values of
! the integrand function.

! Place values of mu and sigma in the extended type
! components:
      mu = mu1
      sigma = sigma1
```

```
! Approximate the integral using a module that
! contains the function fmodule.
     CALL qag2003(fmodule,extend,mu-one,mu+one,approx1)

! A second packaging method is to use
! an external function:
     CALL qag2003(fexternal,extend,mu-one,mu+one,approx2)

! A third alternate packaging is to contain the
! evaluation function fcontained in this
! program unit.
     CALL qag2003(fcontained,extend,mu-one,mu+one,approx3)
     IF (extend%ier==0 .AND. (approx1==approx2) .AND.  &
         (approx1==approx3)) THEN
       WRITE (*,'(A,F5.2,A,F5.2/A,F7.3)') &
         ' Normal cumulative for mu = ', mu,  ' sigma = ', &
          sigma, ' within limits [mu-1,m+1] is = ', approx1
     ELSE
       WRITE (*,'(A)') 'Error -- approximations differ'
       WRITE (*,'(A, E16.8)') 'Using fmodule:     ', approx1
       WRITE (*,'(A, E16.8)') 'Using fexternal:   ', approx2
       WRITE (*,'(A, E16.8)') 'Using fcontained: ', approx3
     END IF
     END ASSOCIATE

   CONTAINS
! Define the integrand function and use the
! passed values of mu, sigma:
     FUNCTION fcontained(x,ex) RESULT (y)
       IMPLICIT NONE
       REAL (wp), INTENT (IN) :: x(:)

       CLASS (quadpackbase), INTENT (INOUT) :: ex
       REAL (wp) :: y(SIZE(x))
! This is the integrand constant scale factor,
! s=1/sqrt(2*pi).
       REAL (wp), PARAMETER :: s = one/sqrt(8.0_wp*atan(one))

       SELECT TYPE (ex)
       TYPE IS (extype)
         ASSOCIATE (mu => ex%mu, sigma => ex%sigma)
           y = (s/sigma)*EXP(-(x-mu)**2/(two*sigma**2))
         END ASSOCIATE
       END SELECT

     END FUNCTION
! Expected results:
! Normal cumulative for mu =  1.00 sigma =  2.00
! within limits [mu-1,m+1] is =   0.383
   END PROGRAM documentExample
```

Listing 8.4. *Routine defined in a secondary module.*

```
!! This code extract is part of the accompanying software
!! that supports Chapter 8. It may be found in the file
!! normalPdf.f90
```

```
! !
      MODULE normalPdf
! This demonstrates the use of qag2003 by integrating
! the function s*exp(-(x-mu)**2/(2*sigma**2)),
! s=1/sqrt(2*pi*sigma**2).  The integration limits are
! from mu-1 to mu+1.
      USE set_precision, ONLY : wp
      USE quadpack2003, ONLY : quadpackbase, fs, qag2003
      REAL (wp), PARAMETER :: zero = 0.0E0_wp, one = 1.0E0_wp, &
         two = 2.0E0_wp

! Extend the base class so that mu and sigma are passed
! to the evaluation function, FMODULE(x(:), EXTEND).
      TYPE, EXTENDS (quadpackbase) :: extype
         REAL (wp) :: mu = zero
         REAL (wp) :: sigma = one
      END TYPE extype

   CONTAINS
! Define the integrand function using the supplied
! values of mu, sigma
      FUNCTION fmodule(x,ex) RESULT (y)
         IMPLICIT NONE
         REAL (wp), INTENT (IN) :: x(:)
         CLASS (quadpackbase), INTENT (INOUT) :: ex
         REAL (wp) :: y(size(x))
! This is the integrand constant scale factor,
! s=1/sqrt(2*pi).
         REAL (wp), PARAMETER :: s = one/sqrt(8.0_wp*atan(one))
         SELECT TYPE (ex)
         TYPE is(extype)
            ASSOCIATE (mu => ex%mu, sigma => ex%sigma)
              y = (s/sigma)*exp(-(x-mu)**2/(two*sigma**2))
            END ASSOCIATE
         END SELECT
      END FUNCTION fmodule
   END MODULE normalPdf
```

The source for the external function *fexternal* (Listing 8.5) could be provided in a separate file or appended to the end of the main program (after the **END PROGRAM** statement). This is similar to the method used with the original QUADPACK routine, *qag*, where the user-supplied function was declared **EXTERNAL**. With the updated software, it is not necessary to declare *fexternal* to be **EXTERNAL** since there is now a precise declaration of the function and its interface: PROCEDURE(fs) :: fexternal, where the interface is use-associated from the primary module *quadpack2003*. We note also that the secondary module *normalPdf* needs to be use-associated within *fexternal* to allow access to the extended type name.

Listing 8.5. *External routine.*

```
!! This code extract is part of the accompanying software
!! that supports Chapter 8. It may be found in the file
!! fexternal.f90
!!
! Define the integrand function externally and use the
! passed values of mu, sigma:
```

```
    FUNCTION fexternal(x,ex) RESULT (y)
! Note that it is necessary to use-associate the
! defined extended base class and other symbols.
    USE set_precision, ONLY : wp
    USE normalPdf, ONLY : quadpackbase, extype
    IMPLICIT NONE
    REAL (wp), PARAMETER :: one = 1.0E0_wp, two = 2.0E0_wp, &
       eight = 8.0E0_wp
    REAL (wp), INTENT (IN) :: x(:)
    CLASS (quadpackbase), INTENT (INOUT) :: ex
    REAL (wp) :: y(size(x))
! This is the integrand constant scale factor,
! s=1/sqrt(2*pi).
    REAL (wp) :: s = one/sqrt(eight*atan(one))

    SELECT TYPE (ex)
    TYPE IS (extype)
       ASSOCIATE (mu => ex%mu, sigma => ex%sigma)
       y = (s/sigma)*exp(-(x-mu)**2/(two*sigma**2))
       END ASSOCIATE
    END SELECT

    END FUNCTION fexternal
```

8.5   Documenting Internal Working Variables

For users of the routine *qag*2003, the *PUBLIC* symbols and the routine arguments
are all that are available for them to use and understand. But for the programmer
who must maintain the code, there is generally a need to have the internal code
variables documented. This is normally provided as a variable dictionary in the
form of comments within the source code and should include the following as a
minimum:

- An alphabetical list of program variables and constant parameters.

- The uses made of these variables and parameters within the module.

- The type, kind, rank, and size of the variables and parameters.

In addition, comments should also give details of the following:

- Any copyright or license agreements.

- References to other work that the software relies on in any way.

- A summary of the algorithms used in each routine.

- Portability testing.

- An audit trail of code changes: date of each change, who made it, and the
  reason for it being made. We also note here that updates and modifications to
  software may also necessitate changes to the associated user documentation.

EXERCISE 8.1. *In the module set_precision, change the precision parameter and recompile the complete package in single precision. Run the examples in single precision and compare the accuracy and the number of integrand function evaluations with the double precision version.*

EXERCISE 8.2. *Define an extended type, extra, of the base class quadpackbase and include the limits of integration, a, b, and the integrand function. Use this to define a scalar function qag2003f so that approx $\approx \int_a^b f(x)\,dx$ is given by the single statement approx=qag2003f(extra).*

Chapter 9

IEEE Arithmetic Features and Exception Handling

Synopsis:

 IEEE arithmetic and exception handling:

- ▶ *IEEE intrinsic modules*

- ▶ *Using IEEE features from Fortran*

- ▶ *Using an efficient algorithm and handling exceptions*

- ▶ *James Blue's pre-IEEE l_2 norm algorithm*

- ▶ *W. Kahan's IEEE l_2 norm algorithm*

- ▶ *Implementing dnrm2 with IEEE exception handling*

- ▶ *Various IEEE module features*

- ▶ *Denormalized numbers, underflow*

- ▶ *Exercises*

9.1 Introduction

The adoption of the IEEE standard for floating-point arithmetic [45] by the major chip manufacturers in 1985 was critical for advancing the state of numerical computing. Prior to that time the diversity of floating-point representations and quirky arithmetic provided by vendors made the production of portable numerical software difficult or even unreliable; see Kahan [51] for an interesting discussion. While the language standards ensured that Fortran software would compile successfully on any conforming compiler, the results obtained from executing the resultant code could vary dramatically depending on the quality of the underlying floating-point arithmetic. This led to a number of problems; for example, single precision codes could not be run reliably on some systems due to large rounding errors, while double precision versions would be inefficient on others.

The IEEE standard not only provides exact specifications for the representation of floating-point numbers in several different precisions, but it also defines precisely how the four basic arithmetic operations and the square root function should operate. In addition, full adherence to the IEEE standard requires the following:

- The provision of a variety of different rounding modes: round down, round up, round toward zero or round to nearest.

- Exception handling—the ability of the programmer to trap "illegal," or perhaps "exceptional," arithmetic operations and deal with them. For example, if division by zero occurs, we may be able to code a recovery step and continue with the computation. Failing at this, we may allow the operating system to handle this situation by terminating the execution.

- The availability of flags that can be set and queried by the programmer to ascertain whether or not certain types of results occurred during a set of numerical operations, for example, floating-point underflow or overflow.

Adoption of the standard also provided numerical analysts with a floating-point model which is a powerful tool for the error analysis of numerical algorithms. William Kahan was instrumental in guiding this standard from conception to acceptance, and a very readable history of the early work and rationale is summarized in [50].

A major problem was the lack of support from the standard Fortran language definition. Indeed, Fortran 77 did not even provide basic support in the form of elemental functions that returned underlying floating-point parameters such as the base of the arithmetic and the precision of the mantissa. These missing features had already led to widespread use of externally defined functions such as $R1MACH$ and $I1MACH$ from the PORT library [30] prior to the introduction of new numeric inquiry functions in Fortran 90 (see Adams et al. [3, p. 504] for details).

The need for access to exception handling within Fortran was recognized with the release of Fortran 95 but, rather than being included in the standard at that time, it was contained within a technical report [77]. This provided clear guidelines that could be implemented by compiler writers as an extension to Fortran 95. A slightly enhanced version of this report has been integrated into the 2003 standard.

Access to the IEEE floating-point facilities is provided in Fortran 2003 through a number of functions and constants defined within the following three *intrinsic modules*: *IEEE_EXCEPTIONS*, *IEEE_ARITHMETIC*, and *IEEE_FEATURES*. An intrinsic module is one that is part of the Fortran language as opposed to a user-supplied module. It is distinguished from a user module by the **INTRINSIC** keyword

```
USE, INTRINSIC :: IEEE_ARITHMETIC , ONLY: IEEE_IS_NAN
```

9.2 Example Problem

We consider a practical example that uses several of the available IEEE arithmetic facilities defined in the latest Fortran standard. Note that as the resulting algorithms become more robust and efficient, the code implementing them increases in length.

We discuss the computation of the l_2 norm of a given vector $\{x_i\}_{i=1}^{n}$. This function is used by many numerical algorithms, for example, in the scaling of intermediate vectors or computing the distance between points in n-dimensional space. Mathematically we wish to calculate

$$\|x\|_2 = \sqrt{\sum_{i=1}^{n} x_i^2}, \tag{9.1}$$

and the Level-1 BLAS [56] routine, dnrm2(n,x,incx), attempts to compute this as robustly as possible given the restrictions of Fortran 66. There are a number of "obvious" ways to implement this in Fortran 2003. For example, with declared values $x(1{:}n)$, $incx{=}1$, we can use the available array manipulation intrinsic functions.

Method 1.

```
dnrm2 = SQRT(SUM(x*x))
```

Method 2.

```
dnrm2 = SQRT(DOT_PRODUCT(x,x))
```

Method 3 (alternatively we could use either a straightforward loop).

```
      dnrm2 = zero
! For the template code we assume incx=1
      DO i = 1, n
          dnrrm2 = dnrm2 + x(i)**2
      END DO
      dnrm2 = SQRT(dnrm2)
```

Method 4 (or, by investing a little more computational effort, *compensated summation*; this is a technique for reducing the total numerical error in a summation by accumulating the small error committed at each step; see Kahan [52] or Higham [38, Section 4.3] for details).

```
      dnrm2 = zero
      s = zero
! For the template code we assume incx=1
      DO i = 1, n
        s = s + x(i)*x(i)
        t = dmrm2
        dnrm2 = t+s
        s = (t - dnrm2) + s
      END DO
      dnrm2 = SQRT(dnrm2)
```

Method 3 is appealing because it is so simple. Why should we consider any of the alternatives? The answer lies in analyzing the interplay of the source with the machine instructions generated by modern compilers. In fact the Intel and AMD machines contain a *floating-point unit* in hardware that essentially does a perfect job implementing Method 3. However, this hardware is not generally utilized when the compiler generates executable code. We have provided a model C function, *l2*, that computes the l_2 norm using Method 3. Our implementation uses an in-line assembler that directly accesses the x87, or floating-point unit, so it is obviously not portable but can be used as a guide for other processors. If we are not concerned about the occurrence of invalid operations, then the assembler function is efficient and accurate when the unit is enabled to use its 80-bit internal registers and standard rounding.

Method 1 may be inefficient, as it could result in the system creating a temporary n-vector containing $\left\{x_i^2\right\}_{i=1}^n$ followed by the sum and square root operations. While all four methods could provide equivalent accuracy, there are problems with each one which illustrate the need for caution in the construction of reliable, robust, general purpose software.

Consider the vector

$$x = \{2y, 4y, 4y, 8y\}$$

where $y = $ SQRT(HUGE(zero)) and $\|x\|_2 = 10y$. While the value of the l_2 norm is within the floating-point range, a naive approach to the computation—such as Method 3 or Method 4 above—will result in an exception occurring, since $x_1^2 = 4y^2 = 4*$**HUGE(zero)** overflows. A similar problem occurs if all the elements of the input vector are less than the square root of the smallest representable number. Here the intermediate values can underflow when squared, causing a value of zero to be returned with a catastrophic loss of accuracy. In fact, the exact result is always at least as large as the magnitude of the smallest nonzero component and is thus representable under these circumstances.

We specify our *goals* for the *dnrm2* function as follows:

> *The routine dnrm2 is a function that evaluates the l_2 norm of a given n-vector x. The calculation should produce a correct value whenever this value is representable. Any nonfinite or not-a-number value in the input vector should be detected and the function should return a mathematically correct result.*

This is partially achievable by performing scaling on the vector. In its simplest form we can prevent overflow by dividing all the elements of the input vector by the largest magnitude element, $|scale|$, and forming

$$\|x\|_2 = |scale|\sqrt{\sum_{n=1}^n \left(\frac{x_i}{scale}\right)^2}.$$

A problem with this approach is that we have to scan the input vector twice: once to find the maximum value and once to form the sum. Blue's algorithm [14] is a one-pass algorithm that takes great care to avoid any unnecessary overflows or harmful underflows. The main body of this method is presented in Figure 9.1. Prior

Figure 9.1. *Blue's pre-IEEE algorithm.*

Input :: $\{x_i\}_{i=1}^{n}$ Computation: Use three accumulators:

$$a_b^2 = \sum \{(x_i \cdot S_b)^2 \quad | \quad |x_i| > B_b\}$$

$$a_s^2 = \sum \{(x_i \cdot S_s)^2 \quad | \quad |x_i| < B_s\}$$

$$a_m^2 = \sum \{x_i^2 \quad | \quad B_s \le |x_i| \le B_b, \text{ "normal" case}\}$$

$$a_b > L \quad : \quad \text{return}\{+\infty\}$$

$$a_b > 0 \quad : \quad \text{return}\left\{\sqrt{\left(\frac{a_b}{S_b}\right)^2 + a_m^2}\right\}$$

$$a_s > 0 \quad : \quad \text{return}\left\{\sqrt{\left(\frac{a_s}{S_s}\right)^2 + a_m^2}\right\}$$

$$\text{otherwise} \quad : \quad \text{return}\{a_m\}$$

where, for $a_b > 0$ and $a_s > 0$, we compute $\sqrt{x^2 + y^2}$ with $|x| > |y|$ by

$$y \le Rx \quad : \quad \text{return}\{x\}$$

$$\text{otherwise} \quad : \quad \text{return}\left\{x\sqrt{1 + \left(\frac{y}{x}\right)^2}\right\}$$

and R, B_b, B_s, S_b, S_s, and L are dependent upon the precision of the floating-point arithmetic being used; values of these parameters are given in Figure 9.2 for IEEE single and double precision formats.

to the appearance of the IEEE standard and accompanying compiler support, this complex algorithm was the best available method for computing the l_2 norm of a vector. William Kahan once remarked that researching methods for completely avoiding exceptions was *misplaced inventiveness*. Our approach is to present Blue's algorithm as a back-up subprogram, *dnrm2_blue*, when there is no effective support for the IEEE standard within the Fortran compiler. However misguided this is, a compiler vendor does have the option of *not* supporting this part of the standard!

When the required level of support for IEEE arithmetic is available, we use the compensated sum loop (Method 4 above) for efficiency reasons, and only if this generates any exceptions do we fall back on a more sophisticated algorithm from Kahan (see Section 9.2.2 for details).

Our resultant hybrid algorithm is summarized in Figure 9.2.

Figure 9.2. *An IEEE–Kahan–Blue hybrid algorithm.*

1. If the required level of IEEE exception support for Kahan's algorithm is not available, compute the norm using Blue's algorithm.

2. Else if the naive loop computation in Method 4 causes an underflow, an overflow, an Infinity, or a NaN, use Kahan's algorithm.

Table 9.1. *Values of the constants in Blue's algorithm—IEEE floating-point arithmetic.*

	Single	Double
B_s	2^{-63}	2^{-511}
B_b	2^{52}	2^{485}
S_s	2^{64}	2^{512}
S_b	2^{-75}	2^{-538}
L	$2^{52}(1 - 2^{-24})$	$2^{485}(1 - 2^{-53})$
R	$\sqrt{2^{-23}}$	2^{-26}

9.2.1   Blue's pre-IEEE Euclidean Norm Algorithm

The constants used by the Blue algorithm to determine when scaling should occur are dependent on the floating-point arithmetic being used. For IEEE format single and double precision, these values are given in Table 9.1. These constants may all be set correctly using the intrinsic functions *SCALE* and *EPSILON*. The values given ensure that

1. if the computed value of the norm is representable, then it is computed without overflow or underflow;

2. the returned results have known error bounds ([see 14, p. 19] for details).

Optimally, we would like to use a hybrid algorithm in order to obtain the best of both worlds: the naive loop for efficiency in the majority of cases and Blue's algorithm when we have difficult data. However, since we are assuming that IEEE exception handling is not available, we choose to trade speed for accuracy and reliability and use Blue's algorithm in all cases.

9.2.2   Kahan's IEEE Euclidean Norm Algorithm

With access to the Fortran IEEE intrinsic modules, an elegant algorithm[1] is now available that is not only accurate, thanks to compensated summation, but also,

---

[1]Private communication from W. Kahan, April, 2012.

Table 9.2. *Values of the constants in Kahan's algorithm using environmental parameters.*

ϵ	EPSILON(kind)	
τ^2	TINY(kind)	
ω^2	HUGE(kind)	
Precision	Single	Double
$h_l = \omega$	2^{64}	2^{512}
$h_u = (\epsilon\tau)^{-1}$	2^{86}	2^{563}
$t_l = \sqrt{\epsilon}/\omega$	2^{-76}	2^{-538}
$t_u = \tau/\epsilon$	2^{-40}	2^{-459}

by scaling, avoids unnecessary overflows and underflows. Furthermore, it is mathematically correct in that if any element of input array *x(1:(n−1)*incx+1:incx)* is an IEEE infinity value, then the method will return the machine representation of positive infinity (*+Inf*) for the appropriate precision and, if none of the elements are infinite but one or more are NaNs, then a NaN is returned.

Since the normal case (no exceptions) is the most likely and because the tests made on each element of the input vector slow down the process, we use the naive loop (Method 4 above) by default and, only if an arithmetic exception is thrown, do we call on Kahan's algorithm. If explicitly required, Kahan's method may be called directly by using the function name *dnrm2kc(...)* with the same parameters as *dnrm2*. In the pseudocode fragment (Figure 9.3), *t_l, t_u, h_l, h_u* are the parameters t_l, t_u, h_l, h_u appearing in Table 9.2.

9.3 Using the IEEE Features from Fortran

We need to be able to set and test the underflow and overflow flags during the computation of the norm so that we can detect whether Kahan's algorithm is required. The final result can overflow only if it is not representable. We also want to set the inexact flag explicitly if this signals during the calculation.

On entry to the program unit, access is provided to a local set of signal flags which are initialized to quiet. On return to the caller unit the flags signaling are the union of those signaling just prior to the call being made and those signaling on exit from the callee. Thus exceptional conditions are propagated back through the call chain.

All modes (halting, rounding, underflow) are inherited by the callee and reset to their original state on exit. Therefore, we need to set up the environment to detect whether the simple loop (Method 4 above) causes underflow or overflow. First, we ensure that the halting mode is set to allow computation to continue if either of these exceptions occur, and we set the relevant exception flags to *.FALSE.*. We do this using the subroutine call as shown in Listing 9.1.

Figure 9.3. *Pseudocode for Kahan's IEEE Algorithm.*

```
dnrm2 = 0; ahat = 0; s = 0; big = h_l/sqrt(n)
DO i = 1, (n-1)*incx+1,incx
    if (x(i) does not test as finite) then
        if (x(i) is a NaN) then
            s = quiet NaN
            cycle ! on i loop
        else ! Know result is Infinity
            dnrm2 = +Infinity; return
        end if
    else
! NaN will propagate here providing it is not a signalling NaN
        ahat = MAX(ahat, abs(x(i)))
        if (ahat >= big) cycle ! on i loop
! compensated summation
        s = s + x(i)*x(i)
        t = dnrm2
        dnrm2 = t + s
        s = (t - dnrm2) + s
    end if
end DO i loop
! Filter NaNs
if (s is a NaN) then
    dnrm2 = s; return
end if
! Set scaling factors if required
if (ahat >= big) then
    sc = t_l
else if (ahat <= t_u) then
    sc = h_u
else ! Normal case - no scaling
    dnrm2 = sqrt(dnrm2) ; return
end if
! Scaling required, still use compensated summation
dnrm2 = 0; s = 0
DO i = 1, (n-1)*incx+1,incx
    s = s + (x(i)*sc)*(x(i)*sc)
    t = dnrm2
    dnrm2 = t + s
    s = (t - dnrm2) + s
end DO i loop
! Might still overflow -- but this is unavoidable
dnrm2 = sqrt(dnrm2)/sc
return
```

Listing 9.1. *Initializing halting modes.*

```
!! This code extract is part of the accompanying software
!! that supports Chapter 9. It may be found in the file
!! dnrm2_ieee.f90
!!
    CALL IEEE_SET_HALTING_MODE(IEEE_ALL, .FALSE.)
```

This overrides any other halting modes that may have been set on entry. Note that *IEEE_ALL* is a predefined array, available from the *IEEE_EXCEPTIONS* module, whose entries are all the exception flags.

Having attempted to compute the norm using the simple loop, we need to use Kahan's algorithm if either of the underflow or overflow flags are signaling. Before this subsequent call takes place, we need to clear any flags that may have been signaling as a result of executing the simple loop.

Listing 9.2. *Saving and resetting flags before the call to Kahan's algorithm.*

```
!! This code extract is part of the accompanying software
!! that supports Chapter 9. It may be found in the file
!! dnrm2_ieee.f90
!!
! Retrieve the underflow and overflow status flags. If
! either of these are signaling then we have a genuine
! scaling problem and we call Kahan's algorithm.
        CALL IEEE_GET_FLAG(IEEE_OVERFLOW , signal(overflow))
        CALL IEEE_GET_FLAG(IEEE_UNDERFLOW , signal(underflow))
        IF (signal(overflow) .OR. signal(underflow) .OR. &
            IEEE_IS_NAN(norm) .OR. .NOT. IEEE_IS_FINITE(norm)) THEN
! If the input vector contained NaNs and no Infs then the
! value of norm is a NaN.
! If there were any Infs and some NaNs, then norm will also be a NaN.
! So we must scan the data again if norm is a NaN.

! The flags ieee_overflow, ieee_underflow also cause this scan.
! Reset flags -- any previously set were only being used
! to steer the computation internally
        signal( (/overflow,underflow,inexact/) ) = .FALSE.
        CALL IEEE_SET_FLAG(IEEE_OVERFLOW , .FALSE.)
        CALL IEEE_SET_FLAG(IEEE_UNDERFLOW , .FALSE.)
        CALL IEEE_SET_FLAG(IEEE_INEXACT , .FALSE.)
        norm = dnrm2kc(n, x, incx)
```

In order to ensure that it is clear when an overflow really occurred during the calculation, we set the return value of the norm to *+Inf* when Kahan's algorithm determines that the final value is too large to be represented.

Listing 9.3. *Returning infinity on genuine overflow.*

```
!! This code extract is part of the accompanying software
!! that supports Chapter 9. It may be found in the file
!! dnrm2_ieee.f90
!!
        norm = IEEE_VALUE(norm, IEEE_POSITIVE_INF)
```

Here *IEEE_VALUE* returns the representation of positive infinity for the floating-point kind signified by the type of *norm*. In addition we set both the overflow and inexact flags to true so that we can update the state we inherited from the caller. Finally we note that for the special case of n equals 1 we just return the absolute value of *x(1)*. The invalid input parameter, *INCX* negative, returns immediately after setting the exception flag *IEEE_INVALID*.

We also need to react correctly if the input vector contains either NaNs or infinite values while minimizing the impact on the execution time for data that uses the simple loop. Two types of NaN are defined: quiet NaN (qNaN) and signaling NaN (sNaN). Typically NaNs are quiet and the IEEE arithmetic model allows them to propagate through the computation without setting either the invalid or the inexact flags. Signaling NaNs are rarely used in practice although some compilers initialize all user-declared variables to sNaN in order to detect the use of unassigned variables at run time, which is generally considered to be a programming error.

Either an infinite value in the input vector or an overflow caused by the value of $(\sum x_i^2)^{1/2}$ exceeding $HUGE(zero)$, where the x_i are in-range floating-point values, will cause the value of $norm$ to be returned as $+Inf$. However, there is a subtle difference between them. In the case of an infinite value in the input vector the overflow flag may NOT be set because the calculation is deemed to be exact; for example, mathematically $\infty \times x = \infty$ when x is a finite positive number.

Thus on exit from the simple loop we have four possible situations:

1. The result returned is a NaN: this implies that there were NaNs in the input vector. However, we do not know whether there were infinite values as well as NaNs in the data, so we need to rescan the input vector.

2. The overflow or underflow flag is signaling: this implies that the input vector contained normal floating-point values, but Kahan's algorithm is required for a reliable result. This calculation can still cause an overflow but not an underflow.

3. The overflow and underflow flags are not signaling but the value returned is $+Inf$: this implies that there were infinity values in the input vector but no NaNs.

4. None of the three conditions above hold: this implies that the simple loop was sufficient.

Inserted after the simple loop, the following code implements this decision process.

Listing 9.4. *Dealing with NaNs in the input vector.*

```
!! This code extract is part of the accompanying software
!! that supports Chapter 9. It may be found in the file
!! dnrm2_ieee.f90
!!
! If any component is infinite, the result is infinite.
! So just return with a positive infinite result.
            IF (.NOT. IEEE_IS_FINITE(x(i))) THEN
! Either Inf or NaN can trigger a .TRUE. above.
! If the result was an Inf, X(I) will not be a NaN.
               IF (IEEE_IS_NAN(x(i))) THEN
                  s = IEEE_VALUE(s, IEEE_QUIET_NAN)
! Even though a NaN was seen there may still be Infs.
                  CYCLE
               ELSE
! Now we know the result is an Inf; set value and quit.
                  y = IEEE_VALUE(y, IEEE_POSITIVE_INF)
```

```
                    EXIT block
                 END IF
              ELSE
...
```

The Fortran standard supports a subset of the features described in the IEEE floating-point standard. Even software that adheres to this subset will only perform successfully if the processor executing the code supports these features. Furthermore, processors may choose not to implement particular elements because they result in an unacceptable run-time performance, for example. Given that the reason for providing access to IEEE arithmetic is to allow programmers to construct more reliable, portable software, it is a challenge to write software using the IEEE modules that is portable without the assurance that each compiler vendor has implemented the required support.

The *IEEE_FEATURES* module defines a set of named constants, each corresponding to a particular feature. If a named constant is accessible via a USE statement, then the corresponding feature must be available for at least one kind of real. These names can be thought of as compiler directives in that if a feature is not available, use of the associated named constant will cause compilation to fail. For example, if the statement

```
 USE, INTRINSIC :: IEEE_FEATURES , ONLY: IEEE_DIVIDE , IEEE_SQRT
```

appears, then the compilation phase will abort if either the floating-point divide or the square root intrinsic is not implemented to the accuracy defined by the IEEE standard.

If the modules *IEEE_ARITHMETIC* and *IEEE_EXCEPTIONS* are available at all, we can assume that all the types, named constants, and module procedures specified in the Fortran standard are accessible even though the target processor may not support all the features. This ensures that software which may potentially use any of these facilities will always compile and link. In the case of an unsupported feature, the relevant support inquiry function is guaranteed to return .FALSE.; attempting to call any associated module procedures under these circumstances will render the software nonstandard conforming, and the effect will be processor dependent. There is no requirement on the compiler to issue even a warning.

When considering portability issues, three situations can occur:

1. The processor does not support IEEE arithmetic, or none of the IEEE intrinsic modules are implemented by the compiler.

2. The processor partially supports IEEE arithmetic, whence either one or both of the modules *IEEE_ARITHMETIC* and *IEEE_EXCEPTIONS* are available along with *IEEE_FEATURES*.

3. The processor is fully compliant as far as the Fortran standard is concerned.

For situation 1 above any mention of the intrinsic IEEE modules will cause the compilation to fail. In these circumstances we need to use the implementation of Blue's algorithm, *dnrm2_blue*, from the module *dnrm2_support*. But there are drawbacks:

1. Any NaN in the input x vector will not be detected and this may cause the execution to be aborted.

2. Any infinite values in the input will not be detected and this may cause the execution to be aborted.

3. If the final mathematical result overflows, the returned result is truncated at the largest floating-point value, *HUGE(zero)*. This often involves a large relative error in the result, and that value must, therefore, be considered as equivalent to an overflow of the mathematical result.

4. As there are no floating-point divides in the algorithm, no consideration need be given to the divide-by-zero exception. For other applications, lack of support for this event may prove a serious hindrance and preclude using stubs.

5. Blue's algorithm has tests in the inner loop that may hamper efficiency, but at least the data is accessed only once.

The Fortran standard suggests two different ways of dealing with a partial IEEE implementation. First, we can force a situation close to that used when no support is available in that we can use *IEEE_FEATURES* to trigger a compilation error if any of the features required by the software are not supported. Thus adding

```
USE , INTRINSIC :: IEEE_FEATURES , ONLY: IEEE_DIVIDE , IEEE_SQRT ,&
    IEEE_DATATYPE , IEEE_HALTING , IEEE_INEXACT_FLAG , IEEE_INF ,&
    IEEE_INVALID_FLAG , IEEE_NAN , IEEE_UNDERFLOW_FLAG
  ...
```

to the body of *dnrm2* will cause the compilation to fail should any of the features be unavailable. Under these circumstances it would again be necessary to use Blue's algorithm from module *dnrm2_support* to ensure both successful compilation and linking.

Although we do not use any of the rounding facilities in the present code, it could be argued that a reasonable approach to portability would be to require the level of conformance provided by *IEEE_SUPPORT_STANDARD*. We note that this does not include underflow control, although there is support for denormalized numbers.

We provide a full implementation of the Fortran 2003 standard specifications for nonintrinsic versions of *IEEE_ARITHMETIC*, *IEEE_EXCEPTIONS*, and *IEEE_FEATURES*. These modules are targeted for use on Intel and AMD x86 architectures, primarily with the *gfortran* compiler [33]. The interface to the machine instructions and register flags use the C interoperability standard (see Chapter 10) to call C functions. These can be found in the source code file *c_control.c*; for the location of codes see Chapter 20.

EXERCISE 9.1. *The level-2 BLAS code DTRSV (see Dongarra et al. [22] for details) solves a system of linear equations $Ax = y$, where A is upper or lower triangular. There is no testing in this routine for division by zero or overflow. Discuss how either a zero diagonal term or an overflow can be detected following the call to DTRSV.*

EXERCISE 9.2. *Use the IEEE_ARITHMETIC intrinsic module and write an efficient and reliable Fortran function that computes the $l_p, 1 \leq p < \infty$, norm of a 2-vector, $q = [x, y]$. This norm is $||q||_p = (|x|^p + |y|^p)^{1/p}$.*

EXERCISE 9.3. *Modify the quicksort algorithm of Chapter 6 so that NaN values are ignored in the sorting. All such values should be moved to the highest indexed end of the sorted list. The flag IEEE_INVALID should be set so that the calling program unit can use this to detect that the input list contains a NaN.*

9.4 Denormalized Numbers and Underflow Modes

The IEEE standard defines two underflow modes, *abrupt* and *gradual*. Abrupt underflow signals whenever the result of an arithmetic operation generates a value that is less than *TINY(x)* in magnitude. In the case when the halting mode is set to continue, the result is set to zero and the inexact flag is set to signaling. Effectively, the floating-point system does not recognize any numbers in the interval $(-v, +v)$ where $v = TINY(x)$.

To provide a more gradual approach to zero, the IEEE standard defines a set of denormalized or subnormal numbers, *denormals*, represented by setting the biased exponent to zero and interpreting the mantissa as a value lying in the range $(0, 1)$, rather than $[1, 2)$ as is the case for normalized numbers; i.e., for denormals there is no hidden bit. Now increasing the number of leading zeros in the mantissa extends the range of the exponent while, at the same time, decreasing the number of bits available to represent the fractional part. Thus in each range $[2^e, 2^{e+1})$, where e is a normal exponent, there are 2^t representable numbers where t is the number of bits in the mantissa (excluding the hidden bit). For denormalized numbers in the range $[2^{emin-d}, 2^{emin-d+1})$, $d = 1, \ldots, t$, there are 2^{t-d} representable numbers. As a side effect of this the relative spacing of denormals increases as the exponent increases in magnitude; i.e., precision decreases from $t + 1$ bits for normalized numbers to a single bit for the exponent $(emin - t)$.

Not all processors may support gradual underflow, and the module function call *IEEE_SUPPORT_UNDERFLOW_CONTROL(x)* may be used to enquire whether this facility is supported, on a particular platform, for reals of *KIND(x)*.

Gradual underflow may be selected using

```
      gradual = .TRUE.
      CALL IEEE_SET_UNDERFLOW_MODE(gradual)
```

Setting *gradual* to **.FALSE.** would select abrupt underflow.

The currently active underflow mode may be obtained using

```
CALL IEEE_GET_UNDERFLOW_MODE(gradual)
```

which sets *gradual* to true, if gradual underflow is set, and false if abrupt underflow is being used.

Neither of these two routines should be called unless the function *IEEE_SUPPORT_UNDERFLOW_CONTROL* returns true for the desired real type. We note that if we choose to ignore this, then the compiler is not required to flag an error and the behavior of the program is compiler dependent.

A gradual underflow is signaled when an arithmetic operation or intrinsic function invocation results in a denormalized number which is not exact within the precision available. While both the underflow and inexact flags signal, we note that the result need **NOT** be zero.

We illustrate this behavior with two small examples; in both cases all real variables and constants are assumed to be of the same precision and t is set to the number of bits in the mantissa for this precision, i.e., $DIGITS(x)-1$. We also assume that the rounding mode is set to *NEAREST* and the halting mode for underflow is set to continue.

```
! Example 1
  x = TINY(x)
! t has been set to DIGITS(x)-1
  DO i = 1, t
    x = x/two
  END DO

  CALL IEEE_GET_FLAG(IEEE_UNDERFLOW , flag)
  PRINT *,'x = ',x, ' underflow flag = ', flag
  x = x/two
  CALL IEEE_GET_FLAG(IEEE_UNDERFLOW , flag)
  PRINT *,'x = ',x, ' underflow flag = ', flag
```

For single precision this gives

```
x =    1.4012985E-45  underflow flag =  F
x =    0.0000000  underflow flag =  T
```

The value of x is initialized to the normal number 2^{emin} and each division in the loop generates a denormal whose exact value is 2^{emin-i}. On exit from the loop x represents the smallest denormal representable in that precision and all the calculations that have taken place are exact. Hence no underflow exception occurs. The final divide by the value two generates an underflow exception since the result is too small to be represented even by a denormalized value; this results in a value of zero. Note also that underflow will occur whatever the rounding mode; for *IEEE_TO_ZERO* and *IEEE_NEAREST* the final divide will result in the value zero while *IEEE_DOWN* and *IEEE_UP* will result in the smallest denormalized number.

```
! Example 2
  x = IEEE_NEXT_AFTER(TINY(x), two)
  x = x/two
  CALL IEEE_GET_FLAG(IEEE_UNDERFLOW , flag)
  PRINT *,'x = ',x, ' underflow flag = ', flag
```

gives

```
x =     5.8774718E-39   underflow flag =   T
```

Now x is initialized to the second smallest normal number $2^{emin-1}(1+2^{-t+1})$ which has a mantissa whose bits are all zero apart from the least significant bit. Division by two in this case generates a denormalized value, and the least significant bit is lost in the resulting right shift of the mantissa. It is the generation of the inexactness of the result that triggers the underflow exception rather than the magnitude of the number.

EXERCISE 9.4. *Repeat Example* 2 *above but use the third smallest normal number. Is the underflow flag now set? Explain your result.*

Chapter 10

Interoperability with C

Synopsis:

▶ *Mixed Fortran and C programming history*

▶ *The iso_c_binding intrinsic module*

▶ *Traps for the unwary*

▶ *Calling by name or pointer reference*

▶ *Storage arrangement for two-dimensional arrays*

▶ *Sharing storage and global data*

▶ *C function pointers used from Fortran*

▶ *Calling C for operating system commands*

▶ *Exercises*

10.1 Introduction

Some of the most important reasons for using Fortran as a programming language are its wide availability, its portability, and the extensive software base and libraries of routines that are available as efficient building blocks for applications.

For many years C and C++ programmers have sought to tap into this wealth of software by calling the Fortran code directly rather than going through the error-prone and expensive task of translating it. This comment also holds in the opposite direction. Fortran programmers often need to call C or C++ routines that interface to applications or other available software, including the operating system. Our examples demonstrate aspects of the interoperation of Fortran and C and are not directly applicable to C++ or other target languages.

For these reasons much effort has been expended to make C and Fortran compilers, often from different providers, interoperate and there has been a long and dismal history of problems associated with this aspect of mixed language programming. Previous to Fortran 2003 the standard was completely silent about how to interoperate with C and programmers were forced to develop *ad hoc* methods for calling the alternate language. The most common problems prior to Fortran 2003 include the following:

1. *Name mangling*: Unlike C compilers, where user-defined names are generally translated into the compiled code without change, most Fortran compilers alter the names of global entities like program unit and **COMMON** block names. This internal name mangling usually takes the form of appending underscores to the front and/or end of a name and forcing the letter in the name into lower- or uppercase. Moreover, different Fortran compilers might generate different name transformations even under the same operating system.

   Thus, to call a Fortran routine *fortSub*, the name used in calling a C function may need to be *_fortsub* or *_FORTSUB_*, with the exact name used entirely dependent on the Fortran compiler being used.

   Making calls in the other direction is just as fraught with problems and generally requires a set of C wrapper routines, whose names are the Fortran compiler-dependent mangled versions of the original C names! This state of affairs is hardly compatible with portability.

2. *Access to global data*: An example of this would be variables stored in Fortran **COMMON** blocks.

3. *Array storage*: Fortran requires two-dimensional arrays to be stored in column major order, while C expects row major storage. A similar incompatibility exists for arrays of dimension greater than two (see also Chapter 18).

4. *Hidden arguments*: Often, when passing character data between C and Fortran, the system would add extra, hidden, length arguments to the Fortran parameter list as seen from C. Therefore,

```
SUBROUTINE example(char, string)
   CHARACTER char
   CHARACTER*5 string
   ...
```

became

```
extern void example_(char* a, char* b, int len_a, int len_b)
```

There are features of one language that have no counterpart in the other. For example, allocatable arrays in Fortran seem similar to their use in C but have very different levels of functionality. For another example, pointers in the two languages are different.

The Fortran 2003 standard, via an intrinsic module, provides a standard mechanism for interoperating between a matched pair of Fortran and C compilers.

The intrinsic module, *iso_c_binding*, contains named constants, derived types, and module procedures that support mixed language programming subject to restrictions that are necessary due to inherent incompatibilities between the two languages.

Data of a particular type may be shared provided that both systems represent and manipulate the data in the same way; for example, both compilers could implement real and double precision floating-point arithmetic according to the IEEE standard. Intrinsic types for which this is true are termed *interoperable*, and the *iso_c_binding* module provides a set of named constants of type default integer containing *kind* parameter information. For each C real, integer, double, complex, logical, and character type the corresponding named constant is set to either the positive value for the interoperating Fortran kind of the same intrinsic type or a negative value if interoperability is not possible. Both Metcalf, Reid, and Cohen [65, p. 250] and Adams et al. [4, p. 565] provide tables detailing all the available constants and type names.

Note that there may be traps for the unwary when a Fortran 2003 compatible compiler is used on mixed Fortran and C code that was written to exploit old platform-dependent mechanisms. We have encountered examples where the combination of a new compiler and *ad hoc* methods cause unexpected run-time errors.

To illustrate some practical aspects of mixing C and Fortran code we begin by looking at calling the BLAS routine *saxpy* [56] from a C program. At the outset we have two choices. Either we change the source code of the original BLAS routine to make it directly callable by C or we provide a Fortran communication routine to do the job.

The first choice has the advantages of using one routine call instead of two and preserving the name by which the function will be invoked from C. But it has two major disadvantages. First, we need access to the Fortran source, and second, we will be generating a "special" version of the function that will possibly be out of step with future releases of the Fortran library.

Therefore, as a general rule, we opt for the second choice, a communication or wrapper routine—we agree to live with the slight inconvenience of a name difference on the C side—and two routine calls. In this case the communication routine has the following form.

Listing 10.1. *Fortran wrapper for BLAS routine saxpy.*

```
!! This code extract is part of the accompanying software
!! that supports Chapter 10. It may be found in the file
!! CInterSaxpy.f90
!!
    SUBROUTINE c_saxpy(n, sa, sx, incx, sy, incy) &
            BIND (C, NAME='C_saxpy')
      USE, INTRINSIC :: iso_c_binding , ONLY: c_int , c_float
      INTEGER (c_int), INTENT (IN) :: n, incx, incy
      REAL (c_float), INTENT (IN) :: sa, sx(*)
      REAL (c_float), INTENT (INOUT) :: sy(*)

      CALL saxpy(n, sa, sx, incx, sy, incy)
    END SUBROUTINE c_saxpy
```

The features to note are as follows:

1. We have added the **BIND(...)** attribute to the subroutine declaration. This specifies that the routine is to be interoperable from C, and it provides the name to be used when it is invoked from C code. If a name is provided, it is case sensitive. If no name is provided, it will default to the lowercase version of the Fortran name. This feature is aimed at obviating the name mangling problem. Any name specified which differs from the default is solely for use from C; i.e., it cannot be used as an alternative name from Fortran. In addition, the C name cannot be the same as any other global name appearing in the Fortran software; thus, we cannot use BIND(C, NAME='saxpy') in this example.

2. The kinds of the parameters to *c_saxpy* have been defined as **c_int** and **c_float**. This is for both robustness and documentation purposes. We are assuming that the **INTEGER** and **int**, and the **REAL** and **float**, data types will interoperate. If this is not the case, there will be a type mismatch in the parameters across the call to *C_saxpy*. Of course the compiler is under no obligation to report actual and dummy argument mismatches of this kind, although many now do. In addition, if the compiler does not support interoperability for a particular type (it is only obliged to support **int**), then the kind value will be set to −1, and this should also be reported by the compiler when attempting compilation.

The argument definitions in the communication routine define the following corresponding C prototype definition.

Listing 10.2. *C Prototype for BLAS routine saxpy.*

```
// This code extract is part of the accompanying software
// that supports Chapter 10. It may be found in the file
// saxpy_main.c
//
void C_saxpy(int *n, float *sa, float sx[], int *incx,
             float sy[], int *incy);
```

Here all parameters, by default, are passed by reference, i.e., a pointer to an object of the defined type. However, we do have some further control over the way we define the interface.

For example, the arguments *n, sa, incx,* and *incy* are all INTENT(IN) and it would be more natural for them to be passed by value from C. The **VALUE** attribute allows such a calling sequence to be generated as follows.

Listing 10.3. *Fortran wrapper for BLAS routine saxpy using call by value.*

```
!! This code extract is part of the accompanying software
!! that supports Chapter 10. It may be found in the file
!! CInterSaxpy.f90
!!
   SUBROUTINE c_val_saxpy(n, sa, sx, incx, sy, incy)
            BIND (C, NAME='C_val_saxpy')
      USE, INTRINSIC :: iso_c_binding, ONLY: c_int, c_float
      INTEGER (c_int), INTENT (IN), VALUE :: n, incx, incy
```

```
      REAL (c_float), INTENT (IN), VALUE :: sa
      REAL (c_float), INTENT (IN) :: sx(*)
      REAL (c_float), INTENT (INOUT) :: sy(*)

      CALL saxpy(n, sa, sx, incx, sy, incy)
    END SUBROUTINE c_val_saxpy
```

This has a matching C prototype function of the following form.

Listing 10.4. *C Prototype for pass by value BLAS routine saxpy.*

```
// This code extract is part of the accompanying software
// that supports Chapter 10. It may be found in the file
// saxpy_main.c
//
void C_val_saxpy(int n, float sa, float sx[], int incx,
          float sy[], int incy);
```

Only simple variables are allowed to have the **VALUE** attribute. Thus, even though its contents are not changed during the execution of the routine, the C array *sx[]* cannot be made a Fortran **VALUE** parameter.

Thus when calling a C function from Fortran or a Fortran procedure from C, there should be an interoperable Fortran procedure interface with the BIND(...) specification and a matching C prototype definition.

10.2   Characters and Two-Dimensional Arrays

To illustrate the passing of characters and two- (or higher-) dimensional arrays we use the Level 3 BLAS routine *dgemm* as an example. As with *saxpy* above, we define a simple communication routine *c_dgemm*:

Listing 10.5. *Fortran wrapper for BLAS routine dgemm.*

```
!! This code extract is part of the accompanying software
!! that supports Chapter 10. It may be found in the file
!! dgemm.f
!!
    SUBROUTINE c_dgemm(transa,transb,m,n,k,alpha,a,lda,b,
  +    ldb,beta,c,ldc)  bind(c,name='C_dgemm')
    USE, INTRINSIC :: iso_c_binding, ONLY : c_char, c_int, c_double
    CHARACTER (c_char), INTENT (IN) :: transa, transb
    INTEGER (c_int), INTENT (IN) :: m, n, k, lda, ldb, ldc
    REAL (c_double), INTENT (IN) :: alpha, beta, a(lda,*), b(ldb,*)
    REAL (c_double), INTENT (INOUT) :: c(ldc,*)

    CALL dgemm(transa,transb,m,n,k,alpha,a,lda,b,ldb,beta,c,ldc)
    END SUBROUTINE c_dgemm
```

This has a matching C prototype function of the following form.

Listing 10.6. *C prototype for BLAS routine dgemm.*

```
// This code extract is part of the accompanying software
// that supports Chapter 10. It may be found in the file
// dgemm_main.c
```

```
//
void C_dgemm(char* transa, char* transb, int* m, int* n,  int* k,
        double* alpha, double a[][LDA], int* lda, double b[][LDB],
        int* ldb, double* beta, double c[][LDC], int* ldc);
```

Here the integer and double precision scalar arguments are dealt with in the same way as with the *c_saxpy* routine. Fortran character parameters of length 1 interoperate with the C **char** type. A character dummy argument of length greater than 1 is not interoperable; only a scalar or array declared as CHARACTER(LEN=1) is interoperable.

However, the standard does allow for an actual character argument of length greater than 1 to be used when the dummy argument is an array of CHARACTER(LEN=1). When processing character strings that have been passed from C to Fortran or conversely, care needs to be taken to ensure that the terminating null character expected or provided by C is processed appropriately. Failure to do so might to lead to fatal run-time errors, for example, attempting to use *strcpy* to copy a nonterminated string obtained as an argument from Fortran.

We illustrate these features in the subroutine *copy_string* below which shows how we may convert between Fortran and C strings. When calling the routine, the actual argument used for *fstring* may be a CHARACTER(LEN=1) array or a character variable with length greater than one. This is a special exception to the usual rules of argument association and is specifically designed to make the use of character strings easier across the Fortran/C interface. In both cases it is essential that the actual argument is declared large enough to accommodate the final result.

Listing 10.7. *C to/from Fortran string converter.*

```
!! This code extract is part of the accompanying software
!! that supports Chapter 10. It may be found in the file
!! charplay.f90
!!
  SUBROUTINE copy_string(cstring, fstring, clen, ftoc) BIND(C)
  USE, INTRINSIC :: iso_c_binding, ONLY: c_char, c_int, c_null_char
  CHARACTER (c_char), INTENT(INOUT) :: cstring(*), fstring(*)
  INTEGER (c_int), INTENT(INOUT) :: clen
  INTEGER (c_int), INTENT(IN) :: ftoc

! If ftoc is set to 1 then converts a Fortran string of length clen
! stored in fstring into a C string stored in cstring. This contains
! the same characters but is terminated by the null character.

! If ftoc is set to 0 then converts a C string stored in cstring
! into a Fortran string stored in fstring. This contains the same
! characters but is NOT terminated by the null character. clen is
! set to the clength of the copied string

  IF (ftoc == 1) THEN
    cstring(1:clen) = fstring(1:clen)
    cstring(clen+1) = c_null_char
  ELSE
    clen = 0
```

```
! The DO WHILE construct has been deprecated :-(
   DO
      IF (cstring(clen+1) == c_null_char) EXIT ! for a WHILE!
      clen = clen+1
      fstring(clen) = cstring(clen)
   END DO
END IF

END SUBROUTINE copy_string
```

The passing of two-dimensional arrays requires alertness from the programmer since Fortran and C store the elements of multidimensional arrays in transposed order in memory. Interoperability for two-dimensional arrays requires compatible C and Fortran array declarations to ensure that the required ordering is preserved. Thus an array declared in Fortran as being of size $(5, 2)$ would need to be declared $[2][5]$ in C. The effect of this is to transpose the array indices used to access specific data when switching languages.

Returning to *dgemm*, suppose we wish to compute $3 * A * B' + 2 * C$, where A and B are 5×2 and C is 5×5. If the Fortran contents of A are to be

$$\begin{pmatrix} 1 & 6 \\ 2 & 7 \\ 3 & 8 \\ 4 & 8 \\ 5 & 10 \end{pmatrix},$$

the array A would need to be declared $a[2][5]$ in the C calling code and the data input as

$$\begin{pmatrix} 1 & 2 & 3 & 4 & 5 \\ 6 & 7 & 8 & 9 & 10 \end{pmatrix}.$$

The implicit redimensioning of the data in Fortran then provides the correct sequence of contiguous elements for *dgemm* to operate on. For more details see the sample driver in *dgemm_main.c*.

We emphasize that a two-dimensional Fortran array is *NOT* interoperable with a C array of pointers to one-dimensional arrays, i.e., `double *a[LDA]`. To make this construction interoperable we need to treat it as an array of type *c_ptr* and use the procedure *c_f_pointer* from the *iso_c_binding* module to access the individual one-dimensional arrays. The Fortran code to do this is of the following form:

```
!! This code extract is part of the accompanying software
!! that supports Chapter 10. It may be found in the file
!! PtrArray.f90
!!
     SUBROUTINE PtrArray(cptr, ncptr, sizes)   &
             BIND(C, NAME='PtrArray')
! Code to illustrate the interoperability of a C array
! of pointers to one-dimensional arrays. cptr is the array
! of ncptr pointers. The length of the array pointed at by
! cptr(i) is sizes(i)
```

```
      USE, INTRINSIC :: iso_c_binding, ONLY : c_int, c_ptr,  &
         c_double, c_f_pointer

      INTEGER(c_int), INTENT(IN) :: ncptr
      INTEGER(c_int), INTENT(IN) :: sizes(ncptr)
      TYPE(c_ptr) :: cptr(ncptr)
      TYPE rows
         REAL(c_double), DIMENSION(:), POINTER :: r
      END TYPE rows
      TYPE(rows),DIMENSION(ncptr) :: carray

         DO i = 1, ncptr
! carray(i)%r will contain the data from the array pointed at
! by cptr(i).
            ALLOCATE(carray(i)%r(1:sizes(i)))
            CALL c_f_pointer(cptr(i), carray(i)%r, (/sizes(i)/))
         END DO
...
```

10.3   Sharing Data Structures and Global Data

C structs and Fortran derived types can interoperate provided the components are themselves interoperable. The use of the **BIND** attribute ensures that components are stored in memory in a way that is compatible for both C and Fortran.

As a simple example we consider a type declaration for the vertex of a two-dimensional polygon. This consists of an ordered pair of real values and an index number

```
TYPE, BIND(C, NAME='Point') :: point
  REAL(c_float) :: x
  REAL(c_float) :: y
  INTEGER(c_int) :: vertexNo
END TYPE point
```

and this derived type then interoperates with the C struct

```
struct Point{
  float *x, *y;
  int *vertexNo;
}
```

The above definitions allow data to be read and written from both languages. A lengthy example of an interoperable derived type is used in Chapter 11 to define a sparse matrix operator, .ip., for solving linear systems. The normal rules apply regarding the global name for a particular type definition; thus for structs of type *Point* the **NAME** specifier is necessary since the default would be to translate the given type name completely into lowercase.

Other global data may be made available either via **COMMON** blocks or through module variables. Data in a named **COMMON** block can be made to interoperate with a C struct which has the same name as the binding label associated with the **COMMON** block. Every item in the **COMMON** block must be interoperable and, if one occurrence of a **COMMON** block has the **BIND** attribute, then all occurrences must have the same attribute. For example,

```
      INTEGER(c_int) :: k
      REAL(c_float) :: f
      COMMON /cblock/ k, f
      BIND(C) :: /cblock/
```

interoperates with

```
struct cblock {
   int *i;
   float *r;
}
```

Global data may also be shared through module variables. Thus

```
      MODULE test
      REAL (c_float), bind(C, NAME='valfrommodule') :: x
      ...
      ...
      END MODULE test
```

associates the variable x with a variable named *valfrommodule* in the associated C code. Changes to a variable in one language will alter the corresponding variable in the other; in most cases the two variables will share the same memory address, although this method of implementation is not mandated by the Fortran standard.

10.4   Function Pointers

Here we wish to call a Fortran routine from C where one of the arguments is a function and the actual function to be used is written in C. An example of this would be a call from C to a Fortran quadrature routine where the function being passed defines the integrand and is written in C.

To do this we create a wrapper routine in Fortran where the external function parameter is replaced by a C procedure pointer (actually, just the address of the C function). We then use the intrinsic function *c_f_procpointer* from the *iso_c_binding* intrinsic module to associate a Fortran procedure pointer with the target of the C function pointer. This Fortran procedure pointer can then either be used as an external argument passed to the quadrature routine, or called directly from Fortran.

The two following code segments illustrate the detail.

Listing 10.8. *Passing a C function to a Fortran routine.*

```
!! This code extract is part of the accompanying software
!! that supports Chapter 10. It may be found in the file
!! c_sam.f90
!!
REAL FUNCTION c_sam(fptr, x) BIND(C)
! Pass a function defined in C to a Fortran
! function where it is used and the result
! passed back to the calling C code
!
```

```fortran
! fptr is the C address of function which
!       is interoperable.
! x is the value to be used for evaluation
USE, INTRINSIC :: iso_c_binding, ONLY: c_float, &
  c_funptr, c_f_procpointer
! Provide interface for a function that is
! interoperable with the C procedure pointed
! at by fptr.

INTERFACE
  REAL FUNCTION f(x)
  REAL :: x
  END FUNCTION
END INTERFACE

TYPE(c_funptr), VALUE :: fptr
REAL(c_float) :: x
PROCEDURE(f), POINTER :: fun

! Associate a Fortran procedure pointer with the target
! of a C function pointer
  CALL c_f_procpointer(fptr, fun)

! Finally we can call the function!
  c_sam = fun(x)
END FUNCTION
```

Listing 10.9. *Calling C code.*

```c
// This code extract is part of the accompanying software
// that supports Chapter 10. It may be found in the file
// funptrs.c
//
#include <stdio.h>

float g (float*);
float h (float*);
float c_sam (float(*fun)(float*), float*);

int main()
{
  float (*fp)(float*);
  float x, y;

  fp = g;
  x = (float) 5.0;

  if (c_sam(fp, &x) == (float) 25.0) {
    printf("Test passed for function g\n");
  }
  else {
    printf("Test failed for function g: expected %f got %f\n",
      (float) 25.0, c_sam(fp, &x));
  }

  fp = h;
  x = (float) 6.0;
```

```
  if (c_sam(fp, &x) == (float) 216.0) {
    printf("Test passed for function h\n");
  }
  else {
    printf("Test failed for function h: expected %f got %f\n",
      (float) 216.0, c_sam(fp, &x));
  }

}

float g(float* x)
{
  return ((*x)*(*x));
}

float h(float* x)
{
  return ((*x)*(*x)*(*x));
}
```

10.5 System Calls

One potentially very useful feature of C interoperability is the ability to make system calls to the host operating system. We illustrate this by providing a C function, *RunSimpleCommand* (Listing 10.10) that runs a user-defined command on a given argument string. We then call the function three times from Fortran (Listing 10.11) where we execute the system calls

1. *mkdir dirname*

2. *mkdir dirname*

3. *rmdir dirname*

These commands were chosen because they are recognizable by both Unix and Windows based operating systems. Note that the second call is expected to fail and may issue a system-dependent error message.

The C function combines the two arguments (command name and command arguments) into an allocated string array and then executes this using the C *system* function. Note that the length of this allocated string array is one more than the combined length of the Fortran strings in order to accommodate the trailing **NULL** character. The string is freed or deallocated after return from the *system* call.

We also provide a second C function, *CommandProcessorAvailable* which checks to see if the *system* function is available for running system calls. A call of the form system() is made, i.e., no command argument is supplied; this will result in a nonzero return value if commands can be run and in zero otherwise.

Listing 10.10. *C code for system calls.*

```
// This code extract is part of the accompanying software
// that supports Chapter 10. It may be found in the file
// csyscall.c
```

```
//
int CommandProcessorAvailable()
{
// See if a command processor is present.
// If it is then system() returns a non-zero value,
// otherwise it returns zero.
  char* s;
  s = 0;
  return(system(s));
}

int RunSimpleCommand(char command[], char argument[])
{
// This builds a command "command argument".
// The code then executes that command and returns
// the status.  The allocated space for the combined
// command is then freed.  The status is 0 for success
// and 1 for failure.

  const char* separator = " ";  // This works for Unix, MS-DOS.
  char* syscommand;
  int status;

  /* Malloc enough space to contain the built command */
  syscommand = (char*)malloc(strlen(command)+strlen(separator)
                              +strlen(argument)+1);
  strcpy(syscommand, command);
  strcat(syscommand, separator);
  strcat(syscommand, argument);
  status = system(syscommand);
  free(syscommand);
  return (status);
}
```

Listing 10.11. *Example use from Fortran.*

```
!! This code extract is part of the accompanying software
!! that supports Chapter 10. It may be found in the file
!! syscall.f90
!!
PROGRAM syscall
USE, INTRINSIC :: iso_c_binding, ONLY : c_char, c_int, c_null_char

INTERFACE
  FUNCTION ComProcAvail() &
     BIND(C,NAME='CommandProcessorAvailable')
  IMPORT :: c_int
  INTEGER(c_int) :: ComProcAvail
  END FUNCTION ComProcAvail

  FUNCTION RunSimpleCommand(command, arg) &
     BIND(C, NAME='RunSimpleCommand')
  IMPORT :: c_char, c_int
  CHARACTER(KIND=c_char) :: command(*), arg(*)
  INTEGER(c_int) :: RunSimpleCommand
  END FUNCTION RunSimpleCommand
```

```
END INTERFACE

CHARACTER (LEN=*, KIND=c_char), &
   PARAMETER :: dirname=c_char_'CreatedFromFortran'//c_null_char, &
                mkdir_com = c_char_'mkdir'//c_null_char, &
                rmdir_com = c_char_'rmdir'//c_null_char
INTEGER :: status

  status = ComProcAvail()
  IF (status == 0) THEN
    WRITE(*,'(''No command processor available'')')
    STOP
  ELSE
    WRITE(*,'(''Command processor available. Status: '',i3)')status
  END IF

! Create a directory (Unix or Windows based systems)
  status = RunSimpleCommand(mkdir_com, dirname)
  IF (status == 0) THEN
    WRITE(*,'(''First mkdir succeeded -- OK!'')')
  ELSE
    WRITE(*,'(''First mkdir failed. Status: '',i3)')status
  END IF

! Try and create it again.  Normally this should not succeed.
  status = RunSimpleCommand(mkdir_com, dirname)
  IF (status /= 0) THEN
    WRITE(*,'(''Second mkdir failed -- OK!'')')
  ELSE
    WRITE(*,'(''Second mkdir succeeded -- WRONG!'')')
  END IF

! Remove it
  status = RunSimpleCommand(rmdir_com, dirname)
  IF (status == 0) THEN
    WRITE(*,'(''rmdir succeeded -- OK!'')')
  ELSE
    WRITE(*,'(''rmdir failed -- WRONG!'')')
  END IF

END PROGRAM syscall
```

10.6 Some Names Are Still Not Allowed

With the modern standards it would seem that Fortran/C interoperability removes all need to understand how Fortran and C compilers interact internally. Unfortunately this is not the case. As an example let us assume that we have a C code, written prior to the newer standards, which makes calls to the Fortran BLAS. Because of name mangling the actual calls from C have an appended underscore, for example *saxpy_*, since this was required on the development machine.

An obvious way to provide portability with a minimum of fuss would be to create a wrapper routine that calls *saxpy* but utilizes the **NAME** specifier in the

BIND attribute to use the mangled name; for example

```
SUBROUTINE csaxpy (......)  BIND(C, NAME='saxpy_')
```

However, attempting to link the C code, the wrapper routine, and the Fortran BLAS library leads to an error which reports that *saxpy_* is multiply defined: once in the **BIND** attribute and once from the Fortran compiler mangling the name of the BLAS library routine.

Thus, we have interoperability provided we avoid making the name used from the calling C code the same as a name that already exists in the Fortran code through name mangling. There are a number of ways around this problem, for example, by using `BIND(C, NAME='Saxpy_')`, where the uppercase S is enough to differentiate, or by just using a consistent version of library names for all the wrapper routines, like *Csaxpy*. Whatever choice is made under the circumstances will probably result in changes being necessary to the C code.

EXERCISE 10.1. *Use an operating system call from a Fortran program that will obtain the names of all routines in a subdirectory and place this list in a file, say file_list. (The system command for a directory listing is typically "ls" under Linux or Unix and "dir" for Windows. This exercise requires writing a matched pair of Fortran and C routines.)*

EXERCISE 10.2. *A Fortran program calls a C routine with a prototype:*

```
extern void C_Code(void* buf);
```

The pointer argument buf can be realized as a rank-1 INTEGER or a rank-1 type REAL array. Write an interface for this C routine and illustrate its usage in this program.

Chapter 11

Defined Operations for Sparse Matrix Solutions

Synopsis:

Defined operations for sparse solving:

- ▶ *The SuperLU library*

- ▶ *The operations .ip. and .pi.*

- ▶ *An ascended type for factoring and solving*

- ▶ *Overloading assignments and defined operators*

- ▶ *Exercises*

11.1 Introduction

In this chapter we combine the use of defined types and overloaded assignment (Chapter 4) with C interoperability (Chapter 10) to create defined operators for solving sparse linear systems of equations.

Rather that writing routines to compute the LU factors and perform the triangular back substitution from scratch, we heed our own advice and call C functions from the SuperLU library [59, 58] (the code we have developed here interfaces with version 4.3 of the package, dated December 14, 2011).

To allow the application code to be more readable we wish to provide defined operators to implement the solution of linear systems of the forms $Ax_k = b_k$ and $y_k^T A = b_k^T$ where A is a sparse matrix. We define two operators .ip. and .pi. (read as *invert then form matrix product* and *invert then form transposed matrix product*) that compute $x_k = A^{-1}b_k$ and $y_k = (b_k^T A^{-1})^T, k = 1, 2, \ldots,$ respectively.

For efficiency reasons we assume that a sequence of solves will be performed, and so we always store the LU factors along with other related information such as the permutation vector. This allows the expensive factorization step to be computed once and the factors reused in subsequent triangular back substitutions to solve for further right-hand sides.

Our new defined type, *slu_dhb_sparse*, which is described in detail in the following section, has components to store the original coefficient matrix in HB format (see Section 4.2), the *LU* factor information, user-settable options for the underlying C package, and other flags. We would like to be able to write statements of the form `x(:,k) = a .ip. b(:,k)` and `y(:,k) = b(:,k) .pi. a` to solve the systems $x_k = A^{-1} b_k$ and $y_k = (b_k^T A^{-1})^T$, respectively, where a is a variable of type *slu_dhb_sparse*. The first time that a is used as an operand, the associated routine should ideally generate and store the *LU* factor information and perform the back substitution. In all subsequent uses of a as an operand only the back substitution should be required.

However, the Fortran 2003 standard mandates that the operands of a defined operation must have the attribute **INTENT(IN)** in the associated subprogram. This means that, in its first use as an operand, we cannot alter a by storing the required *LU* information in one of its components. We, therefore, choose to implement an overloaded assignment of the form `a = b` where b is of type *dhbc_sparse*. This results in computing the *LU* factorization and storing both b and the factor data in components of a. For finalization we define an assignment `a = 0`, where the right-hand side is an integer zero, which clears all the data currently stored in the data structure and releases the allocated memory.

The use of the overloaded assignment for initialization also allows us to provide extra robustness at the factorization stage. For example, while the SuperLU factorization function detects a zero pivot or a rank deficient matrix, its factorization algorithm presumes that the HB coefficient matrix contains entries in every row and column. If the input data is deficient in this sense, then the SuperLU algorithm does not apply and the user needs to be informed. Scanning the rows and column pointers of an HB data structure requires additional code that is very likely to be ignored by the application programmer. Our implementation of the overloaded assignment hides this error checking and passes back a status result via a flag component of a. Checking this flag following the assignment prevents this error from being propagated to a point where it is much harder to diagnose.

11.2   Ascended Harwell–Boeing Sparse Matrices

A new derived type, *slu_shbc_sparse*, is defined that is used to store both data involved in the solution of the sparse system and user options to control the factorization and back solve steps. This *ascended SuperLU* structure (Listing 11.1) contains the following fields:

1. *hbMatrix* of type *dpHBSparseMatrix* stores the original coefficient matrix in HB format. This remains unaltered by both the factorization and solve steps.

2. *options* of type *superLU_options_t* (see Listing 11.2) contains the values of user-controllable parameters to both stages of the computation. To ensure interoperability this data structure needs to be an exact replica of the C structure

of the same name which is defined in the SuperLU include file *slu_util.h* and whose fields are described in detail in the *SuperLU Users' Guide* [59, Section 2.4].

The user may change the default options simply by setting the relevant component of *options*; for example, to turn off the equilibration of the system prior to factorization we would use

```
! Set default options as defined in Chapter 2 of the user manual
  CALL set_default_options(a%options)
! Assumes that NO/YES are available as 0/1
  a%options%Equil = NO
```

where *a* is of type *slu_shbc_sparse* and values associated with the options are mostly defined as enumerated types in *superlu_enum_consts.h*, one of the SuperLU include file.

3. *dropTol* is a value of type *c_double*. This is assigned as component *ILU_DropTol* of the structure *options* within the C wrapper code we provide. Because this is one of the more useful settable options, it is separated out for convenience.

4. *factorData* of type *c_ptr* is a pointer to a C structure that contains the *LU* factorization of the user-supplied coefficient matrix and associated data, for example, the permutation vector. This information is generated at the factorization step and is required for back substitution steps. We therefore need to keep hold of it at the Fortran level. An anonymous pointer is sufficient, as the user has no need to access individual elements of the stored data.

5. *info* of type **INTEGER** is a flag used to communicate the success or failure of the factorization stage. A value of zero following a "factorization" assignment indicates success. A positive value gives the index of the first column of the coefficient matrix that yielded a zero pivot. A negative *info* value indicates a problem with the user-supplied HB coefficient matrix:

   −1: The matrix is not square.

   −2: The matrix has a missing (i.e., zero) row.

   −3: The matrix has a missing (i.e., zero) column.

Listing 11.1. *The ascended SuperLU structure.*

```
!! This code extract is part of the accompanying software
!! that supports Chapter 4. It may be found in the file
!! sparseTypes.f90
!!
    TYPE slu_dpHBSparseMatrix
! This is the sparse matrix involved in the solve step.
        TYPE(dpHBSparseMatrix) :: hbMatrix
! This is the options used in the solve step.
        TYPE(superlu_options_t) :: options
```

```
! This is the drop tolerance used
! in the SuperLU factorization.  It is initialized
! to the value 0.
        REAL(dkind) :: dropTol = zero
! This is the C pointer, where the factored matrix
! and its related data are stored.
        TYPE(c_ptr) :: factorData
! This is the flag value resulting from a factorization
! by the SuperLU package.
        INTEGER :: info = 0
    END TYPE slu_dpHBSparseMatrix
```

Listing 11.2. *The SuperLU options structure.*

```
!! This code extract is part of the accompanying software
!! that supports Chapter 4. It may be found in the file
!! sparseTypes.f90
!!
! This derived type repeats the structure (using the
! same name) that is a parameter for the SuperLU codes.
    TYPE, BIND(C) :: superlu_options_t
        INTEGER (c_int) :: Fact
        INTEGER (c_int) :: Equil
        INTEGER (c_int) :: ColPerm
        INTEGER (c_int) :: Trans
        INTEGER (c_int) :: IterRefine
        REAL (c_double) :: DiagPivotThresh
        INTEGER (c_int) :: SymmetricMode
        INTEGER (c_int) :: PivotGrowth
        INTEGER (c_int) :: ConditionNumber
        INTEGER (c_int) :: RowPerm
        INTEGER (c_int) :: ILU_DropRule
        REAL (c_double) :: ILU_DropTol
        REAL (c_double) :: ILU_FillFactor
        INTEGER (c_int) :: ILU_Norm
        REAL (c_double) :: ILU_FillTol
        INTEGER (c_int) :: ILU_MILU ;
        REAL (c_double) :: ILU_MILU_Dim
        INTEGER (c_int) :: ParSymbFact
        INTEGER (c_int) :: ReplaceTinyPivot
        INTEGER (c_int) :: SolveInitialized
        INTEGER (c_int) :: RefineInitialized
        INTEGER (c_int) :: PrintStat =0
    END TYPE superlu_options_t
```

11.3   C Wrappers Calling SuperLU Functions

The SuperLU package provides some support for the Fortran programmer in the form of a C driver routine that may be used to perform the factorization, back solve, and clearing storage steps via a user-supplied *option* parameter. Calling this driver as provided is reliant on the user being able to induce the C and Fortran compilers to communicate; i.e., it does not use the new interoperability features, and the mechanism for achieving this is, therefore, compiler dependent.

We have separated the functionality of this support code into three separate C procedures, one for each of the core computational steps, and have used additional parameters to provide more flexibility. We have then implemented a set of Fortran interfaces to these C procedures to enable standard conforming interoperability.

The three core C routines are *FACTOR_with_SuperLU*, *SOLVE_with_SuperLU*, and *CLEAR_SuperLU* with Fortran names *factor_superlu*, *solve_superlu*, and *clear_superlu*, respectively. We also provide an interface to the SuperLU function *set_default_options* which effectively initializes the *superlu_options_t* data type; the user is then free to override these values by assigning directly to the relevant fields as described in Section 11.2. Listing 11.3 shows details of the *set_default_options* and *factor_superlu* interfaces; the others are similar.

Listing 11.3. *Interface specifications for C code called in overloaded assignment.*

```
!! This code extract is part of the accompanying software
!! that supports Chapter 11. It may be found in the file
!! sluInterop.f90
!!
! This defines the interfaces to C codes used for the support of
! defined operations .ip. and .pi.
     INTERFACE
        SUBROUTINE set_default_options(options) BIND(C, &
           NAME='set_default_options')
        IMPORT superlu_options_t
        TYPE (superlu_options_t), INTENT (INOUT) :: options
        END SUBROUTINE

        SUBROUTINE factor_superlu(iopt,n,nnz,values,ir,ip,options, &
           drop_tol, f_factors,info) &
           BIND(C,NAME='FACTOR_with_SuperLU')

!    This usage allows changes to arguments due to the
!    LU factorization.

!    FACTOR_with_SuperLU(int *iopt, int *n, int *nnz,
!        double *values, int *rowind, int *colptr,
!        superlu_options_t *options,
!     double *drop_tol, fptr *f_factors, int *info)

        USE, INTRINSIC :: iso_c_binding
        IMPORT superlu_options_t , dkind
        IMPLICIT NONE

        INTEGER (c_int), INTENT (IN) :: iopt, n, nnz
        INTEGER (c_int), INTENT (INOUT) :: info
        TYPE (superlu_options_t), INTENT (INOUT) :: options
        REAL (c_double), INTENT (INOUT) :: values(*), drop_tol
        INTEGER (c_int), INTENT (INOUT) :: ir(*), ip(*)
        TYPE (c_ptr), INTENT (INOUT) :: f_factors
        END SUBROUTINE

        SUBROUTINE solve_superlu(iopt,n,b,ldb,nrhs,options,trans, &
           f_factors,info) BIND(C,NAME='SOLVE_with_SuperLU')
```

```
!   This usage assumes static arguments due to any solve step

!   SOLVE_with_SuperLU(int *iopt, int *n, int *nnz,
!        double *b, int *ldb, int *nrhs,
!        superlu_options_t *options, trans_t *trans,
!        fptr *f_factors, int *info)

        USE, INTRINSIC :: iso_c_binding
        IMPORT superlu_options_t , dkind
        IMPLICIT NONE

        INTEGER (c_int), INTENT (IN) :: iopt, n, ldb, nrhs, trans
        INTEGER (c_int), INTENT (OUT) :: info
        TYPE (superlu_options_t), INTENT (IN) :: options
        TYPE (c_ptr), INTENT (IN) :: f_factors
        REAL (c_double), INTENT (INOUT) :: b(ldb,*)
      END SUBROUTINE

      SUBROUTINE clear_superlu(iopt,options,f_factors,info) &
          BIND(C, NAME='CLEAR_SuperLU')

!   This usage allows changes to arguments due to memory release

!   CLEAR_SuperLU(int *iopt, superlu_options_t *options,
!        fptr *f_factors, int *info)

        USE, INTRINSIC :: iso_c_binding
        IMPORT superlu_options_t , dkind
        IMPLICIT NONE

        INTEGER (c_int), INTENT (IN) :: iopt
        INTEGER (c_int), INTENT (OUT) :: info
        TYPE (superlu_options_t), INTENT (INOUT) :: options
        TYPE (c_ptr), INTENT (INOUT) :: f_factors
      END SUBROUTINE
    END INTERFACE
```

Listing 11.4 gives outline code showing how to use the ascended assignments
and defined operators to solve sparse linear systems using the SuperLU library.

Listing 11.4. *Outline code using proposed assignments and operators.*

```
USE sluInterop, ONLY: OPERATOR(.ip.), OPERATOR(.pi.), &
       ASSIGNMENT(=), set_default_options
...
TYPE (dpHBSparseMatrix) :: h
TYPE (slu_dpHBSparsematrix) :: gg
...
! Form HB coefficient matrix h and right hand side vectors
! rhs1 and rhs2
...
! Set default option values
CALL set_default_options(gg%options)
! Override defaults as required
gg%options%Equil = NO
```

```
   ...
! Factor h via overloaded assignment
  gg = h
! Solve systems using defined operators
  sol1 = gg .ip. rhs1
  sol2 = rhs2 .pi. gg
   ...
! Destroy data and reclaim storage
! Can now reuse gg with a new HB matrix if required
  gg = 0
   ...
```

11.4 The Overloaded Assignments and Defined Operators

As stated in Section 11.1, any operation that requires data in the ascended SuperLU data type to be stored or altered needs to be implemented as an overloaded assignment rather than as a defined operator. There are two core operations that involve altering the content of the data type *slu_dhbc_sparse*: factorizing the user-supplied HB coefficient matrix and clearing the ascended SuperLU data type so that allocated storage may be retrieved and the data structure reused, if required, for a different coefficient matrix. We differentiate between these assignments by allowing two different data types to appear on the right-hand side: type *dpHBSparseMatrix* means that a factorization is requested and type **INTEGER** (specifically the value zero) that the data structure should be cleared. Listing 11.5 provides a code snippet that illustrates the use of these assignments.

The associated operations are implemented in the procedures *slu_dhbc_eq_dhbc* and *clear_slu_dhbc* in the module *sluInterOp* (see Listing 11.6). While the clear procedure just consists of a small amount of bookkeeping followed by a call to the core C function via *clear_superlu*, the factorization code is slightly more complicated. Before calling the C code we take the opportunity to perform extra checks on the user-supplied HB matrix to ensure that it is structurally sound, i.e., there are no missing rows or columns. Such defects as these are commonly caused by errors in the construction of the HB matrix and, as stated earlier, we believe it is highly unlikely that the user will bother to perform these checks. Any errors found are reported via the *info* component of the ascended HB data variable (see Section 11.2 for details).

The two defined operators, .ip. and .pi., are implemented via the two functions *solve_ext_sparse_matrix_dense_rhsv* and *solve_dense_rhsv_ext_sparse_matrix*, respectively. These just perform small amounts of bookkeeping around a call to the core C solve function *SOLVE_with_SuperLU*.

EXERCISE 11.1. *Implement alternate versions of the operators .ip. and .pi. by associating a pointer to the hbMatrix component of slu_dpHBSparseMatrix within the* *overloaded assignment* **A=B** *rather than using a copy of the HB matrix. What are the pros and cons of the two approaches?*

Listing 11.5. *Fragment for overloaded ascension of HB matrices.*

```
USE Sparse_Support
  TYPE(dpHBSparseMatrix) :: h
  TYPE(slu_dpHBSparseMatrix) :: g
...
! Assignment uses defaults for LU factorization and then factors h
    g = h
...
! Clear storage associated with this matrix in SuperLU
    g = 0
...
```

Listing 11.6. *Supporting subroutines for assignment of* TYPE*(SLU_DHBC_SPARSE).*

```
!! This code extract is part of the accompanying software
!! that supports Chapter 11. It may be found in the file
!! sluInterop.f90
!!
      SUBROUTINE slu_dhbc_eq_dhbc(g,h)
        IMPLICIT NONE
        TYPE (slu_dpHBSparseMatrix), INTENT (INOUT) :: g
        TYPE (dphbsparsematrix), INTENT (IN) :: h
        INTEGER :: itemp
! Copy the Harwell-Boeing part into place.
        g%hbMatrix = h
! Get default options for use in SuperLU solve steps.
! Give special treatment to the PrintStat parameter.
! This may have been turned on in user code.
        itemp = g%options%printstat
        CALL set_default_options(g%options)
        g%options%printstat = itemp
! Set iterative refinement to be a default.
        g%options%iterrefine = 1
! Flag that the LU factorization is not available.
        g%options%fact = 0
! Default setting of the LU factorization flag.
        g%info = 0
        CALL factor_sparse_system(g)
      END SUBROUTINE

      SUBROUTINE clear_slu_dhbc(g,i)
        IMPLICIT NONE
        TYPE (slu_dpHBSparseMatrix), INTENT (INOUT) :: g
        INTEGER, INTENT (IN) :: i

        INTEGER :: info, iopt

! Only the specific value I==0 results in clearing
! the storage used by factoring the matrix.

        IF (i==0) THEN
           iopt = 3
```

```
! Unload storage in the C code. The name used here is
! to inform the compiler of changes to the arguments.
! No factorization is performed, only memory release.
        CALL clear_superlu(iopt,g%options,g%factorData,info)
! Flag that the LU factorization is not available.
        g%options%fact = 0
        g%info = info
      END IF
    END SUBROUTINE
```

Chapter 12

Case Study: Two Sparse Least-Squares System Examples

Synopsis:

> *Defined operations in linear algebra with sparse solving:*
>
> ▶ *Two examples: data fitting and Airy's equation*
>
> ▶ *Overloaded assignment for matrix accumulation*
>
> ▶ *The linear system solving operations .p. and .ip.*
>
> ▶ *Exercise*

12.1 Introduction

In this chapter we consider the practical use of the defined operators and overloaded assignments, that we developed in Chapters 4 and 11, in the solution of two problems based on the least-squares method. These implementations demonstrate the efficiency of combining basic operations to construct and solve the resultant sparse linear systems. They also illustrate clearly how efficient application software may be developed in a timely and robust manner by utilizing such building blocks.

12.2 Data Fitting with Continuous Linear Splines

Our first example is a data fitting problem where we seek a least-squares approximation to M given data values $\{(t_j, y(t_j))\}_{j=1}^{M}$ by a piecewise linear function $x(t)$ on the interval $[0, 1]$.

We choose $y(t) = t^2$ and partition the unit interval such that $0 = a_1 < a_2 < \cdots < a_N = 1$. The number of data points, M, is chosen so that the intrinsic Fortran random number generator, *random_number*, places at least one data value in each

141

interval. This constraint is necessary to ensure that the resulting sparse coefficient matrix has at least one nonzero value in each row and column.

Define the piecewise linear approximation by

$$x(t) = \sum_{i=1}^{N-1} x_i(1 - v_i(t)) + x_{i+1}v_i(t), \tag{12.1}$$

where

$$v_i(t) = \begin{cases} (t - a_i)/(a_{i+1} - a_i), & a_i \leq t \leq a_{i+1}, \\ 0 & \text{otherwise} \end{cases}$$

and we require $x(t_i) = y(t_i), i = 1, 2, \ldots, M$.

To compute the values of the parameters $\{x_i\}_{i=1}^N$ we choose to solve the overdetermined least-squares problem $Az \cong b$ as a system of linear equations in $(N + M)$ unknowns of the form

$$B \begin{bmatrix} x \\ r \end{bmatrix} = \begin{bmatrix} b_m \\ 0 \end{bmatrix},$$

where $x = (x_1, x_2, \ldots, x_N)^T$ are the required parameters and $r = (r_1, r_2, \ldots, r_M)^T$ are the residual values $y(t_i) - x(t_i)$ at the data points. The coefficient matrix B is of the form

$$B = \begin{bmatrix} C & I_M \\ 0 & C^T \end{bmatrix},$$

where C is of order $M \times N$ and I_M is the unit matrix of order M (see Björk [12, p. 77] for details).

Row j of the matrix C has only two nonzero values in columns k and $k + 1$ where $a_k \leq t_j \leq a_{k+1}$ and $C_{jk} = v(t_j), C_{j,k+1} = 1 - v(t_j)$. Since C is therefore sparse, the compound matrix B may also be considered sparse. Provided we have access to a sparse linear equation solver package like SuperLU (see Li et al. [59] and Chapter 11) this approach allows us to solve a sparse linear least-squares problem of order N as a sparse linear system of order $(M + N)$.

Using the defined operator .ip. (see Section 11.3) we can compute a solution to our problem while minimizing the amount of detailed knowledge of SuperLU required. Listing 12.1 shows the important part of the code; the full program and associated modules are available from the web site; see Chapter 20.

EXERCISE 12.1. *The perturbed expanded matrix*

$$B_\epsilon = \begin{bmatrix} A & I_M \\ -\epsilon I_N & A^T \end{bmatrix}$$

is nonsingular for $\epsilon > 0$. This fact allows sparse least-squares systems with rank deficient or ill-conditioned matrices to be approximated using a sparse linear equation solver. Prove the nonsingularity of B_ϵ.

Listing 12.1. *Piecewise linear fitting: A Sparse least-squares system.*

```
!! This code extract is part of the accompanying software
!! that supports Chapter 12. It may be found in the file
!! driverPiecewiseLinear.f90
!!
    PROGRAM drivePiecewiseLinear
! Generate the coefficient matrix for a least squares problem
! that comes from piece-wise linear fitting of data with a
! continuous function.  The breakpoints are equally spaced.

! There are N unknowns in the problem and M data values.
! The N unknowns are the values of the linear functions at the
! ends of the each breakpoint interval.

! The M data value are pairs (t_i, y(t_i)) where the t_i
! are random on (0,1).

! The matrix  B=[A : I_M]
!             [0 : A^T] is first defined as a list of triplets.
! This matrix is assembled using overloaded assignment.
! B is then converted to Harwell-Boeing format using overloaded
! assignment between derived types.  The sparse matrix B has
! dimension (M+N) by (M+N).

      USE set_precision, ONLY: dkind
      USE sparseTypes, ONLY: dpTriplet, dpTripletList ,&
         dpHBSparseMatrix, slu_dpHBSparseMatrix
      USE sparseOps, ONLY: OPERATOR(.p.)
      USE sluInterop, ONLY: OPERATOR(.ip.), ASSIGNMENT(=)
      USE sparseAssign, ONLY: ASSIGNMENT(=)
! Pick the required Blas routine up via the library specified in
! the Makefile.inc file -- if not available pick up the module from
! Chapter 3
!     USE BlasModule, ONLY : dnrm2
      IMPLICIT NONE
! Declaration only needed if using a library routine
      REAL(dkind) :: dnrm2
! Real constants
      REAL(dkind), PARAMETER :: one=1.0E0_dkind, zero=0.0E0_dkind
! Set problem size:
      INTEGER, PARAMETER :: n=2000 ! Could make this an input value
! Define arrays for knots, data points, etc
      REAL(dkind), ALLOCATABLE :: a(:), rhs(:), t(:), x(:), r(:)
! iseed is used to store the seed used for the Fortran intrinsic
!       random number generator
! saw_points is used to ensure that every interval in the partition
!       contains at least one point
      INTEGER, ALLOCATABLE :: iseed(:), saw_points(:)
      INTEGER :: m, findInterval
! Define what will be the collection of matrix triplets.
      TYPE (dpTripletList) :: s
! Define the Harwell-Boeing derived type that holds the
! processed triplets.
      TYPE (dpHBSparseMatrix) :: b
! Define the ascended type that holds the Harwell-Boeing
! matrix and factorization quantities.
      TYPE (slu_dpHBSparseMatrix) :: g
```

```
! Define local variables
      REAL (dkind) :: delta, u, v, resid_error
      INTEGER :: errno, i, j, k, sz

      ALLOCATE (a(n), saw_points(n-1), STAT=errno)
      IF (errno /= 0) THEN
        print *, "Allocate fails with errno: ", errno
      END IF
      delta = one/real(n-1,dkind)
! Define the array of breakpoints
      a(1) = zero
      a(n) = one
! Define the knots or inner breakpoints
      DO i = 2, n - 1
        a(i) = a(i-1) + delta
      END DO

! Generate sufficient random values so that each interval
! has at least one value.  We do not store these data values
! here as we don't know the total number of data points required
! yet
      saw_points = 0
      m = 0
! Store the seed so we can regenerate the data points later
      CALL random_seed(size=sz)
      ALLOCATE (iseed(sz), STAT=errno)
      IF (errno /= 0) THEN
        print *, "Allocate fails with errno: ", errno
      END IF
      CALL random_seed(get=iseed)
      DO WHILE (any(saw_points==0))
        CALL random_number(u)
        k = findInterval(u, n, a)
        saw_points(k) = 1
        m = m + 1
      END DO
! Set random number seed so the same sequence results.
      CALL random_seed(put=iseed)

! Allocate local working space
      ALLOCATE (t(m),x(m+n),r(m+n),rhs(m+n), STAT=errno)
      IF (errno /= 0) THEN
        print *, "Allocate fails with errno: ", errno
      END IF
! Generate the random values and write the matrix entries.
! Record the function values in RHS(*).
      DO j = 1, m
        CALL random_number(t(j))
        rhs(j) = t(j)**2
        k = findInterval(t(j), n, a)
        v = (t(j)-a(k))/delta
! Gather up the list of the sparse matrix triplets (S) that
! will define B.  The next assignments (S =) are accumulation
! steps of the list of matrix entries.
! Write adjacent columns of the A matrix, in NW corner of B:
        s = dpTriplet(j,k,v)
```

```
        s = dpTriplet(j,k+1,one-v)
! Write adjacent rows of the A^T matrix, in SE corner of B:
        s = dpTriplet(k+m,n+j,v)
        s = dpTriplet(k+m+1,n+j,one-v)
! Write row of identity matrix I_M, in NE corner of B:
        s = dpTriplet(j,n+j,one)
      END DO
! Use overloaded assigment to convert from a list of
! triplets. Create a Harwell-Boeing matrix representation for B.
! This assignment (B =) converts the S list to a sparse matrix format.
      b = s
! Clear out space occupied by S.  This assignment deallocates
! the space used accumulating the list, S.
      s = 0
! Define the rest of the right-hand side.
      rhs(m+1:n+m) = zero
! Solve for the coefficients of the piece-wise linear spline.
! This defined operation works with a Harwell-Boeing matrix
! and ascends B to be a component of an extended type, G.
! Default settings of pivoting rules and other parameters
! are used.
      x = b .ip. rhs
...
```

12.3 Airy's Equation with Boundary Values

For our second example we look at the numerical approximation of a boundary value problem using a Galerkin procedure (see Strang and Fix [89] for details). The particular equation we consider is known as Airy's equation and is defined by the ODE

$$L(y) = \frac{d^2 y}{dx^2} - xy = 0, \tag{12.2}$$

with the boundary conditions $y(0) = y(1) = 1$.

The exact solution of this equation is given by $y(x) = c_1 Ai(x) + c_2 Bi(x)$; see Abramowitz and Stegun [1, Equation (10.4.1)], where $Ai(x)$ and $Bi(x)$ are Airy functions of the first and second kind. If the required values of these functions are available, we can use the given boundary conditions to solve a linear system of order two for the values of c_1 and c_2 and our solution is complete.

However, we choose to approximate the solution as a sum of piecewise linear basis functions on a partition of the unit interval into $(N-1)$ equal intervals of width $h = 1/(N-1)$. This leads to a numerical solution of the form

$$y_N(x) = \sum_{i=1}^{N} q_i \phi_i(x), \tag{12.3}$$

where $\phi_i(x)$ is zero everywhere on the unit interval except

$$\phi_1(x) = (x_1 - x)/h, \qquad\qquad 0 \le x \le x_1,$$
$$\phi_N(x) = (x - x_{N-1})/h, \qquad\qquad x_{N-1} \le x \le x_N$$

and

$$\phi_i(x) = \begin{cases} (x - x_{i-1})/h, & x_{i-1} \leq x \leq x_i, \\ (x_{i+1} - x)/h, & x_i \leq x \leq x_{i+1} \end{cases}$$

for $i = 2, \ldots, N - 1$ and $x_i = (i - 1)h$.

Applying the Galerkin procedure

$$I_i(y_N) = \int_0^1 L(y_N)\phi_i(x)dx = 0, \qquad i = 1, \ldots, N,$$

with the boundary conditions, $\phi_1(0) = \phi_N(1) = 1$, allows us to derive a system of linear equations in the coefficients $q_1, \ldots, q_N$.

Integrating the term

$$\int_0^1 \frac{d^2 y_N}{dx^2}\phi_i(x)dx, \qquad i = 1, \ldots, N,$$

by parts yields, for each i,

$$\phi_i(1)y_N'(1) - \phi_i(0)y_N'(0) - \int_0^1 \frac{dy_N}{dx}\phi_i'(x)dx.$$

By combining terms and using the boundary conditions we may fix the values $q_1 = q_N = 1$, whence the one-sided divided differences

$$y_N'(0) = \frac{(q_2 - q_1)}{h} \quad \text{and} \quad y_N'(1) = \frac{(q_{N-1} - q_N)}{h}$$

give the equations

$$I_i(y_N) = \frac{(\phi_i(1) + \phi_i(0))}{h} - \frac{(\phi_i(0)q_2 + \phi_i(1)q_{N-1})}{h}$$
$$- \int_0^1 \left(\frac{dy_N}{dx}\phi_i'(x) + xy_N(x)\phi_i(x)\right) dx = 0, \quad i = 1, \ldots, N.$$

So far we have used a standard one-dimensional finite element analysis (for example, see Strang and Fix [89] for more details). However, this has given us N equations but just $N - 2$ free parameters, $q_2, \ldots, q_{N-1}$. We thus choose the remaining parameters, q_i, $i = 2, \ldots, N - 1$, in a nonstandard way by minimizing the vector norm of residuals $I_i(y_N)$ in a *least-squares sense*.

We now have the following computational algorithm:

1. Define $q = [q_1, q_2, \ldots, q_{N-1}, q_N]$. Define the matrix elements of $I_i(y_N)$, $i = 1, \ldots, N$, that are the multiples of the components of q and generate these as individual triplets.

2. Accumulate these triplets to assemble a system of linear equations, $Aq = b$, where A is a sparse matrix of order N with column vectors $A = [a_1, \ldots, a_N]$.

3. On fixing the boundary conditions $q_1 = q_N = 1$, we define the $(N-2)$-vector $z_{N-2} = [q_2, \ldots, q_{N-1}]$. We generate the sparse submatrices $C = [a_2, \ldots, a_{N-1}]$ and C^T from A and, at the same time, form the right-hand side vector $b_N = -q_1 a_1 - q_N a_N + b = -(a_1 + a_N) + b$ using the nonzero elements of a_1 and a_N that are being discarded to create C.

4. Prepare to solve the linear least-squares problem for z_{N-2} and the residual vector r by generating the matrix

$$G = \begin{bmatrix} C & I_N \\ 0 & C^T \end{bmatrix},$$

where C is the $N \times (N-2)$ sparse matrix defined in step 3 above.

5. Finally, solve the linear system

$$G \begin{bmatrix} z_{N-2} \\ r_N \end{bmatrix} = \begin{bmatrix} b_N \\ 0 \end{bmatrix},$$

where r_N is the residual vector (see Björk [12, p. 77] for details).

The terms of each sum of integrals are evaluated for the matrix elements. We note that, using the support of the basis functions, the first row of the product Aq is given by

$$q_1 \int_0^h (\phi_1'(x)^2 + x\phi_1(x)^2)dx + q_2 \int_0^h (\phi_1'(x)\phi_2'(x) + x\phi_1(x)\phi_2(x))dx$$
$$= q_1 \frac{(12 + h^3)}{12h} + q_2 \frac{(-12 + h^3)}{12h},$$

and similarly, for the last row we have

$$q_{N-1} \frac{(-12 + 2h^2 - h^3)}{12h} + q_N \frac{(12 + 4h^2 - h^3)}{12h}.$$

For those components indexed $2 \le i \le N - 1$, the ith term of the product is

$$q_{i-1} \int_{(i-1)h}^{ih} (\phi_{i-1}'(x)\phi_i'(x) + x\phi_{i-1}(x)\phi_i(x))dx + q_i \int_{(i-1)h}^{ih} (\phi_i'(x)^2 + x\phi_i(x)^2)dx$$
$$+ q_{i-1} \int_{ih}^{(i+1)h} (\phi_i'(x)^2 + x\phi_i(x)^2)dx + q_{i+1} \int_{ih}^{(i+1)h} (\phi_{i+1}'(x)\phi_i'(x) + x\phi_{i+1}(x)\phi_i(x))dx$$
$$= q_{i-1} \frac{(-12 + h^3(2i-1))}{12h} + q_i \frac{(12 + h^3(4i-1))}{12h}$$
$$+ q_i \frac{(12 + h^3(4i+1))}{12h} + q_{i+1} \frac{(-12 + h^3(2i+1))}{12h}.$$

The integrations were performed using Maple 11.02 [62]. Since, for Airy's equation, each integrand is a cubic polynomial, these may be performed analytically. Any numerical quadrature algorithm that is exact for cubics could be used as an alternative. It is natural to compute the contributions to the matrix A by accumulating the coefficients as they arise from each integration. This could be performed algebraically, but we prefer to avoid any further tedious and error-prone algebra by using the sparse matrix software we already have to accumulate the numerical values for each row entry.

Note that each matrix and right-hand side entry has the scale factor $1/h$. Our implementation shown in the listing has removed this common factor. The program unit for the solution is not completely listed here but is available on the web site; see Chapter 20.

Listing 12.2. *Piecewise linear solution of the Airy boundary value problem.*

```
!! This code extract is part of the accompanying software
!! that supports Chapter 12. It may be found in the file
!! driverAiryBVP.f90
!!
    PROGRAM driverAiryBVP

! Solve the Airy boundary value problem y''-x * y = 0, y(0)=y(1)=1
! in a least-squares sense.  Use piece-wise linear continuous
! functions with equally spaced breakpoints.

! The interval [0,1] is partitioned into n-1 intervals each having
! width h=1/(n-1). There are n values of the function y(x) at the
! breakpoints. The n-2 unknowns are the values of the piece-wise
! linear functions at the ends of each internal breakpoint
! interval. The left and right values are fixed at the value 1
! by the boundary conditions.

    USE set_precision , ONLY: dkind
    USE sparseTypes , ONLY: dpTriplet , dpTripletList ,&
        dpHBSparseMatrix
    USE sparseOps , ONLY: OPERATOR(.p.)
    USE sluInterop , ONLY: OPERATOR(.ip.)
    USE sparseAssign , ONLY: ASSIGNMENT(=)
    IMPLICIT NONE

! Constants
    REAL (dkind), PARAMETER :: one = 1.0E0_dkind , &
            two = 2.0E0_dkind , four = 4.0E0_dkind , &
            twelve = 12.0E0_dkind , zero = 0.0E0_dkind
! Set problem size -- could make this run-time data
    INTEGER , PARAMETER :: n = 10001

! Define array for the knots
    REAL (dkind) :: b(n), x(n), y(n+n-2), z(n+n-2)
! Declare variables for the collection of matrix triplets and
! the HB matrix for SuperLU
    TYPE (dpTripletList) :: s
    TYPE (dpHBSparseMatrix) :: g
    TYPE (dpTriplet), ALLOCATABLE :: t(:)
! Local variables
```

```
      INTEGER :: i, j
      REAL (dkind) :: h, u, v

! Define the value of h, the interval width.
      h = one/REAL(n-1,dkind)

! Define entries for the matrix of integrals
      DO i = 1, n
! Get the pieces of the integrals for each of the n-1 intervals.
! This defines the sparse matrix by rows.

! Get the contribution of basis function i with the series.
! Each basis function has support that is non-zero on
! [max(0,(i-1)*h),min(1,(i+1)h)].

! Note: All matrix entries and right-hand side values
!       have been scaled by h, the constant increment.
      SELECT CASE (i)

      CASE (1) ! Left end
        u = (twelve+h**3)/twelve
        s = dpTriplet(i,1,u)
        v = -(twelve-h**3)/twelve
        s = dpTriplet(i,2,v)

      CASE (n) ! Right end
        u = -(twelve-two*h**2+h**3)/twelve
        s = dpTriplet(i,n-1,u)
        v = (twelve+four*h**2-h**3)/twelve
        s = dpTriplet(i,n,v)

      CASE DEFAULT ! 1 < i < n
        u = -(twelve-h**3*(two*REAL(i,dkind)-one))/twelve
        s = dpTriplet(i,i-1,u)
        v = (twelve+h**3*(four*REAL(i,dkind)-one))/twelve
        s = dpTriplet(i,i,v)

        v = (twelve+h**3*(four*REAL(i,dkind)+one))/twelve
        s = dpTriplet(i,i,v)
        u = -(twelve-h**3*(two*REAL(i,dkind)+one))/twelve
        s = dpTriplet(i,i+1,u)
      END SELECT
    END DO
! Define the fixed values
    b = zero
    b(1) = one
    b(n) = one

! Use prior estimate of the end derivatives,
! one-sided divided differences for y_n'(0) and y_1'(0).
    s = dpTriplet(1,2,one)
    s = dpTriplet(n,n-1,one)
...
```

Chapter 13

Message Passing with MPI in Standard Fortran

Synopsis:

  MPI software usage:

  ▶ *Two examples*

  ▶ *Simple MPI implementations*

  ▶ *A core suite of MPI codes*

  ▶ *A standard-complying interface to MPI C routines*

  ▶ *Exercises*

13.1 Introduction

The use of message passing as a means of achieving high performance or large-scale computing is one of the success stories of scientific and numerical software development. Many Fortran application codes now use MPI to solve very large problems by harnessing the resources of a number of processors. Such a collection of cooperating processors is often called a virtual machine or work-sharing group. The parallel model used may be referred to as *Multiple Program, Multiple Data* (MPMD), although the majority of MPI applications are run as *Single Program, Multiple Data* (SPMD). In SPMD the computation takes place on a set of independent processors, with each running a copy of the same executable on its own sets of data.

We note here that MPI can be used to run applications on very diverse collections of processors from groups of supercomputers, physically widely separated and connected by the internet, down to multiple threads/cores on the same chip. (Although neither of these extremes is likely to be a very efficient way of using MPI!) Work-sharing is accomplished by the cooperating processors exchanging packets of data, called messages, between one another.

Initial versions of the MPI library were implemented in C, and the port to Fortran 77 was later achieved by writing Fortran wrappers that called the C functions. At first sight this appears to be good software engineering: reusing mature code and having only a single base library to maintain. However, the price paid was the violation of the Fortran standard, which we look at later in this chapter.

13.2 Two Examples

As with most practical subjects, we believe that the best way to start learning the Fortran interface to MPI is to study and run some simple programs. Toward this end we provide two examples that illustrate how more that one processor may be used to improve the execution speed of a computational problem. The code for these examples uses many of the routines listed in Table 13.1.

13.2.1 Approximating π

We use the mathematical identity

$$I \equiv \int_0^\infty (1 + x^2)^{-1} dx = \frac{\pi}{4}$$

to compute the value of $\pi = 4I$ using the very simple midpoint quadrature rule (see Hildebrand [39, p. 95]) to approximate I. The official MPICH2 distribution package includes simple implementations for this problem in Fortran 77, C, and C++. We present a Fortran 2003 version that uses example calls to more MPI routines. While the problem is somewhat contrived, it does help to illustrate a variety of MPI calls and provides a basic example of message passing. An alternate approach using coarrays is presented in Chapter 14.

The midpoint rule computes an approximation to I as

$$\frac{I}{h} \approx \sum_{i=1}^n f\left((i-1)\frac{h}{2}\right) \equiv \sum_{i=1}^n g_i,$$

where $h = 1/n$ and $f(x) = (1 + x^2)^{-1}$. We note that when computing the above summation using IEEE double precision arithmetic, we need to restrict the value of n to be less than $nmax = 67,108,865 = \frac{1}{\sqrt{\epsilon}}$ where $\epsilon = 2^{-52}$, the machine epsilon for this precision. This restriction is necessary to ensure that f is evaluated at distinct points as h gets smaller.

13.2.2 Matrix Vector Multiplication

For this example we consider the computation of the matrix-vector product $y = Ax$. We assume that the matrix A has been partitioned into p groups of consecutive columns, $A = [A_0, \ldots, A_{p-1}]$, where each A_r is of dimension $m \times k_r$. We choose the partitioning so that each process stores as close to the same number of columns as possible; we assume that all the processors are of similar specification, so this approach should ensure that they all have similar amounts of computational work to perform. In particular we have $k_r \geq 0$ and $\sum_{r=0}^{p-1} k_r = n$, but we note that some k_r may be zero. The vector, x, is partitioned in the same way, i.e., $x = [x_0, \ldots, x_{p-1}]^T$ where x_r is of order k_r.

The matrix-vector multiply is then straightforward, each process computes the partial result $y_r = A_r x_r$, and the required vector is then given by $y = \sum_{r=0}^{p-1} y_r$.

13.3 MPI Implementations

13.3.1 Approximating π

Within MPI the default work-group or *communicator* has the default name *mpi_comm_world*. Each process within a work-group of *numProc* processors is allocated a node number, *myId*, in the range $[0, numProc - 1]$ by MPI; the node whose numerical identifier is zero is called the root or master node. The first three calls to MPI routines in most applications are to the following:

1. *mpi_init* to initialize the MPI system. This routine must be called before any other MPI library subprogram;

2. *mpi_comm_size* which returns the number of processes available in the work-group, *numProcs*; and

3. *mpi_comm_rank* which returns the unique integer identifier associated with the executing process within the work-goup, *myId*.

Since we use these calls almost every time we write an MPI application, we choose to place them inside a subroutine, *mpi_startup* (Listing 13.1). We also include calls to two other MPI routines, *mpi_get_version* and *mpi_get_processor_name*, which return information about the version of the MPI library that the executable is linked against along with the name of the processor on which the executable is running.

Listing 13.1. *User routine for initializing MPI system and common values.*

```
!! This code extract is part of the accompanying software
!! that supports Chapter 13. It may be found in the file
!! mpiExampleSubs.f90
!!
    SUBROUTINE mpi_startup
! This is a collection of calls to MPI routines that are
! commonly used in the set up phase of an MPI application.
! We set the variables numProcs (total number of processes in
! the current work-group) and myId (the rank/node number of the
! executing process). In addition we obtain the version of mpi
! being used and the name of the executing processor
    INTEGER :: ierr, nameSize
    CHARACTER :: tempName(mpi_max_processor_name)

! Initialize the mpi system, this must be called before any
! other mpi library routines.
```

```
    CALL mpi_init(ierr)
! Get the number of processes available in the work group
! We are using the default communicator mpi_comm_world
    CALL mpi_comm_size(mpi_comm_world, numProcs, ierr)
! Get the rank of the executing process
    CALL mpi_comm_rank(mpi_comm_world, myId, ierr)
! Get the version of the mpi library the code has been
! linked against. This is given in the form (version.subversion)
    CALL mpi_get_version(mpiVersion, mpiSubversion, ierr)
! Get the name of the executing processor
! This is at most mpi_max_processor_name characters, get
! the name and then store it in a correct sized array
    CALL mpi_get_processor_name(tempName, nameSize, ierr)
    ALLOCATE(processName(nameSize))
    processName(:) = tempName(1:nameSize)

    END SUBROUTINE mpi_startup
```

Although MPI2 provides facilities for multiple processes to read and write to the filesystem, the majority of applications will choose to use only the root node to perform input/output. For input data that is required by all processes, this means that the root process performs the reading and validity checking before broadcasting the values to the rest of the work-group. An example of this is given by routine *readIntBcast* (Listing 13.2).

Listing 13.2. *Routine to read user data and distribute to all processes.*

```
!! This code extract is part of the accompanying software
!! that supports Chapter 13. It may be found in the file
!! mpiExampleSubs.f90
!!
  SUBROUTINE readIntBcast(prompt, val, quit)
  INTEGER, INTENT(OUT) :: val
  CHARACTER(LEN=*), INTENT(IN) :: prompt
  LOGICAL, INTENT(OUT) :: quit
! Routine to input a legal integer, val, from the user
! following the output of the user-supplied prompt. The input
! is performed on the root process and then broadcast to all
! the other processes in the work group.
! quit -- set false for n>0 and true otherwise.

  INTEGER :: ierr, itemp(1)
  LOGICAL :: init
! Check that the mpi system has been initialized if not
! initialize it
  quit = .FALSE.
  CALL mpi_initialized(init, ierr)
  IF (.NOT. init) THEN
    CALL mpi_startup
  END IF
! Only the root node deals with input/output
  IF (myId == rootId) THEN
! Loop until we have a valid integer
getInput: &
    DO
      WRITE(*, '(A)') TRIM(prompt)
      READ(*,'(I10)',IOSTAT=ierr) itemp(1)
```

```
      IF (ierr == 0) EXIT ! Legal integer input
   END DO getInput
END IF

CALL mpi_bcast(itemp, 1, mpi_integer, rootid, mpi_comm_world, ierr)
val = itemp(1)
! If n is zero or less then halt execution.
! Note all processes have the value of n here so all can
! now halt their own execution.
IF (val <= 0) THEN
   quit = .TRUE.
END IF

END SUBROUTINE readIntBcast
```

Note here that, in order to conform to the Fortran standard the first parameter to *mpi_bcast* needs to be an array. We return to this in Section 13.4.

Using *numProcs* the application may calculate how much of the problem-dependent data is to be stored, processed, and distributed by each node. In our implementation process, *myId* computes the partial sum

$$S_r = \sum_{m=1}^{N} g_{(m-1)p+r+1},$$

where $r = myId$, $p = numProcs$, $N = \lceil n/p \rceil$, and $g_k = 0$ for $k > n$. Then, by collecting and accumulating the S_r values from all the processes to form S, we can compute an approximation to π using $\pi \approx 4hS$.

The routine, *computePi*, performs two tasks. First, it computes the partial sum of function values on each processor in parallel and accumulates the *numProcs* values on the root node. It then distributes that value to all the other processes in *mpi_comm_world*, and this code is used to illustrate the case of synchronized sends and receives. This is not the most effective method either in terms of execution speed or in lines of code (see Exercise 13.1).

On exit from *computePi* all the processes have received the computed approximation to π. The root node is then used to output this value along with its relative error and timing information (these routines are not reproduced here but are included within the software that accompanies this book; see Chapter 20).

Finally, we need to call *mpi_finalize* to close down the MPI system. This call does not halt the executable, but it does mean that no more calls to MPI library routines may be made (and this includes *mpi_init*). We use the routine *mpi_shutdown* to gather together all the tidying-up code required and add an explicit stop statement to terminate the process cleanly.

Note that all the Fortran MPI interface routines have an error status parameter whose value is set on exit to *mpi_success* or an implementation-dependent integer error code. Technically we should test this parameter on exit from all MPI routines and react to any failures. The problem here is that, for example, to output an error message means communicating the failure to the root node, and to abort the computation requires informing all the processes of the need to halt execution. This will almost certainly mean greater code complexity and may actually slow down the computation due to the need to synchronize the processes at error check points. For this reason many application programmers choose not to test error conditions from MPI library subprograms.

EXERCISE 13.1. *Rewrite the computePi routine using a single MPI library routine call to replace the mpi_send, mpi_recv, and mpi_reduce calls. Does doing this have any noticeable effect on the execution time for large numbers of quadrature points?*

EXERCISE 13.2. *Modify the subprogram f2003pi so that mpi_comm_dup is used to create a duplicate communicator, myComm. Use this in place of mpi_comm_world as the communicator for all subsequent calls to MPI routines.*

13.3.2   Matrix-Vector Multiplication

For our second example we implement the matrix-vector product described above. What is important here is how the data is distributed among the processes. In our solution we assume a partitioning that results in a straightforward MPI implementation; indeed, the more interesting uses of MPI library routines are in building the test harness. There are many different ways of partitioning this problem, some of which may be more efficient. However, if the matrix-vector product forms only a relatively minor part of the computation, we may be willing to trade nonoptimal code here for a more efficient implementation of the majority of the computation. Unlike sequential programming, where we can pick the best (fastest, minimal memory, etc.) algorithm for the job, parallel programming often forces a set of compromises mainly imposed by the need to balance the cost of comparatively slow data transfers against computational cost.

As with the first example, we have used a number of MPI routines for illustration purposes only. We make the following points and refer the reader to the online code rather than reproducing it here.

1. The values of m and n are input from the user at the root node and broadcast to the other processes using the same routine that was used in the first example (Section 13.3.1).

2. The root node then allocates space for a, the complete array which is part of the test procedure and is only used to generate an oracle value for checking the result of the distributed computation. A complete vector, v, is also allocated, and both a and x are populated with random numbers.

3. Each process computes the partitioning based on the input values of m and n and allocates space to store its own set of columns A_r in b, its share of the vector, x_r, in x, and its partial result y_r in y.

4. The step of sending the partitions A_r from the root node to each processor is part of the testing process and would not normally occur in an application. In this step we illustrate the use of *mpi_isend* on the root and *mpi_irecv* on the other nodes. Illustrative calls to *mpi_wait*, *mpi_waitall*, and *mpi_test* are also used.

5. The routines *mpi_isend* and *mpi_irecv* are both nonblocking, which means that the process does not have to wait until the send or receive has completed before carrying on with the execution. So, after initiating all the sends, the root process may then perform extra computation, such as copying over A_0 and x_0, and computing the model solution $z = Ax$, while waiting for them all to complete.

6. The required result is obtained by summing the vectors y_r using *mpi_reduce*.

7. The result y is checked against the matrix-vector product $z = Ax$, where z is computed with the intrinsic matrix-vector product function z=MATMUL(a,x). The vectors y and z will not agree exactly because of rounding error differences, so we use a tolerance to deal with this difference as part of the test.

EXERCISE 13.3. *Modify the subprogram f2003mv so that the partitioning information of the matrix A is computed only at the root node. Then use MPI_scatter to send this data to the remaining processors.*

13.4 Fortran Standard Code Violations

Listing 13.3 shows a small MPI code fragment that uses the traditional Fortran MPI bindings [86]. Here two processes form a work-group with one ($myId = 0$) sending data comprising a Fortran integer value, *imax*, and a double precision value, *bigmax*, to a second process ($myId = 1$) using two separate messages.

Listing 13.3. *MPI fragment showing violation of Fortran standard.*

```
...
USE SET_PRECISION
include 'mpif.h'

INTEGER :: imax, ierr, myId, tag
REAL(DKIND) :: bigmax
... ! Includes calls that initialize the computation
    ! and define the other parameters
SELECT(myId)

CASE(0)
  CALL mpi_send(imax,   1,mpi_integer,1,tag,comm,ierr)
  CALL mpi_send(bigmax,1,mpi_double_precision,1,tag,comm,ierr)

CASE(1)
  CALL mpi_recv(imax,   1,mpi_integer,1,tag,comm,&
      mpi_status_ignore,ierr)
  CALL mpi_recv(bigmax,1,mpi_double_precision,1,tag,comm,&
      mpi_status_ignore,ierr)

END SELECT
...
```

All the Fortran compilers that we have experience with will compile this code correctly, although it may be necessary to refrain from using certain compile-time

Table 13.1. *MPI core routines interfaced in module Fortran_to_MPI.*

MPI_Abort	MPI_Get_version
MPI_Allgather	MPI_Init
MPI_Allgatherv	MPI_Initialized
MPI_Allreduce	MPI_Irecv
MPI_Barrier	MPI_Isend
MPI_Bcast	MPI_Recv
MPI_Comm_dup	MPI_Reduce
MPI_Comm_rank	MPI_Scatter
MPI_Comm_size	MPI_Scatterv
MPI_Finalize	MPI_Send
MPI_Gather	MPI_Test
MPI_Gatherv	MPI_Wait
MPI_Get_processor_name	MPI_Wtime

options (see Chapter 18). However, this code definitely *violates the Fortran standard*, which states (see [49, Section 12.4.1]) that the actual argument types must match their corresponding dummy argument types. Typically the routines *mpi_send* and *mpi_recv* are precompiled in a library, and there are usually no provided interface definitions or information regarding type, kind, and rank compatibility of the routine's arguments.

A second common standard violation is to use a scalar variable rather than an array of length one, for example, when sending or receiving a single item of data. This whole area is discussed in more detail in Rasmussen and Squyres [76].

We now show how the C interoperability addition to Fortran 2003 may be used to allow a standard-complying interface *where each Fortran routine directly calls the corresponding MPI C function*. It is then not necessary to violate the Fortran standard by using differing data types, and since the C functions are called directly, there may be a slight gain in efficiency. By using such an interface we achieve compliance with the Fortran standard, enable argument checking that can help avoid silly mistakes, and allow direct calls to the C MPI library for that environment.

There is a potential replacement for MPI, known as Fortran *coarrays*, which is included in the 2008 standard. It covers much the same application needs as MPI and we briefly introduce this in Chapter 14, where the two examples presented in this chapter—computing π and matrix-vector products—are repeated using coarrays.

13.5   A Core Suite

The number of routines in MPI is large: there are 128 in MPI-1 and 287 routines in all of MPI [86, p. 395]. The experience of the authors, and other practitioners we have contacted, suggest that 26 routines suffice for most applications. This subset of the MPI library is listed in Table 13.1. We restrict our attention to this core suite and provide interfaces to the corresponding C software.

13.5.1 Defining Parameters Using MPI C Code

We introduce the idea of using the underlying MPI C libraries by rewriting the nonstandard-conforming code fragment in Listing 13.3 using our C binding library; the result is shown in Listing 13.4. Major differences are as follows.

1. We have exchanged the include line for the MPI Fortran header file with a USE statement for the C binding library. This means that we now need to declare and explicitly set via a function call (to an additional C function, *mpi_value*) all the values that we use for describing various data types and flags such as *mpi_double_precision*, *mpi_status_ignore*, etc. These values are dependent on the particular implementation of the C MPI library.

2. The calls to the MPI library routines are now function calls (rather than subroutines) which return the integer status flag (instead of this being the last parameter in the argument list).

3. Message arguments which, with the Fortran bindings, can be of various types and rank, are replaced by calls to *c_loc* which returns a *c_ptr* containing the C address of its argument. This removes one of the nonstandard features of the Fortran bindings.

Listing 13.4. *MPI fragment showing standard-conforming code.*

```
...
USE set_precision , ONLY : wp
USE Fortran_to_MPI

INTEGER :: comm , mpi_integer , mpi_double_precision , &
           tag=0
INTEGER , TARGET :: imax , mpi_status_ignore
REAL(wp) , TARGET :: bigmax
... ! Includes calls that initialize the computation
comm                  = mpi_value ('mpi_comm_world')
mpi_integer           = mpi_value ('mpi_integer')
mpi_double_precision  = mpi_value ('mpi_double_precision')
mpi_status_ignore     = mpi_value ('mpi_status_ignore')
...
SELECT(myId)
CASE(0)
 ierr = mpi_send(C_LOC(imax),   1,mpi_integer ,1,tag , comm)
 ierr = mpi_send(C_LOC(bigmax),1,mpi_double_precision ,1,tag , comm)

CASE(1)
 ierr = mpi_recv(C_LOC(imax),   1,mpi_integer ,1,tag , comm, &
                 C_LOC(mpi_status_ignore))
 ierr = mpi_recv(C_LOC(bigmax),1,mpi_double_precision ,1,tag , &
                 comm , C_LOC(mpi_status_ignore))
END SELECT
...
```

13.5.2   Defining the C Bindings

For each routine in our core list, an interface is provided to the underlying C function; this bypasses the need to have separate Fortran wrapper routines that call their parent C functions. In addition we now satisfy the Fortran standard, and missing or mistyped arguments may be detected during the development of an application. Finally, this interface can assist in writing portable MPI applications. Normally the Fortran interoperability function $C\_LOC(...)$ is used for those arguments that are called by reference or pointer value, and this is a fixed type even though *its* target can be any interoperable data type. Any parameter that is an argument for $C\_LOC(...)$ must, therefore, have the **TARGET** attribute. First, consider the Fortran use of *mpi_send* whose interface is in the module *Fortran_to_MPI* and is shown in Listing 13.5. We note that all arguments are passed by value, and the C external name is defined by using the parameter *Name='MPI_Send'* in the binding specification. Maintaining the exact mixed case is necessary so that this name will match the C internal name which is case sensitive. Most of our MPI routines return an error flag for the function value; here *IERR* is used.

Listing 13.5. *Fortran interface to mpi_send.*

```
!! This code extract is part of the accompanying software
!! that supports Chapter 13. It may be found in the file
!! fortran_mpi.f90
!!
    FUNCTION mpi_send(buf, bufCount, datatype, dest, tag, comm) &
                  BIND(C,NAME='MPI_Send') RESULT(ierr)
      IMPORT c_int, c_ptr
      TYPE (c_ptr), VALUE :: buf
      INTEGER(c_int), INTENT(IN), VALUE :: bufCount, datatype, &
                                        dest, tag, comm
      INTEGER(c_int) :: ierr
    END FUNCTION mpi_send
```

The second interface to *mpi_recV* is different because one of its arguments may be of two different data types. The C specification for this routine is

```
int MPI_Recv(void* buf, int count, MPI_Datatype datatype,
             int source, int tag, MPI_Comm comm,
             MPI_Status *status)
```

The arguments *MPI_Datatype* and the communicator handle *MPI_Comm* are normally C integers, but the argument *MPI_Status* can be either a particular C integer value, *MPI_STATUS_IGNORE*, or a C structure of type *status*. This C structure corresponds to the Fortran derived type *MPI_Status*, defined with a C binding.

Listing 13.6. *Fortran derived type mpi_status.*

```
!! This code extract is part of the accompanying software
!! that supports Chapter 13. It may be found in the file
!! fortran_mpi.f90
!!
TYPE,BIND(C):: MPI_Status
   INTEGER(c_int) :: statusCount
   INTEGER(c_int) :: canceled
```

```
! These are the three mandatory components
   INTEGER(c_int) :: mpi_source
   INTEGER(c_int) :: mpi_tag
   INTEGER(c_int) :: mpi_error
END TYPE
```

The MPI specification mandates that the integer fields *MPI_ERROR*, *MPI_TAG*, and *MPI_SOURCE* be components of *status*, but vendor-specific implementations may include additional components. In the case of MPICH2, there are extra components *statusCount*, the number of bytes in the message, and a flag, *canceled*. For routines that use arguments of type *MPI_Status*, the corresponding Fortran specification of this structure must match that for the particular MPI library. In the module *Fortran_to_MPI* we have included several versions of this structure which we have come across in our work. While we are certain these alternatives will not cover all implementations, they should provide a template for new variants.

This is the only place where knowledge of this structure is required for our version of the Fortran interface. The whole issue could have been avoided if the three required components had been defined as being the *first* in the structure, with any additional components following.

The interface to *mpi_recv* can have two data types for the final argument, *status*, so for that argument we need to use the function *c_loc(...)* with an argument *mpi_status* or *mpi_status_ignore*.

Listing 13.7. *Fortran interface to mpi_recv.*

```
!! This code extract is part of the accompanying software
!! that supports Chapter 13. It may be found in the file
!! fortran_mpi.f90
!!
! The STATUS argument can have a derived type or an integer as the
! last argument. So a generic interface is provided that allows for
! either of these two argument types in that position.
   FUNCTION mpi_recv(buf, bufCount, datatype, source, tag, &
                     comm, status) &
                     BIND(C,NAME='MPI_Recv') RESULT(ierr)
      IMPORT c_int, c_ptr
      TYPE (c_ptr), VALUE :: buf
      INTEGER(c_int), INTENT(IN), VALUE :: bufCount, datatype, &
                                           source, tag, comm
      TYPE(c_ptr), VALUE :: status
      INTEGER(c_int) :: ierr
   END FUNCTION mpi_recv
```

Chapter 14

Coarrays in Standard Fortran

Synopsis:

    Coarrays as an alternative to MPI:

      ▶ *Introduction with an example*

      ▶ *Core features of coarrays*

      ▶ *Approximating π with coarrays*

      ▶ *Matrix-vector products with coarrays*

14.1 Introduction

One important new addition to the Fortran 2008 standard was a parallel computing feature based on the *coarray* (note that the expected hyphen "-" is not present in the name, analogous to *cosine*). The main aim of coarrays is to allow the programmer to write portable parallel code with minimal effort. The key attribute is the ability to copy or exchange information between executing program images using assignment notation and a new subscripting convention. Although MPI [86] is in widespread use, it is an unnatural way to write parallel code, as there is a perpetual need to recall routine names, argument order, and key words for data types and functionality. There is no suggestion of concurrency when examining the source language that calls MPI subprograms, and there is the matter of inherent Fortran standard violations. Much of the complexity and messiness of MPI programming is potentially swept away with the promise of coarrays.

The coarray specifications rely on the notion of p *images* of a single program. How the value of p is provided, and how the simultaneous execution of these images is started is not specified by the standard. Hence, this aspect of coarrays is processor dependent and will most likely be provided at an operating system level.

The following code fragment illustrates how coarrays may be used to perform the same task as that used as an example of the Fortran standard violation inherent in using MPI (Chapter 13). As before, the executable with image number one is transferring one integer and one real scalar value to image two. The image numbers are specified by the values appearing in square brackets in the two assignment statements, and this notation highlights code that requires data transfers to take place. We note that, for coarrays, the image range is $[1, p]$ rather than $[0, p-1]$ as favored by MPI.

Listing 14.1. *Coarray fragment showing simple transfer of data.*

```
...
INTEGER  ::  imax[*]
REAL  ::  bigmax[*]
...
imax[2]=imax[1]
bigmax[2]=bigmax[1]
```

14.2   A Core Suite of Coarray Intrinsic Functions

We look briefly at some of the more important features of coarrays that have been included in the Fortran 2008 standard; a fuller summary is available in the working document [78].

14.2.1   Specifying Data Objects

Listing 14.1 illustrates the use of *codimensions* in the declaration of *imax* and *bigmax*. Just like a sequential Fortran program, each image has access to its own set of data objects; these are local to the image and cannot be accessed or altered by any other images. Objects that are declared with codimensions are also distinct entities within each image, but data stored in these entities may be transferred from one image to another via assignment statements.

A codimension index in square brackets, *coindex*, maps to an image in the same way as a normal array index, in round brackets, maps to a memory location. Codimensions of nonallocatable objects are specified in the same way as an assumed-size array in that the final dimension is always an asterisk; an assumed size *equal to the number of images*. Thus *imax[*]* defines a coarray whose *corank* is one.

Codimensions may be associated with any object that may be declared in a standard-conforming program, and coarrays may have coranks greater than one; for example,

```
REAL, DIMENSION(10), CODIMENSION[20,*]  ::  a
REAL  ::  b(3,4)[10,*]
```

specify array coarrays where the codimensions are modeling a grid of images. It is thus possible to define different "processor geometries" using codimensions.

However, the cosize of a coarray is *always* equal to the number of images; this means that we need to exercise caution when using loops to specify coindices to prevent out of bounds problems; [see 65, Section 19.4] for details.

Each coindex must be a scalar integer expression and coarray sections are not allowed. i.e., *imax[1:2]* is illegal. Array subscripts must be used whenever an array coarray is accessed; for example, *a[2,3]* is not permitted as a shorthand for *a()[2,3]*.

14.2.2 Allocatable Coarrays

A coarray may be allocatable and the allocate statement has been extended to allow cobounds to be specified, for example,

```
REAL , ALLOCATABLE :: a ( : ) [ : , : ]
:
ALLOCATE ( a ( 10 ) [ 20 ,*] )
```

The cobounds must always be included in the allocate statement, and the upper bound for the final codimension must still always be an asterisk; for example, the following are not permitted:

```
ALLOCATE ( a ( 10 ) ) ! Not allowed (no cobounds)
ALLOCATE ( a ( 10 ) [ p ] ) ! Not allowed (cobound not *)
```

In addition, the value of each bound, cobound, or length type parameter is required to be the same on all images; for example, the following is not permitted because the bound would vary on each image: *allocate(a(this_image())[20, *])*.

Furthermore, when allocating coarrays, the allocate statement acts as an implicit synchronization point; all images must complete the allocate before any may proceed to execute any subsequent statements. A similar synchronization applies to deallocate statements. Without these rules, it might be possible for one image to refer to data in another that has not yet been allocated or has already been deallocated.

In executing an allocate statement, communication is required only for synchronization; specifically, the compiler is not required to enforce any of the rules regarding coarrays, such as bounds and cobounds being the same on all images, nor is the compiler responsible for providing any assistance with the detection or resolution of deadlock problems. If allocated coarrays, without the **SAVE** attribute, are still allocated when a return or end statement is executed, they are implicitly deallocated before the subprogram exits and this also requires a synchronization point.

14.2.3 Referencing Images

There are three intrinsic functions that provide run-time information about the number of images and architectural position of an image.

1. *num_images()* returns, as an integer, the total number of images available to the application. Normally this value will be specified at the operating system level via the command that initiates the execution. The maximum number of images available is system dependent.

2. *this_image()* returns, as an integer, the index of the image that called the function. This will be in the range [1, *num_images()*]. The function may also

be called with a coarray argument and an optional dimension parameter when it returns coindex information about the value of the invoking image index. As an example, if a was declared as an array coarray using $a(10, 20)/8, -1{:}5, 0{:}*/$, then a call to *this_image()* from image 132 would return the rank-1 integer array $[4, 0, 1]$.

3. *image_index(coa, ind)* returns an integer scaler in the range $[0, num\_images()]$. Here *coa* is a coarray of any type and *ind* is a rank-1 integer array of subscripts corresponding to a coindex. If *ind* is a valid subscript, then the value returned is the corresponding image index; otherwise zero is returned. For example with a declared as above *image_index(a,[4, 0, 1])* would return 132. If the number of images available was less than 132 the result would be zero.

14.3   A Coarray Alternative for Computing π

We now present (Listing 14.2) an implementation of the algorithm for computing π given in Chapter 13. Here image one reads the value of n, the number of quadrature points required, and broadcasts it to all the other images via a coarray assignment. The *numim* images then collect the partial sums in the same way as the individual processes in the MPI implementation.

We note some of the key points of the code:

1. The number of the image, r, is obtained using the intrinsic function *this_image()*.

2. The intrinsic function *num_images()* returns the total number of images available, p.

3. The **SYNC ALL** statements create synchronization points for all the images, i.e., no image executes beyond these points until all the images have reached it. These statements ensure that

   (a) all the images have acquired the value of n before any processing begins, and

   (b) all the partial sums are available for image one to accumulate.

Listing 14.2. *Computation of π: Using coarray fortran.*

```
!! This code extract is part of the accompanying software
!! that supports Chapter 14. It may be found in the file
!! approximatePi.f90
!!
    PROGRAM approximatePi
      USE set_precision , ONLY : wp
      IMPLICIT NONE
      REAL(wp), PARAMETER :: zero = 0.0e0_wp, one = 1.0e0_wp, &
        four = 4.0E0_wp, half = 0.5e0_wp
! The number of panels and partial sums are coarrays
      INTEGER :: n[*]
      REAL (wp) :: partialSum [*]
```

```fortran
! Variables that are local to all images
      INTEGER :: i, myimage, numim
      REAL (wp) :: h, pi, total
! Use the intrinsic functions this_image() and num_images() to get
! the number of this image and the total number of images
      myimage = this_image()
      numim = num_images()
      IF (myimage==1) THEN
        WRITE (*, '(A)') 'Input the number of quadrature points:'
        READ (*, *) n
      END IF

! <= First synchronization point
! Other images wait here until the number of points is defined
      SYNC ALL
      n=n[1]
! Compute the panel size
      h = one/REAL(n, KIND=wp)
      partialSum = zero
! Compute individual pieces of the quadrature
      DO i = myimage, n, numim
        partialSum = partialSum + f(h*(REAL(i,KIND=wp)-half))
      END DO

! <= Second synchronization point
! Add the pieces from all the images when they are ready
      SYNC ALL
      IF (myimage==1) THEN
        total = partialSum
        DO i = 2, numim
          total = total + partialSum[i]
        END DO
! Scale the approximation to get the approximate \pi
        total = four*h*total
        WRITE (*, *) 'Using ', num_images(),' images, and n = ', n
        WRITE (*, *) 'Approximate Value of PI = ', total
! Check the result with an accurate value of \pi
        pi = four*ATAN(one)
        WRITE (*, *) 'Relative error = ', (pi-total)/pi
      END IF

    CONTAINS

    FUNCTION f(x) RESULT (y)
      REAL (wp), INTENT(IN) :: x
      REAL (wp) :: y
      y = one/(one+x**2)
    END FUNCTION f
  END PROGRAM approximatePi
```

14.4   Matrix-Vector Products Using Coarrays

For our second example we look again at the matrix-vector product example we
considered in Chapter 13 (page 152) and reimplement it using coarrays.

The complete program is available online, and here we mention some of the more important features:

- Values of m and n are input from the user on image one and these values are broadcast to all nodes with a coarray assignment.

- The partitioning is computed on each image. The distinguished image, image one, may have up to $num\_images()$ -1 more columns than the alternate images.

- Each image allocates space to hold its partition A_r, its vector x_r, and its partial result, y_r. A_r and x_r are populated with random numbers.

- All nodes compute $y_r = A_r x_r$ using the intrinsic matrix product function $MATMUL$, and the required result is obtained by summing the vectors y_r over all the images and placing the sum on image one.

- The result y is checked against the actual matrix-vector product $z = Ax$, where z is computed on image one. This requires first copying the submatrices A_r and the corresponding x_r to image one from all the other images. This is purely for checking purposes and would not make sense for problems so large that A could not be allocated on a single image.

- If a memory allocation error occurs, that image prints an error message. This output, if it is required, is enclosed by the coarray directives *critical* {...} *end critical* to avoid the output from more than one image becoming jumbled.

Chapter 15

OpenMP in Fortran

Synopsis:

- ► *Elementary concepts of threading*

- ► *Introduction with examples*

- ► *Core directives for OpenMP*

- ► *General thread models with Pthreads*

- ► *Exercises*

15.1 Introduction

The specification for *OpenMP*, short for Open Multi-Processing, describes a methodology for programming multiple CPUs that share memory. The nomenclature of parallel computing tends to be confusing, with different approaches using different sets of vocabulary. The specification of OpenMP is based on *threads* (short for *threads of execution*) which may be synonymous with a processor, or a core, or neither! OpenMP programmers really don't have to worry about exactly what constitutes a thread; they just need to understand how threads interact with the shared memory and how this affects the way in which software needs to be constructed to make it *thread-safe*.

Our description and illustration of some aspects of OpenMP is restricted to its use in Fortran software [69]; alternate specifications for its use in C and C++ are also available. By use of simple examples we illustrate some of the features and pitfalls of this important software technology. To use OpenMP in application development, we recommend the book by Chapman, Jost, and van der Pas [18], and the summary guide to the operations [70].

In Fortran, OpenMP consists of a set of *sentinel comments* that act as directives to the compiler. If the compiler has not been configured to process them, they are treated as any other comments and the source code becomes a straightforward sequential program. Like MPI, OpenMP is not a part of the Fortran standard and its availability is at the discretion of the compiler writer.

We mention a few pros and cons about this design strategy:

- The specifications for OpenMP allow a programmer to take advantage of parallelism when the underlying hardware has multiple execution threads that share memory. The Fortran compiler creates an executable that can take advantage of these threads to improve run-time efficiency. (Pro)

- Installing the directives in the source code can be performed incrementally. (Pro)

- The use of sentinel comments, as compiler directives, sidesteps the standard committee's review process. Thus the Fortran standard is silent about OpenMP and compiler writers are free to add or ignore features. (Con)

- While the use of the directives appears simple, it is very easy to generate code that does not function as intended. New types of errors, for example, *race* and *deadlock* conditions, are possible and these are difficult to both avoid and remove. (Con)

- In this chapter we give some elementary hints that can be used to alleviate the occurrence of errors. (Pro)

We consider a work-group of $1 \leq t \leq t_{max}$ threads that execute sections of a simple program unit in parallel, sharing access to the available memory. The order of execution within the work-group is arbitrary.

A program unit is declared *thread-safe* if, for all $t > 1$, the results obtained by a particular data set are numerically equivalent to those obtained when the code is run sequentially ($t = 1$). It is worthwhile to mention the following points regarding thread-safe code.

- There is no requirement that the results obtained for $t = 1$ and $t > 1$ be identical. This would be too strict due to the differences in rounding errors when the work-group performs floating-point calculations.

- Comparing a result for $t = 1$ and $t > 1$ requires the result for $t = 1$ to be correct. This may often mean debugging a serial version of the software before testing with OpenMP.

- If the program does not terminate for a value of $t > 1$, then we probably have a deadlock condition.

- If the program does terminate for values $t > 1$ but does not generate numerically equivalent results, then we probably have a race condition. This is generally caused by access to data in memory not being synchronized correctly.

15.2   Examples

Our examples get progressively more interesting.

15.2.1   An Array Update

Consider the ubiquitous computation of overwriting an n-vector y with the operation $y \leftarrow ax + y$, where $a \neq 0$ is a scalar and x is a different n-vector of the same size. This operation may be computed in parallel in an obvious way: suppose $n = 100$ and four threads are available that share the memory used by the two vectors. Then each thread $1 \leq p \leq 4$ may compute the new values of the elements $25(p-1) + 1 \ldots 25p$ completely independently of all the other threads. Moreover, since each element of y may be computed independently, any partition of the n elements will allow a parallel execution.

The following Fortran code fragment provides the simplest OpenMP implementation for performing the computation

```
...
        INTEGER :: i, n
        n = 100
        REAL(wp) :: a, x(n), y(n)
!$OMP PARALLEL DO
        DO i = 1,n
           y(i)=a*x(i)+y(i)
        END DO
!$OMP END PARALLEL DO
```

although, in this case, the mapping of the loop indices to threads will not be portable when comparing different compilers!

There is an important implicit point in the above code; while the scalars n and a and the vectors x and y are shared by the threads, each thread must have its own private copy of the loop variable, i. The OpenMP specification requires the compiler to take care of this important detail, but we could be explicit when we write the loop

```
        INTEGER :: i, n
        n = 100
        REAL(wp) :: a, x(n), y(n)
!$OMP PARALLEL DO PRIVATE(i) SHARED(n,a,x,y)
        DO i = 1,n
           y(i)=a*x(i)+y(i)
        END DO
!$OMP END PARALLEL DO
```

Some applications may need to monitor a parallel loop for exceptions; for example, in the above loop, components of the output vector may be assigned NaN or $\pm\infty$ (see Chapter 9 for more about NaNs and infinities).

We might expect this to be a rare event so we have a first loop that makes no tests on the elements. Only if this leads to an exception do we resort to a more detailed analysis. We complicate the loop by summing the components of the updated vector, y; this calculation is not used for its value but rather to classify any exception that occurs. We assume that the extra floating-point additions will not have much of an effect on performance, but, in any case, this extra overhead will cost far less than testing each component. By use-associating the module *ieee_arithmetic* and declaring a variable of derived type *ieee_class_type* we may use the overloaded comparison operator == to test whether *s* is a quiet NaN or infinite.

```
        USE set_precision , ONLY : wp
        USE, INTRINSIC :: ieee_arithmetic
        TYPE(ieee_class_type) :: cls
        LOGICAL :: exception
        INTEGER :: i, n=100
        REAL(wp) :: a, s, x(n), y(n)

        s = 0.0E0_wp
!$OMP PARALLEL DO PRIVATE(i) SHARED(n,a s,x,y) &
!$OMP REDUCTION(+:s)
        DO i = 1,n
           y(i) = a*x(i) + y(i)
           s = s + y(i)
        END DO
!$OMP END PARALLEL DO

! See what the result is for s, as an IEEE class variable.
        cls = ieee_class(s)
! If a NaN or infinity was noted, analyze the input.
        exception = (cls == ieee_quiet_nan) .or. &
           (cls == ieee_negative_inf) .or. &
           (cls == ieee_positive_inf)
        ...
        IF (exception) THEN
           ...
        END IF
```

15.2.2   Output and Input with One Thread

Output Only

We now show an instance of our parallel loop where one of the threads generates output. We want to know which of four threads will process the last index when n = 101. The OpenMP integer intrinsic function *omp_get_thread_num* returns the thread number in the range $[0 \ldots nthreads - 1]$ where *nthreads* is the number of threads in the work-group.

The type declarations of the OpenMP intrinsic functions are provided through use-association with the intrinsic module *omp_lib*. This module will be available if the compiler is configured to recognize OpenMP sentinels. The working precision, *wp*, is use-associated from our module, *set_precision*.

```
!! This code extract is part of the accompanying software
!! that supports Chapter 15. It may be found in the file
!! Example2.f90
!!
        USE omp_lib , ONLY : omp_set_num_threads , omp_get_thread_num
        USE set_precision , ONLY: wp
        IMPLICIT NONE
```

```
      INTEGER :: i
      INTEGER, PARAMETER :: n = 101
      REAL (wp) :: a, x(n), y(n)

! Use four threads
      CALL omp_set_num_threads(4)
      x(1:n) = 1.0E0_wp
      y(1:n) = 1.0E0_wp
      a = 2.0E0_wp

!$OMP PARALLEL DO
      DO i = 1, n
        y(i) = a*x(i) + y(i)
        IF (i == n) THEN
           WRITE (*,'(''Thread '', i3, '' processes index '',i5)')&
              omp_get_thread_num(), n
        END IF
      END DO
!$OMP END PARALLEL DO
```

Input with One Thread, Output with All Threads

We next use thread 0 for an example of a single thread inputting data. The logical variable, *flag*, initialized to **.false.**, is shared by all the threads and is set to **.true.** by thread 0 once it has completed its input. Each thread will eventually execute the statement

```
!! This code extract is part of the accompanying software
!! that supports Chapter 15. It may be found in the file
!! Example3.f90
!!
      CALL subt(time(i),flag)
```

whereupon it will spin for *time(i)* seconds before testing *flag*. This example illustrates how each instance of the subprogram can perform useful work while thread 0 is busy with input. Note that the variable *mythread* must be declared **PRIVATE** for each thread to ensure that it preserves its thread-dependent value.

In the subprogram *subt* the logical variable *flag* is given the additional attribute **VOLATILE**. Specifying this attribute indicates to the compiler that *flag* may be accessed and/or set from outside the executing thread. Each reference to this volatile variable will cause the value to be read from memory, rather than storing and retrieving it from, say, a register or local cache.

This is necessary because the contents of this variable will be changed by thread 0 only after the input is completed. Without specifying this attribute for *flag*, the subprogram would not be reliable. The compiled code would be free to replace the test by equivalent logic if *flag* were not to be reloaded to test its volatile and currently stored value.

```
!! This code extract is part of the accompanying software
!! that supports Chapter 15. It may be found in the file
!! Example3.f90
!!
```

```
      USE omp_lib , ONLY : omp_get_max_threads , omp_get_thread_num

      IMPLICIT NONE
      INTEGER :: i, istat , k, mythread , nthreads
      REAL (skind), ALLOCATABLE :: time(:)
      LOGICAL :: flag

      nthreads = omp_get_max_threads ()
      ALLOCATE (time(nthreads))
      CALL random_number(time)
      flag = .FALSE.

!$OMP PARALLEL DO PRIVATE(mythread) SHARED(flag)
      DO i = 1, nthreads
         mythread = omp_get_thread_num ()
         IF (mythread==0) THEN
            WRITE (*,'(A)',ADVANCE='No') 'Enter an integer -- '
            READ (*,*,IOSTAT=istat) k
! This has the VOLATILE attribute within the routine subt().
            flag = .TRUE.
         END IF
! All threads call subt()
         CALL subt(time(i),flag)
      END DO
!$OMP END PARALLEL DO
```

```
!! This code extract is part of the accompanying software
!! that supports Chapter 15. It may be found in the file
!! Example3.f90
!!
    SUBROUTINE subt(time ,flag)
      USE set_precision , ONLY : skind
      USE omp_lib , ONLY : omp_get_thread_num
      IMPLICIT NONE

      REAL (skind), INTENT (IN) :: time
      LOGICAL , VOLATILE :: flag
      INTEGER , SAVE :: istart , iend , irate , mythread

!$OMP THREADPRIVATE(istart, iend, irate, mythread)
      mythread = omp_get_thread_num ()

      IF (mythread > 0) THEN
         CALL system_clock(COUNT = istart ,COUNT_RATE = irate)
         DO
! Spin Elapsed TIME S before testing FLAG.
            CALL system_clock(COUNT = iend)
            IF ((iend - istart) >= time*irate) EXIT
         END DO

         DO ! Spin until FLAG==.TRUE.
! Since FLAG is VOLATILE, this loop will not be removed
! or changed in the executing code.
            IF (flag) EXIT
         END DO
         WRITE(*, '(''Thread '',I3, '' waited '','' // &
            'F6.3, '' secs before FLAG was tested'')') mythread, time
```

```
      ELSE
         WRITE (*, '(''Thread    0 did no waiting after input.'')')
      END IF

   END SUBROUTINE
```

15.2.3   The Atomic and Critical Constructs

The *atomic* and *critical* constructs are both used for what is called *mutual exclusion synchronization* and are primarily employed to ensure a thread is guaranteed exclusive access to shared data.

As a simple example, consider the following code to form the dot product of a pair of vectors:

```
!! This code extract is part of the accompanying software
!! that supports Chapter 15. It may be found in the file
!! dotp.f90
!!
        s = zero
!$OMP PARALLEL DO
        DO i = 1, n
! Possibility of race condition between reading and
! writing s from/to memory
        s = s + x(i)*y(i)
        END DO
!$OMP END PARALLEL DO
```

When a thread updates s, it reads the current value from memory, forms the sum by adding $x(i)*y(i)$, and then writes the result back to memory. If between the read and write another thread reads s, then it will pick up the same value of the partial sum, and one of the two resulting updates will be lost.

What we need is for each thread to update s as an atomic operation. This means that once a thread starts to update, all other threads are locked out until the first thread has finished, and the memory location of s is effectively locked until the update is finished.

This action can be achieved by using the *atomic* directive

```
!! This code extract is part of the accompanying software
!! that supports Chapter 15. It may be found in the file
!! dotpAtomic.f90
!!
        s = zero
!$OMP PARALLEL DO
        DO i = 1, n
! Possibility of race condition between reading and
! writing s from/to memory
!$OMP ATOMIC
        s = s + x(i)*y(i)
        END DO
!$OMP END PARALLEL DO
```

There are rules about the form of the statement that can be controlled by an atomic directive ([see 69, Section 2.8.5] for details).

We often need to call a subroutine from within a parallel loop and it is essential that the called routine is thread-safe, i.e., it contains no deadlock or race conditions. If we are calling a library routine and have no knowledge of or access to the source, we need to exercise great caution. The only reliable course of action is to forego parallelism and force each thread to have exclusive access to the subprogram; effectively we serialize the calls.

We do this by enclosing the subprogram call within a *critical section* within the parallel directive:

```
    ...
!$OMP PARALLEL DO
         DO i = 1,n
! Do most of the work in parallel, up to the critical section.
! The routine subx is needed but unknown with respect to
! thread-safety. so call the routine subx, one thread at a time:
!$OMP CRITICAL
           CALL subx
! Save or use results of call to subx.
!$OMP END CRITICAL
    ...
! If the intended work must wait until all threads have
! returned from subx, insert the OpenMP barrier directive:
!!$OMP BARRIER
! Do some more work with the results.
    ...
         END DO
!$OMP END PARALLEL DO
```

As each thread reaches the *!$omp critical* directive it waits until no other thread is executing the critical section, at which point it gains exclusive access. The thread order of execution of a critical section is unspecified.

Finally, we note that a commented line in the above code shows the potential use of the *barrier* directive. On meeting this directive each thread waits until all threads have reached this point, and only once they have all arrived does execution proceed through the barrier. This construct should be used sparingly.

Two distinct subprograms may be executed in parallel using a simple parallel directive. However, there must be prior assurance that *any potential race conditions in either routine have no side effects that could impact the other*. Suppose this applies to the subprograms *suba* and *subb*; then two threads, designated with the OpenMP option *num_threads(2)*, can be used with a directive to execute the routines in parallel.

```
!$OMP PARALLEL num_threads(2)
      CALL suba
      CALL subb
!$omp end parallel
```

15.3   Tips on Writing Thread-Safe Routines

We stress the need to develop new software with a view to it being used at some stage with an OpenMP model of parallelism. Converting existing subprograms to be thread-safe is difficult but not impossible. Based on our experiences we offer some hints that have proved helpful in this process, although these are very much general guidelines rather than specific solutions to the many particular problems that are likely to be encountered in practice.

1. Before starting any conversion, gain a full understanding of the source code and the way in which the data is accessed and manipulated.

2. Classify all the local variables into two distinct categories, *shared* or *private*. Variables that either acquire a value that is provably assigned only once by an executing thread or are provably thread-safe are classified as shared; all other should be designated private.

3. Declare all variables classified as private using directives of the form *!$omp threadprivate(<list>)*.

4. Install parallel threads incrementally and test each increment thoroughly. Unexpected changes in the results following an increment are most likely to be due to a race condition. Do not be lulled into a false sense of security; race conditions can still be lurking, undiscovered by the current test suite.

15.3.1 Your Own Private Variables

Fortran language elements can be used to create thread-private objects without these being obliged to have the **SAVE** attribute. This illustration gives hints as to how the OpenMP thread-private directives are compiled into the executing code, but it provides more flexibility. The key idea is to recast a variable as an **ALLOCATABLE** array of the same type and kind. A new dimension or an extra rank is created whose run-time index will depend on the thread number. The size of this additional dimension is the maximum number of threads that are possible, obtained using the OpenMP intrinsic function, *omp_get_max_threads*. This example program uses that idea in the creation of a scalar private variable, here called vt. Access to this private scalar is through the array element *vt(omp_get_thread_num() + 1)*. Note the critical section in the interior of the loop. Exactly one thread enters this section and then allocates the array *vt*. As alternate threads enter this section, they encounter the test and, since the array has already been allocated, this test evaluates to false.

```
!! This code extract is part of the accompanying software
!! that supports Chapter 15. It may be found in the file
!! Example5.f90
!!
      USE omp_lib
      IMPLICIT NONE
! Illustrate creating your own private variables.
      REAL (wp), ALLOCATABLE :: vt(:)
      INTEGER , SAVE :: natural
      INTEGER :: i, maxt
!$OMP THREADPRIVATE(NATURAL)
      maxt = omp_get_max_threads()
```

```
!$OMP PARALLEL DO
      DO i = 1, maxt
! Only one thread allocates vt(:).
!$OMP CRITICAL
      IF ( .NOT. allocated(vt)) ALLOCATE (vt(maxt))
!$OMP END CRITICAL
      natural = omp_get_thread_num() + 1
! This vt() value is private to each thread:
      vt(natural) = natural
      END DO
!$OMP END PARALLEL DO
      WRITE (*,'(A,/,(I5,F6.2))') &
         'Natural Numbers for Each Thread = ', (i,vt(i),i=1,maxt)
```

15.3.2   Avoiding Memory Fragmentation Failures

This section is based on our hard-won personal experience with applications. It is a
warning of potential problems in otherwise correct threaded codes. In the simplest
form, consider a routine SUBROUTINE subw(n). In particular this routine allocates space
in the local array *work(:)*.

```
SUBROUTINE subw(n)
   USE set_precision
   USE omp_lib
   IMPLICIT NONE

   INTEGER , INTENT(IN) :: n
   REAL(wp), ALLOCATABLE , SAVE :: work(:)
!$OMP THREADPRIVATE(work)
 . . .
   ALLOCATE(work(n))
 . . .
   DEALLOCATE(work)
END SUBROUTINE subw
```

We draw attention to the array *work(:)*. Other elements of the routine are
not important here. Suppose the routine *subw(n)* is called a number of times with
different values of n. Each entry and return allocates and then deallocates the
array. This creates a potential for a run-time error. The potential error lies in the
fact that new run-time addresses for the array may be found with each entry to
the routine. There is no guarantee that the memory deallocated on a previous exit
can be recovered and reused. Current computers typically have a lot of memory, so
this potential failure can remain undiagnosed until a stressful computation occurs
that repeatedly calls the routine, particularly with varying values of n. The code
can crash because no contiguous block of memory of size n is available—memory
addressing has become *fragmented*.

There is a fix for this potential catastrophe. It requires rewriting the subprogram and modifying the call. The space for the array *work(:)* is allocated in the
calling program unit that has knowledge of the range of values for n and the maximum number of threads that will call the routine. We illustrate this with a main

program and a new routine *subz(n, allwork)* that passes the total block of working space as an argument. A thread-private pointer within *subz()* picks a segment of *allwork(:)* to use as the local array *work(:)* for each thread.

```fortran
!! This code extract is part of the accompanying software
!! that supports Chapter 15. It may be found in the file
!! Example6.f90
!!
      USE omp_lib
      IMPLICIT NONE

      INTERFACE
        SUBROUTINE subz(n,allwork)
        IMPORT wp
          INTEGER, INTENT (IN) :: n
          REAL (wp), TARGET, INTENT (INOUT) :: allwork(:)
        END SUBROUTINE
      END INTERFACE

! Illustrate passing work space to multiple threads.
      REAL (wp), ALLOCATABLE, TARGET :: allwork(:)
! Here nmax is the largest value for n:
      INTEGER :: n, nmax = 10001
! Allocate one block of working storage.
      ALLOCATE (allwork(nmax*omp_get_max_threads()))
!$OMP PARALLEL
      DO n = 1, nmax
! The array allwork(:) is re-used as work space
! with each call to the routine subz().
        CALL subz(n,allwork)
      END DO
!$OMP END PARALLEL
```

```fortran
!! This code extract is part of the accompanying software
!! that supports Chapter 15. It may be found in the file
!! Example6.f90
!!
    SUBROUTINE subz(n,allwork)
      USE omp_lib
      USE set_precision
      IMPLICIT NONE
      INTEGER, INTENT (IN) :: n
      REAL (wp), TARGET, INTENT (INOUT) :: allwork(:)
      INTEGER :: i
      REAL (wp), POINTER, SAVE :: work(:)

! Designate an n - segment of the working array
! allwork(:) passed to subz as the local
! array, work(:).
!$OMP THREADPRIVATE(work)
      work => allwork(omp_get_thread_num()*n+1:)

! Assign work(:) some values.
!$OMP CRITICAL
      DO i = 1, n
         work(i) = REAL(i, wp)
      END DO
```

```
! Make sure this assignment is thread-safe:
      DO i = 1, n
        IF (work(i) /= i) THEN
          WRITE(*,'(''Assignment appears not to be thread-safe!'')')
        END IF
      END DO
!$OMP END CRITICAL
      END SUBROUTINE
```

15.4   A Mention of More General Threading Models

Other threading models exist, for example, *Windows threads* and POSIX threads
or *pthreads*; a discussion of these may be found in Breshears [15, Chapter 5]. While
the functionality of these C and C++ libraries appears very similar to OpenMP,
their syntax is quite different. The interoperability of Fortran with C, using the
methods of Chapter 10, means that we can at least use C libraries directly from
Fortran and thus maintain portability.

   We now consider a class of problems where the number of threads is limited
by the size of the problem and not the number of CPUs or other restrictions. One
can think of this as the creation of a family of threads that do their work and then
die. However, there is no upper limit to their number. Again, we use the example
of a matrix-vector product $y = Ax$, with A of order $m \times n$. The columns of A are
partitioned into p groups of consecutive columns, $A = [A_1, \ldots, A_p]$, where each A_r
is of dimension $m \times k_r$. The partitioning is chosen based on a divide-and-conquer
method, and a solution and example implementation may be found in Hanson,
Breshears, and Gabb [36, Section 4.1].

   The essential idea is to use a recursive subroutine, $THREADING\_PRODUCT$,
which, depending on the number of matrix columns in the product, either evaluates
the product directly or divides the problem into two balanced subproblems. The
product computation uses a locked *pthreads mutex* to prevent a race condition when
forming the accumulating sums. When the problem is divided, two new threads are
created, one for each subproblem.

EXERCISE 15.1. *Explain why there is a need for an OpenMP CRITICAL section in the routine subz() in Section 15.3.2. Why is this critical section not needed
if the calling program uses a !$OMP PARALLEL DO sentinel instead of !$OMP
PARALLEL?*

EXERCISE 15.2. *A !$OMP PARALLEL DO section may also have an additional
qualifier that suggests how the loop indices are mapped to the threads. This qualifier then takes the form !$OMP PARALLEL DO SCHEDULE(<type>). There are
five values for <type> permitted: STATIC, DYNAMIC, GUIDED, RUNTIME, AUTO.
Execute example2.f90 with each of these scheduling types. (Note that the first three
of these also allow an optional parameter, CHUNKSIZE, that suggests the number
of loop indices to use in each thread assignment.)*

Chapter 16

Modifying Source to Remove Obsolescent or Deleted Features

Synopsis:

Dealing with dusty decks:

▶ *Identifying deleted and obsolescent features*

▶ *Substituting deleted features*

▶ *Replacing **GO TO** statements for language conversion*

▶ *A Newton method solver, before and after*

16.1   Introduction

There are a number of features from earlier versions of Fortran that are now redundant due to the introduction of new and better methods in later standards. With Fortran 2003, five features marked as obsolescent in earlier Fortran versions were finally deleted and nine more have been marked as obsolescent, meaning that they may be withdrawn from future standards. As a practical matter most Fortran compiler vendors continue to recognize these constructs and correctly compile source code that uses them. Most compilers provide user options to generate compile-time messages when these deleted features are encountered; this makes detecting their use extremely straightforward (see Chapter 18 for examples).

The first and second sections of this chapter provide suggestions for modifying source code to replace these obsolescent and deleted features by new standard-conforming code. Depending on the size or complexity of the source files, following these suggestions may require considerable editing and retesting. Software tools are available that perform code restructuring, but these need to be used with care as the resultant transformed code may often be unreadable. Hand editing is error prone but does allow the programmer full control over the conversion. Whatever

course is taken it is essential that a comprehensive set of tests be available to ensure
that the transformed and original codes produce equivalent results.

The third section illustrates a "before" and "after" example using a simple
Newton method code for solving a single nonlinear equation $f(x) = 0$. We illustrate
how to replace **GO TO** statements and the obsolescent alternate return construction using **DO**, **CYCLE**, and **SELECT CASE**. The removal of **GO TO** statements
and labels can help considerably when converting a Fortran code to a language that
does not support a particular form of **GO TO** statement, for example, Java [28,
p. 96]. However, the **GO TO** statement is a part of standard Fortran and is likely to
remain so in the foreseeable future. In our example, the conversion process yields
an equivalent code but requires changes both to the subroutine implementing the
Newton iteration and to the calling program unit. It is a common feature of code
transformation that changes to one routine cause a cascade of changes throughout
the package. This is another reason for having a solid regression test suite.

16.2   On Replacing Obsolescent Features

Using the list found in Adams et al. [3, p. 684], the obsolescent features are the
following:

1. *Fixed form of source file.*

   Conversion to free format requires attention to the format of comments and
   continuation lines. Software is available for performing this transformation
   automatically; see Chapter 19 for details.

2. *Arithmetic-**IF** statement.*

   This ancient form of the **IF** statement is defined as

   ```
           IF (arithmetic expression) L1, L2, L3
   ```

   where the arithmetic expression is evaluated and control jumps to label L1 if
   the result is less than zero, L2 if equal to zero, and L3 if greater than zero.
   Very often either

   (a) the next executable statement is labeled L1, L2, or L3; or

   (b) two of the labels are the same.

   Removal of this statement is best performed by translation into a block-**IF**,
   although this can often be simplified to a logical-**IF** by taking (2a) or (2b)
   above into account. For example,

   ```
           IF (i−j) 10,20,10
   20      CONTINUE
   ```

   can be transformed into

   ```
           IF (i−j /= 0) GO TO 10
   20      CONTINUE
   ```

Removing the labels generally involves a deeper analysis of the logic of the software and may require some serious restructuring of the code. While this will invariably improve the readability and, hence, the maintainability of the application, the choice of whether or not to restructure is, unfortunately, most likely to be determined by time and cost considerations rather than code quality.

3. *Some forms of DO-loop termination.*

   Prior to Fortran 90, good programming practice dictated that all **DO**-loop termination statements should consist of labeled **CONTINUE** statements. In the case of nested loops, each loop should have its own **CONTINUE**. However, old practices die hard and it is very common in older codes to find nested loops terminating on a single labeled executable statement. For example,

   ```
          sum=zero
          sum2=zero
          DO 10 i = 1, n
          DO 10 j = 1, n
             IF (a(i,j) .GT. zero) GO TO 10
             a(i,j) = -a(i,j)
             sum2 = sum2 + a(i,j)
      10     sum = sum + a(i,j)
   ```

   This construct is only standard-conforming if any branch to the common label occurs in the innermost loop. Other restrictions also apply to the use of newer statements like **CYCLE** and **EXIT** with this type of labeled, nonblock loop. For these reasons it should be avoided in new code and replaced in old code; for example, the code segment above could be rewritten as

   ```
          sum=zero
          sum2=zero
          DO i = 1, n
            DO j = 1, n
              IF (a(i,j) <= zero) THEN
                a(i,j) = -a(i,j)
                sum2 = sum2 + a(i,j)
              END IF
              sum = sum + a(i,j)
            END DO
          END DO
   ```

   This transformation also removes the clutter of labels.

4. *Alternate return statement.*

   The alternate return allows control to jump to one of a set of specified labels on return from a subroutine call. Each possible label is signified by $m \geq 1$ asterisks in the dummy argument list; these are numbered left to right from 1 to m. For example, the routine, *newt*, in Listing 16.1 allows two alternate return labels to be specified as actual arguments. A **RETURN** statement is allowed to have an optional integer expression and the value of this expression selects which alternate return is used. Actual arguments corresponding to dummy alternate return arguments are of the form $*n$ where n is a target label in scope in the calling procedure. In Listing 16.1 the call to *newt* specifies that control will jump to label 10 when the statement

```
        RETURN  1
```

is executed, to label 20 if the optional expression evaluates to 2, and to the statement following the call if the **RETURN** does not have an optional argument or one is present but its value is greater than 2.

Use of this construct is almost guaranteed to produce code that is difficult to understand and, therefore, difficult to maintain and change.

5. *Computed-GO TO statement.*

   This statement has the form

```
        GO TO(L1, L2,  ...  , Lk), i
```

   where i may be a simple integer variable or an integer expression. On execution, if i evaluates to n in the range $[1 \ldots k]$, then a branch to label **Ln** occurs, otherwise the next executable statement is taken. A label may occur more than once in the list.

   The simplest replacement is to use a cascade of if-statements of the form

```
        IF (I == 1) THEN
            GO TO  L1
        ELSE IF (I == 2) THEN
            GO TO L2

        . . .
        ELSE IF (I == k) THEN
            GO TO Lk
        END IF
```

   which may be made more efficient by ensuring that the most frequently taken branches occur at the head of the cascade.

   A more readable alternative is to use a **SELECT CASE** construct and to gather the blocks of code corresponding to each branch into the associated **CASE** clause. However, there is no guarantee that the different branches all lead to independent blocks of code, and this means that it may be necessary to untangle logic and to duplicate code. Finally, be aware that, while there is no fall-through in the sequence of **CASE** clauses, this can occur in a computed-**GO TO**, for example,

```
        GO TO (10, 20, 30), i
C Skip if i not in range
        GO TO 40
10      j = 1
C Case i == 1 falls through into i == 2 code
20      a(j) = x
        j = j + 1
        GO TO 40
30      a(j) = −x
40      . . . .
```

executes the code from label 10 to the branch to label 40 when `i == 1`. This leads to an equivalent **SELECT CASE** statement of the form

```
    SELECT CASE (i)

    CASE (1)
       a(1) = x
       j = 2
    CASE (2)
       a(j) = x
       j = j + 1
    CASE (3)
       a(j) = -x

! Add a default case for completeness
    CASE DEFAULT
       CONTINUE
    END SELECT
```

We provide a more extended example of this in Section 16.2.

6. *Statement functions.*

   A statement function is a one-line function definition that appears in the specification section of a subroutine or main program. For example,

```
C Define a statement function to evaluate a quadratic
C polynomial. The names a, b, c and x need to be declared in
C the declarative section of code.
      evalq(a,b,c,x) = c + x*(b + x*a)
```

   where the types of the function name itself and its dummy arguments are of default type or are declared explicitly in the declaration statements around the function definition. This statement dates back to before Fortran 66 and is now well past its sell-by date! In the vast majority of cases it can easily be replaced with an internal procedure placed at the end of the program unit. Doing this also provides the opportunity to improve the documentation of the code by explicitly defining the function and parameter types. Thus,

```
    CONTAINS
    ...
    REAL FUNCTION evalq(a,b,c,x)
    REAL, INTENT(IN) :: a, b, c, x
       evalq = c + x*(b + x*a)
    END FUNCTION
```

7. ***DATA*** *statements occurring within executable statements.*

   These may simply be moved to a position following the declaration section. However, **DATA** statements should be replaced by variable initializations or **PARAMETER** statements. Suppose that the type **REAL** variables *fac* and *fourth* are declared in a **DATA** statement but it is known that the value of *fac* will change from its initial value while *fourth* remains static. The statement

```
    DATA fac/1.0/, fourth/0.25/
```

may then be replaced by initialization as the variables are typed:

```
REAL , SAVE :: fac=1.0
REAL , PARAMETER :: fourth=0.25
```

8. *Assumed-length result from a character function.*

The Fortran 77 standard allowed a character function to declare its return value to be of assumed length, i.e.,

```
CHARACTER *(*) silly(string)
.....
END
```

However, calls to such functions were restricted in that an explicit length declaration of the function name was required in each calling program unit:

```
SUBROUTINE one
CHARACTER*10 silly
...
END

SUBROUTINE two
CHARACTER*6 silly
...
END
```

This restricts the "dynamic" potential to the scope of a program unit.

From Fortran 2003, allocatable scalar values were standardized; in particular, this allows us to declare allocatable character variables with deferred length which may be returned via a function name. Thus we may write

```
      FUNCTION doubleString(arg) RESULT (res)
! Result of function is declared with deferred length
      CHARACTER *(LEN=:), ALLOCATABLE :: res
      CHARACTER *(LEN=*) :: arg
! We use automatic reallocation to generate a return
! value of the required length. In this case double the
! length of the input parameter, arg
      res = arg//arg

      END FUNCTION doubleString
```

and the function may now be called from anywhere in an application with an argument of any length.

9. **CHARACTER*** *form for a character declaration*

The obsolescent declarations

```
CHARACTER *1 A
CHARACTER B
CHARACTER *(*) C
```

should be replaced by standard declarations:

```
        CHARACTER (LEN=1) :: A,B
        CHARACTER (LEN=*) :: C
```

Software tools are available to perform some of these transformations; others will need to be done manually; see Chapter 19 for more details.

16.3   On Replacing Deleted Features

The following five obsolescent features were deleted from Fortran 95. These features are typically still recognized by Fortran 2003 compilers, but there is no guarantee this will continue. A prudent approach would be to replace all occurrences of these deleted constructs by modern equivalents.

1. **REAL** and **DOUBLE PRECISION** loop variables.

2. Branching to an **END IF** statement which has a statement label.

3. The **PAUSE** statement.

4. The **ASSIGN** statement and its accompanying assigned-**GO TO** statement.

5. The **nH** edit descriptor of **FORMAT** statements for input and output.

16.4   On the Removal of GO TO Statements

Through many decades and standards the **GO TO** statement was an essential part of the Fortran programming language. Fortran 66 did not even have a block-**IF** statement; hence a simple IF-THEN-ELSE construct needed **GO TO** statements to implement it:

```
        IF (i .NE. j) GO TO 10
C ELSE block -- i == j
        ... block of statements ...
C Jump over the IF block
        GO TO 20
C IF block -- i /= j
10      ... block of statements ...
C END IF
20      CONTINUE
```

Such templates were easily recognized by experienced programmers. However, uncontrolled use of **GO TO** statements can soon lead to unreadable and unmaintainable code. Constructs like the alternate return, assigned-**GO TO**, and computed-**GO TO** require associated labels and branches and offer unlimited possibilities for producing obfuscated code.

With the control structures and facilities available in Fortran 2003 there should be no need to use any labels or **GO TO** statements. Software tools exist that attempt to restructure code to remove labels or **GO TO** statements. While these tools are generally successful with template code like the IF-THEN-ELSE construct above, they will often fail to improve the readability of true "spaghetti" code. In cases where a rewrite is necessary, for example, when translating into another language that does not have **GO TO** statements, the programmer may be forced to unravel the logic and reimplement the code to obtain a translation.

Here we illustrate how legacy code using **GO TO** statements, statement functions, and alternate returns may be transformed to use the improved features available in modern Fortran. We also show how to improve readability by using constant names rather than numerical values to document the code.

The sample single-variable Newton method code *test_alt_ret* solves $f(x) = 0$ using reverse communication to request values of $f(x)$ and the derivative $f'(x)$. The two alternate returns transfer control to the appropriate statement, and the Newton method code is re-entered. If no alternate return is used, the code drops through to the next statement in the normal way.

Studying the code we see that the calling program unit repeatedly calls the routine *newt* until convergence is obtained and the loop is terminated. Besides handling convergence, there are three other distinct computational tasks performed in the caller: initialization phase, evaluation of the function, and evaluation of the derivative. On completion of each of these tasks *newt* is called.

Internally, *newt* needs to remember where it is in the calculation so that it can pick up the computation again at the relevant step, i.e., initialization, request a function value for a newly computed value of x, request a derivative evaluation, or perform an update step on x. We implement this in the new code by using a local variable with the *SAVE* attribute which we initialize to the *initial* state in the declaration statement. It is reset to this state when convergence is signaled so that the routine will start up correctly if another problem is to be solved in the same program.

The distinct computational tasks in both *newt* and the calling program unit translate simply into **SELECT CASE** constructs, replacing the leapfrog code resulting from the use of computed-**GO TO** and alternate return statements. The final code, we believe, is more structured and understandable and, hence, easier to maintain than the original.

Although the reader may consider this example to be contrived, our experience has been that such code not only exists in legacy systems but is still being produced by diehard Fortran 77 programmers today!

Listing 16.1. *Newton method code with alternate returns: test_alt_ret.*

```
!! This code extract is part of the accompanying software
!! that supports Chapter 16. It may be found in the file
!! test.f
!!
      PROGRAM test_alt_ret
      INTEGER igo
      REAL x,f(2), fun, fderiv, ftrue
      fun(x) = x**2 - 0.81
      fderiv(x)  = 2.0*x
```

```
       ftrue () = 0.9

       igo = 0
       x = 0.81
       GO TO 30

C Compute f(x)
   10 CONTINUE
       f(1) = fun(x)
       GO TO 30

C Compute the derivative of f(x)
   20 CONTINUE
       f(2) = fderiv(x)

C Perform the next step
   30 CONTINUE
       CALL newt(x,f,igo,*10,*20)

C newt executes a simple return on convergence
C which executes the next statement after the call
       WRITE (*,'(A/ 3E12.4)') 'Solution, X and absolute error = ',
     +   x,x - ftrue()

       END

       SUBROUTINE newt(x,f,igo,*,*)
       INTEGER igo
       REAL x,f(2),dx

       GO TO (10,20),igo
C igo == 0 does not branch; acts as an initialization
C Request f(x) in f(1)
       igo = 1
       RETURN 1

C igo == 1 request derivative of f(x) in f(2)
   10 CONTINUE
       igo = 2
       RETURN 2

C igo = 2 we have both function values
C perform a Newton iteration
   20 CONTINUE
       dx = f(1)/f(2)
C Update solution
       x = x - dx
C Continue if change to x is still large
       igo = 1
       IF (ABS(dx).GT.EPSILON(x)*ABS(x)) RETURN 1
C Signal that solution has been found, plain return.
       RETURN

       END
```

Listing 16.2. *Transformed Newton method code: test_alt_ret2.*

```
!! This code extract is part of the accompanying software
!! that supports Chapter 16. It may be found in the file
!! test2.f90
!!
     PROGRAM test_alt_ret2
        INTEGER :: callerstep
        REAL :: x, f(2)
        INTEGER, PARAMETER :: evalf=1, evalfderiv=2,   &
                 converged=3, initialize=0

        callerstep = initialize

LOOP: DO
          SELECT CASE (callerstep)
          CASE (initialize)
! Initialization step
! Set initial estimate of root
             x = 0.81E0
          CASE (evalf)
! Compute f(x)
             f(1) = fun(x)
          CASE (evalfderiv)
! Compute f'(x)
             f(2) = fderiv(x)
          CASE (converged)
! Convergence
             WRITE (*,'(A/ 3E12.4)') 'Solution and error: ', x,  &
                x - ftrue()
             EXIT LOOP
          END SELECT
! Call the Newton iteration
          CALL newt2(x,f,callerstep)
        END DO LOOP

     CONTAINS

        REAL FUNCTION ftrue()
        ftrue = 0.9E0
        END FUNCTION ftrue

        REAL FUNCTION fun(x)
        REAL, INTENT(IN) :: x
        fun = x*x - 0.81E0
        END FUNCTION fun

        REAL FUNCTION fderiv(x)
        REAL, INTENT(IN) :: x
        fderiv  = x+x
        END FUNCTION fderiv

     END

     SUBROUTINE newt2(x,f,callerstep)
        INTEGER, INTENT(OUT) :: callerstep
        REAL, INTENT(INOUT) :: x
        REAL, INTENT(IN) :: f(2)
```

```
      INTEGER , PARAMETER :: evalf=1, evalfderiv=2,  &
               converged=3, initialize=0, getderiv=1, &
               updatex=2
      REAL :: dx
      INTEGER , SAVE :: nextstep=initialize

      SELECT CASE (nextstep)
      CASE (initialize)
! Initialization step
! In this case just get f(x) for the initial x
         callerstep = evalf
         nextstep = getderiv
      CASE (getderiv)
!  f(x) is saved in f(1) -- get f'(x)
         callerstep = evalfderiv
         nextstep = updatex
      CASE (updatex)
! Compute Newton step, f(x)/f'
         dx = f(1)/f(2)
! Update solution
         x = x - dx
! Continue if change to x is still large
         IF (ABS(dx)>EPSILON(x)*ABS(x)) THEN
! Start the cycle again by getting f(x)
            callerstep = evalf
            nextstep = getderiv
         ELSE
! Signal that solution has been found
            callerstep = converged
            nextstep = initialize
         END IF
      END SELECT

      END
```

Chapter 17

Software Testing

Synopsis:

▶ *What makes a good test?*

▶ *Testing metrics: How good is the test suite?*

▶ *Other testing strategies*

▶ *Equivalence partitioning*

▶ *Example of building a test suite*

17.1 Introduction

Typically the purpose of numerical software is to compute approximations to a wide class of mathematical problems, for example, general systems of real linear equations, the roots of polynomials with real coefficients, etc. Before releasing code for general use, we need to be certain, as far as we possibly can, that our code is fit for purpose. This means that our software should either generate approximations that are accurate in some prescribed way or inform the user that an accurate result could not be computed for a particular problem. Given that we cannot generally prove our codes correct for all valid input values, it is essential that testing should form a major component of any software development.

While it is impossible for testing to prove that software is error-free under all circumstances, it is essential that we perform thorough, systematic, and effective testing to increase confidence in our code. Basically the more varied tests that run as expected the more confidence we have that our software will operate correctly for the general case. To paraphrase Dijkstra, *testing shows the presence, not the absence of bugs.* In this chapter we will look at what constitutes a good test, when tests should be created, how suites of tests should be constructed, how we decide

193

when code has been adequately tested and, finally, we provide a concrete example based on code presented in Chapter 9. We will be restricting our discussion of testing to numerical software, although much of what we say is relevant to many other application areas. However, the testing of artifacts such as graphical user interfaces (GUIs) is more complex in the derivation of the tests, their execution and the checking of the *"results"* obtained.

EXERCISE 17.1. *Exhaustive testing of computer software is impossible. Consider the following scenario: you have been told to check the integer add on your company's new computer by checking all possible sums. The range of integer values available is $\left[-2^{31}, 2^{31} - 1\right]$. By assuming you can perform a single integer add and check the result in one nanosecond, convince yourself (and your manager) that this is not viable. [Hint: to within 0.5% there are π seconds in a nanocentury (attributed to Tom Duff, Bell Labs).]*

17.2   What Constitutes a Test?

In its simplest form a test consists of two parts:

1. data required to define a particular problem that the software should be capable of solving or, possibly, recognizing as illegal.

2. the expected results of running the software on the data provided in 1.

   For example, for *dnrm2*, Chapter 9, we could use:

1. data $= (3.0, 4.0)$,

2. expected result $= 5.0$.

EXERCISE 17.2. *How does the data $(0.3, 0.4)$ with expected result 0.5 differ from the above data set? Why may this data make checking the computed result more difficult?*

17.3   When to Start and Stop Testing

The generation of test cases should start as soon as we begin designing our software. Thinking about suitable test data often provides us with insight into special cases and peculiar circumstances that we need to account for when coding the main algorithm. Generating testing material as we write the code improves our productivity by giving us a wide variety of well-understood executable test cases that we may use throughout the code production and maintenance phases of our software development.

We should aim to make each test case we generate count in some way. Remember that the point of testing is to increase confidence; running a large number of very similar test cases is unlikely to achieve this. As an example, if we were to test the *dnrm2* function from Chapter 9, with $(3.0, 4.0)$, performing further tests with data $(4.0, 5.0)$ and $(5.0, 6.0)$ is unlikely to tell us anything new, except for the occurrence of a floating-point rounding value. In fact we will be executing exactly the same sequence of statements in all three cases; hence, if there were an error in this section of the code, the first data set would fail and alert us.

Each data set, therefore, should either execute different sequences of statements or produce unusual numerical behavior, for example, extreme or even infinite intermediate numerical values. We return to choosing suitable data sets in Section 17.6 on equivalence partitioning.

In order to decide when to stop the testing process, we need to be able to define a metric (means of measuring) that allows us to compute how much of the process we have completed using our current test suite. One of the simplest definitions of completeness is that the test suite causes all executable statements in the software to be executed at least once. After all, if we haven't executed a block of code, how can we possibly have confidence that it will operate correctly when it is executed? A relevant metric could be

$$T_s = \frac{Number\ of\ Executable\ Statements\ Executed}{Total\ Number\ of\ Executable\ Statements}, \qquad (17.1)$$

although a more accurate measure would be

$$T_b = \frac{Number\ of\ Blocks\ of\ Executable\ Statements\ Executed}{Total\ Number\ of\ Blocks\ of\ Executable\ Statements}, \qquad (17.2)$$

where a block of statements is defined as a straight line set of statements, for example, a consecutive sequence of assignment statements.

While many may consider this to be a minimal requirement for testing before release, Barnes and Hopkins [9] showed that for the Lapack release 3.0 the accompanying test suite executed 86.9% of the basic blocks, leaving around 2000 blocks unexecuted.

A major drawback of the T_b metric above is actually performing the measurement. How do we compute this value easily and efficiently for a particular test suite? The simple answer is that we need an automated way of logging and accumulating each block of code as it is executed during the running of the test suite. It would also be useful if all the blocks that were never executed could be easily identified so as to provide insight into how to create further tests. Some compilers provide support for this data logging, for example, the *gfortran* compiler. We discuss how to use some of these profiling tools in Chapter 18.

Even 100% statement coverage is quite a weak form of coverage; for example, consider the following block of code:

```
IF (i == 1) THEN
   A=1
END IF

IF (j == 2) THEN
   A=2
END IF
```

If the test suite executes the two **IF**-statements and their associated blocks the same number of times, we can obtain 100% statement coverage, but we never test the cases where the relational expressions are false. A more comprehensive measurement would be to ensure that our tests force all Boolean expressions used to control the flow of execution to evaluate to both *true* and *false*. This is *decision coverage*, and the associated metric is

$$T_d = \frac{Decision\ Outcomes\ Executed\ by\ Tests}{Total\ Number\ of\ Decision\ Outcomes}. \tag{17.3}$$

Note that attaining 100% decision coverage ($T_d = 1.0$) implies that we have full block coverage ($T_b = 1.0$). While we should always strive to obtain 100% branch coverage, many sources suggest that $T_d > 0.8$ is sufficient. Our opinion is that if you felt the need to write the code, you should be able to test it using either an example from the problem domain or an erroneous problem that the software is designed to detect and report.

A test suite should never be considered complete as long as the software is being used and maintained. Any confirmed errors, i.e., any errors that cause changes to be made to the source code, should always be reflected by a new test which illustrates the error in the old version and provides continued evidence that any future versions still fix the problem. The new test does not need to be the exact case reported as a fault but should be a simplified version which clearly illustrates the "situation" that caused the original error to be revealed. It is also good practice when applying maintenance fixes to software to consider whether similar errors could occur elsewhere in the code. The reason for always adding tests which illustrate reported bugs is to guard against these fixes "disappearing" due to poor record-keeping.

All testing material aimed at exercising the code at the package level (calls to user-level subprograms) should be included with the software when it is released. If correctly produced, i.e., the tests are self-checking and *Makefiles* (see Section 19.2) are provided, this material yields a simple way for new users to check their installation of the package. This is especially helpful when the software is being implemented using untried compilers or new hardware. The fact that considerable effort will have been expended during the code development stage to make the tests easy to execute and validate should mean that little effort is required to add test material to the released package.

17.4   Other Types of Testing

Many types of testing have been proposed in the software engineering literature (see Hutcheson [44] for examples) although most of the distinctions are probably of no interest to the author of numerical codes. We will mention three sorts of testing, *white box*, *unit*, and *soak*, because we feel these are the ones most likely to help generate solid, reliable software. *White box* testing just means that we have access to the source code being tested and can, therefore, use the code to help us construct the test cases. This also allows us to measure how well tested our software is by using metrics like those defined in Section 17.3. Each valid test should consist of an example from the problem set that the software is expected to solve; this allows us to link particular sections of code to specific problems.

When developing software packages that consist of many ancillary subprograms, it is useful to test these units separately. This is *unit* testing, and the idea is to localize any errors within small sections of code. The fewer lines of code we have to consider, the more easily bugs should be found. Unit testing consists of writing tests for each individual subprogram in the package, and these tests generally form a hierarchy; we test the lower-level routine first so that we have confidence in the building blocks we use for the higher level subprograms.

Generating test data sets for these lower-level routines is often more time consuming or error-prone than for user-callable codes since the lower-level software is usually solving intermediate computational problems for which it is harder to generate input data. Testing at this level may also involve populating private derived types rather than the more familiar user-level types. However, such conditions also make it more likely that these sections of code will contain difficult-to-locate errors, and thus the effort expended on unit testing these routines is often handsomely repaid.

Unit testing material associated with non–user-callable routines is rarely included as part of the public release of source code, although it may be provided to users who have problems implementing the software on new platforms. These tests should form part of the day-to-day testing of the package during the development and maintenance phases.

Since almost every word in the English language can appear before the word *testing* and still have a definition in software engineering, we define our own form of *soak testing*! In the context of this book, *soak* testing consists of running a very large number of, usually randomly generated, data sets through the software both to increase our confidence in the code and to provide some measure of run-time efficiency. Be careful how timings obtained from this type of testing are used, especially if you are comparing the performance of one code against another (see Hockney [42] for a fuller discussion on the complexities of benchmarking and how to compare fairly the performance of competing codes).

It is useful if soak testing can be made self-checking by using some form of *oracle*, for example, a consistency check on the computed results or a comparison with results obtained from alternative software using a different, possibly less efficient, algorithm. If neither of these is available, running a large number of test problems with all available run-time checking utilized is still worthwhile; see Chapter 18.

While performing checks during soak testing it is useful, if possible, to report the spread of differences between the delivered and oracle results. When measuring these differences any suspicious values should be flagged and the associated data sets preserved; try to write data in binary or hexadecimal format so that the exact test may be rerun. All suspicious results should be investigated, even if this only results in a redefinition of "suspicious"!

The Lapack test suite uses a number of sophisticated consistency checks to allow the automated checking of many of its user-callable routines for randomly generated tests (see Blackford and Dongarra [13] for examples).

17.5   Problems with Constructing Test Data

When constructing test data we seek to generate values that define a valid example from the general problem set that our software is designed to solve. Where possible we choose example problems with either exact or very accurately determined solutions.

For example, consider the testing of a real linear equation solver; here we aim to compute the solution vector x of $Ax = b$, where A is a given real matrix of order n and b is a given real n-vector. We choose a simple matrix

$$A = \begin{bmatrix} 7 & 11 \\ 5 & 13 \end{bmatrix}$$

and construct the vector $b = (3, 15)^T$ by setting the solution to be $x = (-1, 2)^T$. Should we expect the software to compute a solution vector $\hat{x} = (-1, 2)^T$? We need to remember that we are using floating-point arithmetic and that some of the intermediate computations will not be exact. Even though the compiler's output routine may well print $(-1, 2)^T$ as the solution, internally it may be an approximation. Printing the difference between the computed and exact solutions is often more informative.

Here we have an example where the data defining the problem (and the solution) may be represented exactly using binary floating-point, but rounding errors in the intermediate calculations ensure that the exact result will not be returned.

We hope that these rounding errors are controlled by the algorithm (and its implementation) so that the computed values returned are close to the exact solution of the problem. When constructing tests for our software we need to define an acceptable difference between the exact and computed solutions as part of the test data. This information can then be used to make the tests self-checking.

Not all linear equation problems have computable solutions, of course. Discovering an occurrence of an ill-conditioned or unstable system may be one desired output for the solver. As mentioned in Chapter 19, a stiff ODE solver may increase its step-size to a point where the Jacobian matrix may become singular or nearly so. The ODE solver may then decrease the step-size and get back on track. This requires that the linear solver provide exception information that can be interpreted by the ODE solver, without terminating the execution. Testing this functionality should be included as part of a test suite.

17.6   Equivalence Partitioning and Boundary Value Analysis

One useful technique for creating a small number of test examples that will, hopefully, provide high code coverage is called *Equivalence Partitioning* [16, p. 623]. This is a rather grand name for a method that is simple to understand—and reasonably easy to apply—for small to medium-sized pieces of software. It is often considered in the literature to be only a black-box testing technique; i.e., it should be used with just the problem definition and without knowledge of the actual software implementation. However, in our opinion, its effectiveness may be improved if it is combined with a knowledge of the code.

The idea is to split all the possible sets of input data into sets, known as *equivalence classes*, such that it would be expected that every data set defined in a particular class would execute the same path through the code. The argument then proceeds that choosing just one sample from each class provides maximum code coverage at almost minimal cost.

Boundary value analysis is a means of guiding the choice of data sets from each equivalence class and is based on the observation that many programming errors tend to occur at the boundaries of the input domain. Such errors frequently occur when, for example, $<$ is used instead of $\leq$ (or even $>$) or loops are run from 1 to n rather than from 1 to $n-1$.

We will illustrate the use of these techniques to help generate a test suite for our implementation of the l_2 norm code, *dnrm2()*, which we developed in Chapter 9.

From the definition of the problem (page 104) we can split the input domain into a number of "obvious" classes:

1. Inputs which generate a representable result.

2. Inputs which generate a nonrepresentable floating-point result.

3. Input data that includes nonfinite values.

4. Input data that includes not-a-number values.

5. Trivial input data.

6. Illegal input data.

We start by dealing with classes 5 and 6 since these are small classes. As we are aiming to deal with any possible input for the input vector, i.e., both valid floating-point numbers as well as infinite and NaN values, the only illegal data is obtained by setting *incx* to be less than one. The only trivial data is the case of a null array, which we assume is being signaled if the value of n is set to be nonpositive. In both cases we choose to return the value zero for the norm and, in the case of *incx* less than one, we raise *ieee_invalid_flag*. Thus our first two sets of test data are as follows:

Test 1: $n = 0$, $incx = 1$, $x = \{\} \Rightarrow result = 0.0$.

Test 2: $n = 1$, $incx = 0$, $x = \{\} \Rightarrow result = 0.0$ (*ieee_invalid_flag* set).

We choose n and *incx* to be boundary values; i.e., they are values closest to legal values.

For classes 3 and 4 we choose an input vector of size three that contains an infinite or NaN value in position two. For completeness we use both positive and negative infinity along with signaling and quiet Nan values.

Test 3: $n = 3$, $incx = 1$, $x = \{2.0, +Inf, -1.0\} \Rightarrow result = +Inf$.

Test 4: $n = 3, incx = 1, x = \{2.0, -Inf, qNaN\} \Rightarrow result = +Inf$.

Test 5: $n = 3, incx = 1, x = \{2.0, qNaN, -1.0\} \Rightarrow result = qNaN$.

Test 6: $n = 3, incx = 1, x = \{2.0, sNaN, -1.0\} \Rightarrow result = qNaN$.

For class 2 we need to consider a vector of size at least two since, for $n = 1$, if we can represent the floating-point value, we can represent the value of the l_2 norm as it is just the absolute value of the input and all valid negative IEEE values have a valid positive value of the same magnitude. An obvious test would be the following:

Test 7: $n = 2, incx = 1, x = \{maxReal, maxReal\} \Rightarrow result = +Inf$ (*ieee_overflow* set).

We should, however, be looking to use boundary values where possible. Our first thought may be to choose $x = \{maxReal, anyReal\}$ on the grounds that the second value can only increase the value of the norm and, since this is at least $maxReal$ from the first value, we must generate an unrepresentable floating-point result. But we have to remember that we are dealing with floating-point arithmetic, which means that our second value must be large enough to register when the addition is performed. Thus we require x_2 to be the smallest number that will cause an overflow to occur. For any representable floating-point number, x_2, we have

$$res = \sqrt{(maxReal)^2 + (x_2)^2} = maxReal\sqrt{\left(1 + \frac{x_2^2}{maxReal^2}\right)}. \qquad (17.4)$$

If the software is performing to its specification, we should obtain an infinite result only if $(1 + x_2^2/maxReal^2) > 1$; otherwise a value of $maxReal$ should be returned. Thus an unrecoverable overflow would occur if $x_2^2 \geq maxReal^2 \times macheps$ which, for IEEE double precision arithmetic using $maxReal = 2^{1024}$ to obtain an exact power of two, gives $x_2 \geq 2^{998}$.

This leads to two further tests:

Test 8: $n = 2, incx = 1, x = \{maxReal, 2^{998}\} \Rightarrow result = +Inf$ (*ieee_overflow* set).

Test 9: $n = 2, incx = 1, x = \{maxReal, 2^{997}\} \Rightarrow result = maxReal$.

The question now is: *Do we keep all three of Tests 7–9 in our test suite?* After all, the idea of partitioning the input data is to reduce the number of test cases being run to an absolute minimum. In our opinion it is always useful to have a "simple" test, in addition to boundary values, to act as part of a "smoke" test, that is, a set of examples that will signal a serious problem with the software if any fail. This subset of the test suite may then be run first to ensure that there are no glaring errors, while the rest of the suite is designed to exercise the code to the full.

We should also check that we do not have any problems with underflows. It may be necessary to add extra tests if gradual underflow is allowed. Here we assume that it isn't.

Test 10: $n = 4$, $incx = 1$, $x = \{tiny, tiny, tiny, tiny\} \Rightarrow result = 2 * tiny$.

Next we consider the class of inputs for which a representable result will be returned. We start with the simplest of cases; as before, this could be used in a smoke test. Here the data and the result are all exactly representable using floating-point arithmetic.

Test 11: $n = 2$, $incx = 1$, $x = \{3.0, 4.0\} \Rightarrow result = 5.0$.

We should really have an example for which n is larger than two; again this is not adhering strictly to the rules for minimizing the number of tests, but we also want to increase our confidence in the software. Ideally, we should like to have a way of generating example data with a known solution, and sometimes we may need to do some research to find suitable examples. For example, we have

$$\sum_{i=0}^{k-1}(a + i)^2 = \sum_{i=0}^{k-1} r_i^2 = b^2, \tag{17.5}$$

where $k = v^2$, $a = (v^4 - 24v^2 - 25)/48$, $b = (v^5 + 47v)/48$, and v is any integer not divisible by 2 or 3 (see Hirschhorn [40] for details).

This provides us with a source of examples, but which one (or more) should we choose? We note that as we increase v, both the starting value, a, and the number of terms increases. We also note that all the values are integer and, hence, provided we choose v small enough, the sum of squares should be collected exactly. The largest value of v to allow this is $v = 85$ for IEEE double precision arithmetic. Hence Test 12 below would provide an extended test.

Test 12: $n = 85^2 = 7225$, $incx = 1$, $x = \{r_0, r_1, \ldots, r_{n-1}\}$ from equation (17.5) $\Rightarrow result = 92438690$

We should also add the following:

Test 13: $n = 89^2 = 7921$, $incx = 1$, $x = \{r_0, r_1, \ldots, r_{n-1}\}$ from equation (17.5) $\Rightarrow result = 116334659$ (*ieee_inexact* set).

This ensures that the IEEE flags are set correctly on exit from *dnrm2*. In fact Tests 12 and 13 allow us to split class 1 into two subclasses: one where the data generates an exact result and another for data that results in rounding errors and hence in the setting of the inexact flag.

By reading the code, we note that $n = 1$ is treated as a special case. While this is unlikely to be a common practical occurrence, we can provide much simpler and efficient code for this case. To check this we generate the following cases:

Test 14: $n = 1$, $incx = 1$, $x = \{3.0\} \Rightarrow result = 3.0$.

Test 15: $n = 1$, $incx = 1$, $x = \{-maxReal\} \Rightarrow result = maxReal$.

Test 16: $n = 1$, $incx = 1$, $x = \{-tiny\} \Rightarrow result = tiny$.

Test 17: $n = 1$, $incx = 1$, $x = \{+Inf, \} \Rightarrow result = +Inf$.

Test 18: $n = 1$, $incx = 1$, $x = \{-Inf\} \Rightarrow result = +Inf$.

Test 19: $n = 1$, $incx = 1$, $x = \{qNaN\} \Rightarrow result = qNaN$.

Test 20: $n = 1$, $incx = 1$, $x = \{sNaN\} \Rightarrow result = qNaN$.

If we run the above tests on our software with code coverage, we find that we have 100% block and decision coverage for *dnrm2*; the routine *dnrm2_kc* has two unexecuted blocks and two missing conditionals. However, the data required to obtain 100% coverage in the latter case is actually being dealt with by *dnrm2*, and hence explicit calls to *dnrm2_kc* would be needed to obtain complete coverage. If all these tests pass, should we be reasonably confident that our code is functionally correctly?

EXERCISE 17.3. *Change the DO-loops in the routines dnrm2kc and dnrm2 from*

```
DO i = 1, (n-1)*incx +1, incx
```

to

```
DO i = 1, (n+1)*incx -1, incx
```

and rerun Tests 1–20 above. Are you still confident in the completeness of the test suite?

So, despite our coverage statistics, we would still have a serious, undetected error in the code. We have ignored a whole class of problems where *incx* is greater than 1. We, therefore, add the following simple test:

Test 21: $n = 3$, $incx = 2$, $x = \{2.0, 5.0, 3.0, 9.0, 6.0\} \Rightarrow result = 7.0$.

We also add the following, which should trip the inexact flag:

Test 22: $n = 2$, $incx = 3$, $x = \{2.0, 3.0, 4.0, 5.0\} \Rightarrow result = \sqrt{29}$ (*ieee_inexact* flag set).

Finally we might also consider testing a vector that contains an infinite value and a quiet NaN in positions in the vector that do not form part of the l_2 norm computation:

Test 23: $n = 3$, $incx = 2$, $x = \{2.0, +Inf, 3.0, qNaN, 6.0\} \Rightarrow result = 7.0$.

EXERCISE 17.4. *Is the test suite devised in this section also suitable for testing the implementation of Blue's algorithm? Run the tests and obtain the coverage metrics. If necessary add new tests to improve these values.*

17.7   Final Word

Testing numerical software is not easy to do well even for relatively small pieces of code performing straightforward calculations on a sequential machine. The amount of testing effort required increases rapidly for larger codes and for parallel implementations. However, as tedious as some programmers find testing, it remains an essential part of software development and needs to be performed with as much attention to detail as the writing of the application code itself.

With current programming languages, large pieces of software operating on large data sets form extremely complex systems. Even with thorough testing, bugs may always remain in such codes. Our goal should be to minimize the number still hiding and try to ensure that those remaining will appear only under very exceptional circumstances. Good luck!

EXERCISE 17.5. *Testing a large application will necessitate the running of a vast number of tests and will require a substantial amount of resources. The idea of a smoke test is to use a small number of tests to detect any serious programming errors quickly.*

Which subset of the tests suggested above would you choose to form a smoke test for dnrm2? Give reasons for each of the tests you include.

EXERCISE 17.6. (i) *Write a soak test for dnrm2 that uses Blue's algorithm as an oracle. This should use reproducible random numbers to generate the input data. Run your test and calculate the code coverage metrics T_b and T_d. If necessary improve your input generator to increase these values.*

(ii) *Calculate the maximum and minimum differences between the results produced by the two algorithms. Devise a "failure" test and implement it so that, as well as printing out a warning message, it captures any suspicious data.*

(iii) *How would you go about testing your soak test code?*

Chapter 18

Compilers

Synopsis:

- ▶ *Know your options*
- ▶ *Compile-time checks*
- ▶ *Run-time checks*
- ▶ *Code optimization*
- ▶ *Algorithm optimization*
- ▶ *Dusty decks*

18.1 Introduction

Compilers should be your friends! A good compiler can be of great help when developing and later maintaining software. Most compilers offer to perform a large number of code checks which can pinpoint potential bugs and other problems.

Most modern Fortran compilers have many (some well over 100!) options that the user can set when compiling source code, although the vast majority of these are irrelevant during software development and maintenance. Many are, to say the least, esoteric and likely to make a difference only in very exceptional circumstances. However, there will generally be a handful that are extremely useful and all users should take the time to study the compiler options available with their compiler and make a note of any potentially helpful settings.

We describe some of the more commonly available options and how these may assist programmers in uncovering potential problems in their code. We then give some general advice on code optimization and describe what actions a user can take if the code still does not execute quickly enough.

18.2   Commonly Available Checks and Options

Array Bound Checking. One of the most useful and commonly available options is the one that turns on array bound checking. Attempting to access elements of an array outside of the declared bounds is an extremely common error to make when developing code. The behavior of code that accesses out-of-bounds data is entirely dependent on the compiler being used (and, possibly, on other option settings such as the level of optimization). For example, the 32-bit real assignment b = a(n+1), where a has been declared to be of length n, will generally result in the system interpreting the 32 bits of memory immediately following the space reserved for $a(1{:}n)$ as a floating-point number and assigning it to b. The content of these bits is entirely dependent on the compiler and options being used and is not covered by the Fortran standard. This often leads to erroneous final results and a bug that is difficult to locate. These are the types of errors that array bound checking finds easily, and their location requires no additional work by the programmer other than setting the correct option during compilation.

Unassigned Variable Checking. Neither the current Fortran standard nor any of its predecessors has stated what should happen if a variable is used before it has been assigned a value. It is therefore up to the compiler writer to determine what action is to be taken. Many compilers will provide a default value, typically zero for numerical data, but some compilers will just use random bit patterns, and others may act differently depending on the compiler options being used. Whatever your compiler does should not be relied upon, and all variables should be explicitly initialized before they are used.

Checking all variables have been initialized before use is all but impossible without compiler support. A large percentage of all the Fortran codes either accepted before 1993 or submitted after 1993 to the ACM's Collected Algorithms (CALGO) failed when the use of unassigned variable checks were enabled (see Hopkins [43]). At the present time not all compilers offer this support, although the increasing availability of IEEE arithmetic makes its provision somewhat easier by allowing the default assignment for floating-point numbers to be a signaling NaN. The run-time system may then provide tracebacks when these values are used in floating-point expressions.

The use of both array bound checking and unassigned variable checking is not cheap; using either or both will increase execution times dramatically (possibly by an order of magnitude). However, given how difficult these coding errors are to find, they are well worth the expense during the development stage and when running the test suites.

Unused Variable Checking. We recommend that all variable names are explicitly declared. However, during the development of software it is common that the need for a previously declared variable disappears completely and all references to that name are removed apart from the benign, dangling, type declaration. This is certainly not a programming error, but it may cause future confusion when the code is under maintenance. Often software outlasts the involvement of the original authors, and code clutter like this (see also Section 18.3) may well perplex future readers. So, if your compiler will flag variables that are declared but never used, locate them and remove them.

Deleted and Obsolescent Feature Checking. In Chapter 16 we noted features that have been marked as redundant and consequently removed. Other features have been marked as no longer needed but are still part of the standard. As a practical matter, while most compilers continue to accept these features and compile correct code, it may be desirable to transform an existing code and replace such fragments. Using a compiler flag that identifies these source fragments is especially helpful for large codes.

EXERCISE 18.1. *Find out whether your compiler provides support for array bound checking (often -C but -fcheck=bounds for gfortran) and for unassigned variable checking (see -finit-real for gfortran and -C=undefined for the NAG compiler [67]). Recompile and rerun some of your codes with these checks enabled. Record the number of errors that you uncover. Compare the execution times of your programs with and without checking enabled.*

The following are other run-time checks that may be available and are certainly worth using:

1. Procedure references: these check that in calls to subprograms the actual parameters agree in number and type.

2. Dangling pointers: these report on the attempted use of a pointer whose target has been deallocated. For example,

```
PROGRAM dangling
INTEGER , POINTER :: aptr (:)
INTEGER , ALLOCATABLE , TARGET :: val (:) , temp (:)
INTEGER :: i
  ALLOCATE ( val (10) , temp (10))
  val (:) = [( i , i=1 ,10 )]
  aptr => val (:)
! Deallocating val now leaves aptr 'dangling'
! i.e., its target has disappeared.
  DEALLOCATE ( val )
! Compilers that generate run-time checks for
! dangling pointers will report the next assignment
  temp (:) = aptr (:)
END
```

This option is very useful for detecting problems in more complicated situations, such as in the manipulation of complex list structures, since it detects problems early.

3. DO-loops: these check for zero step values or changes to a loop iteration variable within the loop it controls.

4. Optional references: these check that any reference to an optional argument refers to an actual argument that was present in the call. This may sound

simple but it is possible to pass optional arguments through a chain of routine calls when it becomes very difficult to check this condition by eye.

5. Pointer references: these check that all pointers are defined and associated before use.

6. Invalid recursions: these detect recursive calls to a subprogram that has not been defined as **RECURSIVE**.

Many compilers provide an option switch that triggers a battery of these additional checks, for example, *-C=all* for the NAG compiler. In other cases some of the checks (for example, checking procedure references) may be performed by default, at least inside individual modules.

18.3   Other Useful Commonly Available Options

The checks detailed above are principally concerned with removing errors and clutter from the source code. Other common options allow checks to be performed that may assist in improving software portability and quality as well as making life easier for the programmer. Here we discuss a few commonly available options that we have found useful over the years.

Debuggers.   During both software development and maintenance there will almost always be coding errors that prove extremely difficult to locate and correct. Any Fortran compiler worth using will offer some level of debugging support. Typically this allows the program to be run under the control of the user, who may stop the execution at particular points in the code and then examine (and sometimes change) the contents of key variables.

These facilities require the compiler to insert extra information into the executable code which invariably impacts negatively on both run times and size of executable files. Thus when debugging, the programmer needs to select the compiler options to generate this additional information; often this is a combination of flags which usually includes *-g*.

For a more detailed discussion of debugging see also Section 19.5.

Standard Conformance.   Because the Fortran standards have only ever defined what compilers must provide as a minimum (i.e., extra features are not precluded from a standard-conforming compiler), portability may be compromised by programmers who use nonstandard constructs available from a particular compiler. Most compilers can be persuaded to report on the use of nonstandard language features (*gfortran* provides the *-std* option), and some will allow the user to define the language standard to be used (for example, 95, 2003, 2008). Both facilities can be useful when preparing code for export to other systems.

Implicit None Option.   Throughout the code available with this book we have used the IMPLICIT NONE statement to ensure that all variables have been explicitly declared. This prevents the possibility of mistyped variable names (for example, $f1$ instead of fl) going undetected.

Most compilers will check for undeclared variables (the *gfortran* compiler provides *-fimplicit-none*, although *-u* and *-U* are also common). Use of this compiler option can be helpful for imported source code that may not use IMPLICIT NONE explicitly or as a "belt and braces" approach to your own code.

Floating-Point Precision. Changing the precision of pre-Fortran 95 software can be tedious in that this generally requires changing the declarations of, for example, *REAL* variables to *DOUBLE PRECISION* as well as checking that all *REAL* variables have been explicitly declared. In addition, it may be necessary to adjust the definition of various constants to ensure double precision accuracy. Such problems may be avoided by the use of compiler options that perform this precision change automatically.

Clutter Removal. Finally, we note that compilers often report useful information within the optional warning and information messages that they may be asked to generate. Two of the most common forms of clutter reported in this way are variables that are declared but never used (as noted in the previous section) and variables that are assigned values but never used. While neither of these is an error, such occurrences are confusing to readers and maintainers of the software and as such should be tidied up.

It is always good practice to switch on all levels of compiler generated messages throughout the development of the software as, although many are not relevant, some messages may help clarify the code or point to potential problems. One problem is that most compilers do not provide any means of filtering these messages. Thus effective use of this information may require the user to write a simple script to sift out messages of interest if the compiler does not provide the required facilities. Perl [84] and Python [61] are ideal languages for constructing such scripts.

EXERCISE 18.2. *Consider an array a(:) of declared length n. Is the statement*

```
IF (i<=n .OR. a(i)>tol) THEN
```

standard-conforming Fortran under all circumstances?

What does your compiler do when $i = n+1$ and array bound checking is switched on? Try this with several different compilers.

18.4 Optimization

The original Fortran language was designed to allow a high degree of compiler optimization. Indeed, the first compiler produced in 1957 by Backus and his team at IBM contained a host of optimization techniques [7]. This set the standard for all the compilers that followed. In its early years, Fortran was almost invariably regarded as the language of choice for numerical applications solely on the basis of the highly efficient executable code generated by the compiler.

However, code optimization is something that should only be used once the software is considered to be ready for production runs, but even then it is a good idea to run some smaller examples with all available run-time checking enabled just to increase confidence in the code. We are certainly well aware of the execution time overheads that are inherent with such checks, and these can make the running of large problems prohibitively expensive.

When releasing executables it is always advisable to use compiler optimization to ensure that your software operates as efficiently as possible. Some compilers offer just one level of optimization so all that is required is to recompile the complete application using the relevant optimization flags. The resulting executable should then be used to run the complete test suite; if you are using floating-point numbers, you should not expect the results to agree exactly with those obtained without optimization, but if the tests have been well chosen, the results should be very similar. Large differences in test results between optimized and unoptimized executables need to be carefully checked and understood.

When there is more than one level of optimization, many programmers just choose the highest level available without any thought of what this might involve. Generally speaking, increasing the level will increase the compilation time while, at the same time, decreasing the rate of gain in efficiency of the generated code. This is because higher level optimizations are often specialized and are relevant only under specific circumstances. It is also possible that some forms of optimization may increase either the execution time or the size of the executable or both. Others may require time and effort to apply as they use *typical execution patterns* obtained using execution profiles to fine-tune the code produced. Always consult the compiler documentation for clues and pointers as to which level of optimization would be appropriate. Timing tests should be used to ensure that higher levels of optimization are generally effective for each particular piece of software.

There is much folklore surrounding the writing of efficient Fortran code, and many older programmers were raised on a plethora of programming tips that were designed to squeeze the last drop of efficiency out of the compiled code. Such advice included minimizing array accesses by saving a reused element in a simple variable, common subexpression elimination, and **DO**-loop unrolling [21], along with clever ways of reusing memory with **EQUIVALENCE** statements. Code of the form

```
DO  i = 1 , n
   a(i) = SIN(b(i)) + b(i)*b(i)
   c(i) = d*SIN(b(i)) + COS(b(i)) + b(i)**3
END DO
```

would become

```
DO  i = 1 , n
   bi = b(i)
   bi2 = bi*bi
   sbi = SIN(b(i))
   a(i) = sbi + bi2
   c(i) = d*sbi + COS(bi) + bi*bi2
END DO
```

making it very difficult to read. Any commercially competitive compiler will be able to perform these types of common subexpression optimization for itself and, with the complex memory caches on modern processors, it may well be the case that user-performed optimizations actually prevent the compiler from doing the best job! So, in general, trust the optimizer and write clearly what you want to compute.

However, *some* source code optimizations *should* be done by the user. The classic example is accessing data stored in multidimensional arrays. The Fortran standard mandates that the elements of an array must be stored contiguously using *column major order*. This means that the contents of a multidimensional array are flattened into a vector by varying the first subscript most rapidly, followed by the second, with the final dimension varying most slowly. For a two-dimensional array, *a(m,n)*, the order is thus

$$a(1, 1), a(2, 1), \ldots, a(m, 1), a(1, 2), \ldots, a(m, 2), \ldots, a(m - 1, n), a(m, n).$$

This is different, for example, from the C programming language where elements are stored in *row major order*, which can cause some problems with interoperability with Fortran (see the comments in Section 10.2). These problems are typically resolved by transposing arrays, or modifying loop order, or changing the increments between array elements.

Thus when processing blocks of array data the programmer should endeavor to access elements so that the first subscript is incremented the fastest, as this will ensure that data transfers between the main memory and caches will be as efficient as possible. As an example, suppose we wish to compute the sums of the rows of a two-dimensional array; then

```
DO i = 1, n
  rowsum(i) = zero
  DO j = 1, n
    rowsum(i) = rowsum(i) + a(i,j)
  END DO
END DO
```

will be far less efficient, for large n, than

```
DO i = 1, n
  rowsum(i) = zero
END DO
DO i = 1, n
  DO j = 1, n
    rowsum(j) = rowsum(j) + a(j,i)
  END DO
END DO
```

This type of optimization must be performed at the algorithmic level and is not something that a compiler can be expected to do.

One important optimization strategy is allowing the compiler to *in-line* function or subroutine calls (see Chapter 6 for a detailed example and a discussion of the execution time improvements). Calls to Fortran subprograms require setting memory addresses, placing data onto internal working stacks, and branching. These steps frequently can be eliminated by the compiler inserting the entire routine as a replacement for the call or function invocation. Fortran does not have a standard way to allow for this form of in-lining, but Fortran compilers usually make aggressive attempts to perform such optimizations. As usual, improvements to execution speed are dependent on the compiler and options used!

18.5   My Code Doesn't Run Fast Enough!

A common problem facing many application programmers is what to do when software cannot complete its required task in a reasonable amount of time. Code optimization can only take you so far, and once it has been applied there is little more that can be achieved. The next step is usually to use some form of parallelism either by taking advantage of multiple cores or by using multiple machines (see Chapters 13, 14, and 15). Any of these approaches is likely to require a substantial effort—especially the distributed solution—which will almost inevitably involve major restructuring of the software to obtain even a moderate speed-up factor. Some compilers offer an automatic parallelization option, which is usually aimed at using OpenMP, or a variant to improve execution speed. Generally the improvement produced by this approach is very disappointing mainly because programmers do not write sequential code with automatic parallelization in mind! A useful side effect of this option on some compilers is a commentary giving details of which loops could not be parallelized and why. Such information can be helpful in producing a handcrafted OpenMP version of the code.

Here we make a plea: before you set out to optimize your application, spend some effort in finding out where most of the computational effort is being expended. This may be done relatively easily and cheaply by using a run-time profiler (see Chapter 19). There have been scores of anecdotes over the years of programmers spending huge amounts of effort in optimizing sections of code only to find the real bottleneck is somewhere else entirely. Once you are certain where the majority of the execution time is being spent, the first thing to consider is whether it is possible to speed up that part of the computation by using a more efficient algorithm; for example, replacing an $O(N^2)$ sorting routine by an $O(N \log N)$ routine will, particularly for large data sets, have a far greater effect on the run time than any code optimization. It may be that you have used the most effective algorithms and have generated an extremely efficient parallel version of the software yet your application still does not run fast enough; the only answer at this point is to wait for faster hardware with more cores!

18.6   Dealing with Dusty Decks

One of the reasons that Fortran continues to flourish as a programming language is that, due to the efforts of the standards' committees, it is still possible to reuse very old source code. Such code is often referred to as a *dusty deck*.[2]

However, new standards have deprecated (removed from the standard) a number of constructs and features of earlier versions of the language, for example,

---

[2]From the bygone days of dealing with trays or boxes of (dusty) punch card source code images.

Hollerith constants and the assigned-**GO TO** statement (a full list of the features deprecated at successive standards may be found in [65, Appendix B]). Most compilers provide an option—often by default—that allows code containing these deleted features to be compiled and linked against modern code. In addition, it may be possible to compile software that contains extensions that were commonly available in commercial compilers but were never part of any Fortran standard, for example, double precision complex and byte size declarations such as **REAL*4** and **REAL*8**. Note that it may sometimes be necessary to use more than one option depending on which deprecated features or extensions have been used.

We offer more advice on transforming dusty deck code in Chapter 16.

Chapter 19

Software Tools

Synopsis:

> *Useful tools; time savers; better quality software*
>
> ▶ *Make avoids unnecessary recompiling*
>
> ▶ *SVN keeps source in-sync*
>
> ▶ *Source code documentation*
>
> ▶ *Using debuggers, profilers*
>
> ▶ *Error processing; readable output*
>
> ▶ *Source code stylers, converters*

19.1 Introduction

An old adage says that "bad workmen always blame their tools" but our experience suggests that "bad software engineers never use tools"!

We mention a number of specific tools in this chapter, although we do not claim that these are the only, or the best, examples of their type. Several high quality tools are freely available for downloading to a wide range of platforms, and these are definitely worth investigating. While we have not used all the applications described on a regular basis, we believe that they all have the potential both to save time during code development and to improve software quality. Two in particular that have proved of critical help throughout the writing of this book are *make* [63] and *SVN* [73].

Examples of software tools include

- language-aware editors for writing source code;

- programs that build applications [63] and documentation [91] efficiently and accurately;

- applications that track changes to the source code, documentation, etc. [73];

- run-time debuggers to assist in the discovery of coding errors;

- source code profilers for showing which statements have not been exercised during testing and where efficiency gains may be made; see Chapter 17 for more on testing;

- subprograms that provide output, understandable by practitioners in the application field;

- subprograms that manage a range of error or exceptional conditions encountered during execution;

- programs that format source code in a consistent and readable manner.

An important tool available to the Fortran programmer is the Fortran compiler. In fact its facilities are often so underused that we have dedicated a complete chapter to it and how it may be used more effectively; see Chapter 18.

We are convinced that time invested in learning how to use software tools will be handsomely repaid. Many are extremely powerful and contain myriads of features resulting in very large user manuals, which often deter first-time users. In most cases it is possible, by learning a few simple features, to perform mundane and repetitious programming tasks easily and accurately. Once a programmer is confident about using the simpler features, it is then relatively easy to pick up the more complex facilities as they are required. As with programming itself, it pays to study how other developers exploit particular applications, for example, by examining other programmers' *Makefiles* and reading the introductory documentation and tip lists available on the web.

19.2   Application Building Using *make*

Producing an executable from a set of Fortran source files is straightforward; we just compile all the separate files and link them together. On many systems this can be reduced to a single command of the form

```
gfortran -o driver *.f
```

However, this could become a time consuming operation during the development of code. A single, simple change to one file means that all the source files in the application are recompiled. Many compilers allow the generation of intermediate files, often with a suffix like *.o* or *.obj*, and these can then be linked together as in Section 2.2, for example. This is more efficient for developers who only have to recompile files that have been altered and to relink them (assuming that they can always remember which files have been changed)!

The tool *make*, originally written by Stuart Feldman at Bell Labs, allows the user to describe—in a so-called *Makefile*—the steps necessary to build one or more *target* files from a set of files. These rules are known as *dependencies*. In the day-to-day use of *make* by programmers the end targets are often executable files, but *make* may be used to rebuild any sort of files, for example, user manuals and test-results files.

As an example we look at a simple *Makefile* that could be used to produce an executable directly from a set of source files:

```
driver: driver.f subs.f
        gfortran -o driver driver.f subs.f
```

The first line is interpreted as *the target file driver depends upon the two files driver.f and subs.f.* The following lines, **which must start with the ASCII tab character**, describe the steps required to create the target from the dependency files. In this case we just invoke the compiler on all the dependent source files.

So what is the difference between *make* and a simple script? The *make* tool will use the hidden time-stamp information on the targets and dependency files to minimize the amount of work that needs to be performed to generate the target file. When *make* is invoked it determines if any target file is out-of-date with respect to its dependencies; i.e., it uses the time-stamp information associated with each file to see if any of the dependency files have been rewritten since the target was last generated. If so, the target is regenerated; otherwise *make* does nothing.

The real power of *make* is that it allows us to define rules, or use *make*'s built-in rules, to generate intermediate target files that themselves are used as dependencies. This chaining allows complex sets of commands to be executed with little effort on behalf of the *Makefile* author.

For a more realistic example we consider the following simple *Makefile* which builds one of the Quicksort executables from Chapter 6.

```
F90 = gfortran
F90FLAGS = -Wall -fcheck=all -g
F90LINKFLAGS = $(F90FLAGS)

%.o:%.f90
        $(F90) $(F90FLAGS) -o $@ -c $<

%: %.o
        $(F90) $(F90LINKFLAGS) -o $@ $^

ConcreteMain: set_precision.o concrete.o sortElements.o

ConcreteMain.o: set_precision.o concrete.o sortElements.o
concrete.o: sortElements.o set_precision.o
sortElements.o:
set_precision.o:
```

The first three lines define variables that are set to the name of the Fortran compiler and options to be used when compiling and linking. In this example we set both the compile and link options to be the same.

The next two blocks define *Makefile* rules which detail how certain files are to be derived; in the majority of cases we generate one type of file (say *.o* files for linking) from another file with the same file stem but a different suffix (for example, the equivalent *.f* source file).

The two rules define how to generate an object file (*.o*) from a free format Fortran source file (*.f*90) and an executable file from a set of *.o* files. For a particular platform and compiler we will generally use the same rules whenever we build an application; we therefore tend to write these rules just once and store them in a rule file which we *include* in all our *Makefiles*. These rules may appear opaque to a first time reader; for more details on their construction see Mecklenburg [63, Chapter 2].

The final set of statements provides a list of all the dependencies that exist between the files; for example, *concrete.o* is dependent upon both *set_precision.o* and *sortElements.o* because it uses both the modules contained within these files. If, for example, the content of *sortElement.f*90 were altered, then we would need to recompile *sortElement.f*90 before recompiling *concrete.f*90 and *concreteMain.f*90 and then, finally, relinking. *make* can determine the minimum number of files to recompile by using the dependency list along with time and date information. Properly constructed, this dependency list means that the compilation cascade may be dealt with efficiently and accurately. In addition the list also provides documentation of intermodule use within an application.

Note that the use of *make* is not restricted to just building executables; it can also be used to ensure that, for example, documentation is kept up to date, and the current authors have used it to rebuild both separate chapters and the complete book from the LATEX sources.

The code accompanying this book contains a, we hope, well documented make include file that provides a more comprehensive set of rules along with examples of how *make* may be persuaded to use a range of different compilers and sets of compiler options. Makefiles are also included with the software for each chapter; these use the make include file to build all the executables.

Here we have discussed only a very simple form of *Makefile* which is suitable for compiling small to medium size applications. Large applications may require the compilation and linking of hundreds of module files totaling many hundreds of thousands of source lines. In these circumstances rebuilding the required executables following a source change may take many hours, and the associated *Makefiles* need to be made as efficient as possible.

A discussion of the problems of compilation cascades caused by changes to low-level modules leading to the, possibly unnecessary, recompilation of program units that USE these modules may be found in [65, Appendix D]. Also included are a sample *Makefile* and a shell script illustrating how to avoid unnecessary recompilations when using the NagWare compiler [67].

While *make* was originally written for a Unix system, its modern reimplementation *gmake* [63] is available under Linux, MacOS, and Windows. Microsoft Visual Studio provides a comprehensive application builder, *MSBuild*, that has many of the features of *make* but is far more automated.

19.3   Source Code or Text Control Systems

How many times have you made extensive changes to source code only to find that they were ill-conceived and needed to be undone? How many times have you not kept a copy of the original version? A source code control system, like SVN [73], is designed to ensure that backing out of situations like the above is both simple and (almost) foolproof.

However, systems like SVN are not confined to operating just on source code; they may be applied to any complex development task, for example, writing documentation, managing testing material, or writing a book. Indeed, part of their strength is that they may be used to ensure that a dispersed group of workers can access and update material efficiently and without conflict.

During the writing of this book, one author was in New Mexico, USA and the other was in Kent, UK. Personal communication was conducted primarily by email and telephone, but the text for the book and the associated software was transmitted and maintained via an SVN repository. Our goal was to avoid both of us writing or editing the same material simultaneously, then posting back the results, without realizing that conflicts existed. Each time one author submitted a change to the text of a chapter, or to any of the Fortran codes, the system sent out an email alert. This signaled the other author to update his local copies.

The potential for working at cross purposes is present for the developer of software. For example, one of us (Hanson) has worked for a company that develops and licenses libraries of mathematical software. It is standard practice in that process for an individual developer to implement an algorithm and then for other developers to review the software, tests, or documentation, and make further changes. This process often see-saws through several iterations, and each time changes are made, the resulting updated code, tests, and documentation are committed to an SVN repository. All developers are expected to update their local copies of the material, typically at the start of each working day or as alert messages are received. They will then either make further changes or incorporate the new content directly.

Using a source control system such as SVN might, at first glance, seem to be of use only when two or more parties participate in the creation of various types of source text. In that case we believe it is essential. Both authors have been involved with projects that had only one other participant who declined to use a control system such as SVN. Without fail there were instances where both parties edited the same source files and, as a result, important changes were lost or confusion ensued. As with *make* (see Section 19.2 above) knowledge of a relatively small subset of the commands available in SVN can allow the user to benefit greatly from the use of the system. Other facilities may then be explored as confidence in using the tool increases.

19.4   Source Code Documentation Systems

Keeping code documentation current is a challenge, and our experience suggests that many developers are less than enthusiastic about this part of the software development process. A major problem is that documentation commonly lags behind changes to the software, often because the development process requires two sets of files to be edited, the code and the associated documentation.

One particular system that is gaining in popularity is *Doxygen* (see van Heesch [91] for details). By recognizing special forms of comments, Doxygen can extract content from a variety of programming languages, including fixed and free format Fortran, and generate documents in a variety of output formats including LaTeX and HTML. The system recognizes a host of "special commands" which effectively act as mark-up and these may be used to create comprehensive routine documentation. The author of Doxygen has even "abused" the system to generate the Doxygen user manual.

19.5 Debuggers

With a suitable combination of option flags, most compilers can be induced to report where a fatal error has occurred within an executing program along with the calling sequence that led to that particular statement. Some may even be coaxed into revealing the values of local variables when the code terminated.

The term *debugger* may be applied to any tool that assists in the location of errors in a program, although nowadays it is generally reserved for one that provides some form of interaction with a running program.

These tools may vary from a command-line driven debugger running on a single core (for example, gdb [87]) to GUI-based applications running on multinode systems using MPI (see, for example, [81]). Basic facilities include the setting of breakpoints (places within the code where the user wishes to temporarily halt the execution), viewing the values of user-selected variables at breakpoints, halting the program if certain conditions occur (for example, a variable exceeds a user-supplied value), and even altering the values of variables at breakpoints and continuing with the computation. The features available and the way in which the interaction takes places differ with each compiler and debugger.

As with most software tools it pays to start simple; learning how to set a breakpoint and interrogate variables are probably the most useful features to begin with. Mastering just these can be a great step up from inserting print statements and can save much time and effort on behalf of the programmer. Additional features may then be tried out as confidence in using the tool increases.

Use of a debugger requires the compiler to embed extra information into the final executable; this is achieved by setting compiler-dependent flags and will almost certainly require turning off any form of code optimization. For example, if we wish to use the gdb debugger [87], we would modify our compilation *Makefile* and include the "-g" option.

```
driver:  driver.f subs.f
       gfortran -o -g driver driver.f subs.f
```

In order to obtain the greatest flexibility when using a debugger it is advisable to recompile all the source files with the required compiler flags.

19.6   Profiling

A *profiler* is concerned with analyzing the dynamic or run-time behavior of a correctly executing application. Two topics, *coverage* and *execution time*, are of vital concern in making a robust and efficient version of the application. Ensuring that the primary lines of source code are actually covered by the program execution flow is important for testing, maintenance, and building confidence in the reliability of the software. The foremost concern of an application is usually to be efficient, which means that execution time is generally of primary concern.

19.6.1   Execution Time Profiler

This is a software tool that provides information about the time taken to execute segments of a running program. Here segments may be routines or blocks of code or even a single statement. Care needs to be taken with any results obtained; runs need to be long enough to register segment times accurately, and the use of instruction sampling means that timings are generally more accurate for larger sections of code. Also, remember that different sets of data are liable to generate different execution time profiles, certainly for more complex codes.

The main use of this type of profile is to show where we should look to improve code in order to make efficiency gains. Experience has shown that programmers rarely know where bottlenecks in their code actually are (although many claim to know!) and often spend copious amounts of time tuning the wrong sections of code. Execution time profiles are the only way to pinpoint accurately where savings in run time can be made. Remember the 80/20 rule: as a rule of thumb, 80% of the run time is spent in 20% of the code. Don't optimize until you know where to concentrate your effort.

Compilers have improved executable code optimization to a degree where it is increasingly rare that major saving can be made by tweaking the source code. Instead, improved performance requires either better algorithms or more computing power (e.g., parallel computation).

One of the commonest execution time profilers is the Unix tool *gprof*. Obtaining the profile is a two stage process: first, the code needs to be compiled with a special flag (typically *-pg*) to turn on run time profiling. Running this version of the executable produces a data file which may then be postprocessed with *gprof* to generate a user friendly report.

19.6.2   Source Code Profiler

Statement and branch coverage (see Section 17.3) data may sometimes be obtained by setting extra flags during compilation to include counters in the relevant places within the executable. Running the code on test data sets then allows the executable to accumulate the number of times each block and branch has been executed, and a separate tool may then used to merge these counts with the source code to form a readable report at either a file or a routine level.

Such facilities are not available with all compilers and, when they do exist, will invariably require a different procedure for each compiler. For *gfortran* all source files that are to be analyzed need to be compiled with the *-coverage* flag, for example

```
gfortran −c −g −coverage subs.f90
```

Optimization flags should not be used in conjunction with the *-coverage* flag as the optimizer may hinder the production of accurate counts. The compiler generates a *.gcno* file for each source file and running the executable produces additional *.gcda* files. Finally, coverage reports for a particular source file may be produced using

```
gcov −a −b subs.f90
```

when the data collected during the execution in the *.gcno* and *.gcda* files is merged with the source code to form a human readable text file. More details about *gcov* may be found in [32, Chapter 10].

The coverage data is cumulative so complete test suites may be run to produce overall coverage information without further intervention.

19.7   Sample Output and Run-Time Error Processors

Dealing with error conditions is an important part of all forms of software development but is often critical for numerical codes. When generating a user-callable routine no trappable conditions should lead to the routine terminating. While it may, at first sight, appear reasonable to halt execution if a program is about to generate an undefined operation such as divide by zero, this is highly dependent on the context in which it occurs. It could be a fatal error or it could be an issue that is resolvable by analysis at a higher level of the software. The most flexible way of handling exceptions is to return to the calling program unit signaling an error condition. In its simplest form this may be achieved by returning a user-testable error flag. The user may then decide whether or not the situation is recoverable.

As an example consider the case where a stiff ODE solver calls a library routine to compute the solution of a linear system. The occurrence of a near-singular system of linear equations may mean that a step-size selected by the ODE solver needs to be made smaller. This is an exception that can be handled by the ODE code, and the linear solver should not halt just because a singular system has been detected.

When debugging or developing code, programmers often resort to using Fortran write statements. In this context it is useful to have a consistent way of displaying data structures such as vectors and arrays, with convenient control over labels, the number of significant digits output, and the length of each displayed line as well as the ability to output from either an executing image or a specific thread within an image.

One way of obtaining both flexibility and consistency is to use an error message and output processor. An example of such a tool is the subprogram *messy* [54].

19.8 Source Code Stylers

There are many tools available to help Fortran programmers with the day-to-day chores associated with managing source code. In this section we concentrate mainly on applications that can change the appearance and/or structure of code without changing the output generated when the software is executed.

19.8.1 Pretty Printers

Many individual programmers have a preferred way of laying out their code; this could include things like the width of indentation for nested constructs, the case used for keywords, spacing around numerical operators, etc. Indeed, many organizations impose a house style to ensure consistency across programming teams.

Imposing a style manually is tedious and this is just the job for a software tool. Two commercial examples which provide a host of user options are the NAG Fortran compiler [67] (Release 5.3 or later using *polish* mode) and *Spag*, part of the plusFORT suite of tools [74]. Both produce a user-controlled source code layout using either a configuration file or command line options. The NAG compiler is unusual in that it provides other functionality using information obtained during the early stages of compilation rather than having separate applications.

As far as the authors know, there are no comparable public domain source formatting tools available for versions of Fortran 90 and beyond.

19.8.2 Converting Fixed Format Source to Free Format

Both of the commercial tools mentioned in the previous section will convert old fixed format source code into the modern free format, taking care of comments and continuation lines. In addition both will change old style relational operators (for example, .EQ., .GT.) to the new form (for example, ==, >) and ensure that all **DO**-loops are rewritten without labels and terminated with **END DO** statements.

Two public domain tools, Metcalf's *convert* [64] and Miller's *to_f90* [66] are also available to perform a basic conversion from fixed to free format as well as indenting code for **DO**-loops and assigned-**GO TO**. Miller's tool will also convert relational operators.

19.8.3 Deleted Features

Deleted features are constructs that were available in older versions of the standard but which have now been officially removed from Fortran. These are discussed in detail in Chapter 16.

To replace many of these deleted features by their new counterparts in a nonnaive way often requires a major analysis of the source code. It is thus perhaps not surprising that only commercial tools appear to do a thorough job.

Spag [74] is an extremely powerful and comprehensive restructuring tool which will use techniques like code movement and code duplication in an attempt to remove as many **GO TO** statements and their associated labels as possible. If the original code has been written in a controlled manner, then *Spag* is able to generate very clean, modern code. However, if the original code is highly convoluted (as a lot of old Fortran code appears to be), then *Spag*'s restructured code may be almost as hard to follow as the original.

That said, *Spag* allows very fine control of what restructuring is to be attempted, and this mode does allow the user to process a number of deleted constructs:

1. Arithmetic-**IF** statements are replaced by block-**IF** statements.

2. Computed-**GO TO** statements are replaced by **SELECT CASE** constructs.

3. Old style **DO**-loops are replaced by **DO-END DO** blocks (the Nag compiler in polish mode will also do this).

4. Hollerith constants are replaced by character strings in **FORMAT** statements. Use of other data types (for examples, integers) to store and manipulate character data needs to be dealt with outside of the tool.

Spag leaves a number of control flow structures completely unmodified; these include assigned-**GO TO** statements and alternate returns. It also makes no attempt to deal with **DATA** statements and statement functions.

Miller's application replaces all **DO**-loops by **DO-END DO** blocks (Metcalf's *convert* only replaces terminating **CONTINUE** statements). It also converts arithmetic-**IF** statements in a very naive fashion; for example,

```
    IF (i) 10,20,30
    ...
```

is translated into

```
    IF (i < 0) THEN
       GO TO    10
    ELSE IF (i == 0) THEN
       GO TO    20
    ELSE
       GO TO    30
    END IF
10    ...
```

which, while not particularly helpful, does at least provide a template for further manual changes.

On the other hand, *Spag* will endeavor to pull the associated code into the if-block, leading to the far more readable translation

```
    IF ( i<0 ) THEN
       i = 3
    ELSEIF ( i==0 ) THEN
       i = 5
    ELSE
       i = 6
    ENDIF
```

Finally, both *Spag* and *to_f*90 will attempt to generate **INTENT** declarations for all dummy arguments. Neither of the tools attempts to perform any deep analysis of the call tree, so these declarations cannot be obtained with absolute reliability in the case of INTENT(IN). When not enough information is available, the tool will err on the side of caution and generate INTENT(INOUT).

19.8.4 Listing Tools

Some compilers have options to generate listing files; these generally have numbers at the start of each line or statement and may use bold fonts or color to distinguish between keywords, variable names, and strings.

The publicly available utility *a2ps* [20] may be used to convert Fortran source into a PostScript listing file where Fortran keywords are output in bold.

To insert Fortran source into a LATEX document, the *listings* package [37] may be used. All the source listings in this book have been produced using this package which provides fine user control over the appearance of the text, for example, font size, color of keywords and variables, outline boxes, etc. The main drawback of both tools is that they have not been updated since Fortran 95.

Finally, it is worth noting that many editors, for example, *vi* [80] and Emacs [17], may be made (or just are!) language aware. This means that keywords, comments, etc. may be color coded, and minor syntactic errors, such as forgetting a closing quote, may then easily be detected and corrected.

19.9 Other Software Tools

Finally, we mention briefly a number of other tools and facilities that programmers may find useful.

1. *Callgraph generators* show the calling relationships between procedures within an application. This is useful when changing the source of a routine, as the programmer can identify all the places the program unit is called from, and can thus determine whether the proposed changes are appropriate in all circumstances.

2. *Symbol table generators* typically list all the user-defined symbols with the line numbers within the source in which each symbol appears. Some offer more detail, for example, whether or not the symbol is assigned to, whether it is a parameter in a routine call, etc. This information may be used to inform the debugging process, among other things.

3. *Makefile generators* are programs, typically written in Perl [84] or Python [61], which first scan a collection of Fortran source files looking for use-statements, and then generate the dependency rules required by *make* (see Section 19.2 for a more detailed description of *make*). Examples of available applications are the NAG Fortran compiler [67] (used in *depend* mode) and the freely available *makemake* [94] and *fmkmf* [75].

Chapter 20

Fortran Book Code on SIAM Web Site

20.1 Downloading the Software

Here we list package summaries and a web address for the principal Fortran software provided with the book. *All the web addresses will use the prefix*

http://www.siam.org/books/ot134/

So this prefix string, on the front end of the string **Chapter02**, for example, will guide your web browser to the directory at the SIAM web site that has the code for the packaging of routines from the LAPACK and BLAS suites in Chapter 2.

20.2 Topical Headings for the Software

Brief descriptions of the major packages' contents are given below. To access them, use the above instructions for downloading the software.

Chapter02 Suggested packaging for existing collections of Fortran 77 codes. Illustrated using a subset of LAPACK and BLAS routines. Also included is a helper module for specifying floating-point precision.

Chapter03 Generic packaging of Airy functions. Generic interfaces enable the use of the same names for single and double precision, and complex and double complex, versions of the linearly independent solutions of Airy's equation, $w'' - zw = 0$. This gives the Airy functions the same look and feel of other Fortran elementary functions such as $\cos(z), \sin(z), \exp(z)$, etc.

Chapter04 Defined operations and overloaded assignment for sparse matrix operations. Derived types are defined that accumulate lists of matrix triplets representing row and column indices and their value. These lists are converted to HB format sparse representations. Then products, transposes, and sums of HB format matrices are available as the defined operations using the respective symbols *****, **.p.**, **.t.**, **+**. Overloaded assignment clears or deallocates the created objects.

Chapter05 Defines a class object, interior to a numerical code, as an extension of a derived type. The class object may contain problem data, procedure pointers, or even a pointer to a final procedure called as the object goes out of existence. Includes an illustration using a classic one-dimensional zero solver. This routine is transformed to use this class object, including a finalization step.

Chapter06 Develops a general framework and packaging for the efficient Quicksort sorting algorithm. As a result this algorithm can be applied in a variety of contexts, thereby avoiding the proliferation of different routines for differing data types. Recursion, in standard Fortran, is used in the basic structure of the algorithm.

Chapter07 The classic Fortran 77 QUADPACK routine *qag* is transformed to use Fortran 2003 features. This numerical quadrature algorithm is extended to new application areas by using optional arguments, recursion, and extended derived types. These new capabilities include array evaluation of the integrand, multi-dimensional integration, and vector function integration, particularly complex line integrals. A derived type for QUADPACK is defined that has default parameters for the integration. This type can then be modified or extended by the user. Using an extended type as a class argument enables passing data and procedure pointers to the integrand evaluation function.

Chapter08 Documentation examples are provided for the use of the QUADPACK package. Show use of internal and external function subprograms called by the quadrature routines. Examples are a Bessel function evaluation and a normal probability computation. Data is passed to the evaluation function using extended derived types.

Chapter09 An algorithm is developed for computing the l_2 norm of a vector. This is presented in the context of implementing the Level-1 BLAS function *dnrm2*. Usage of the IEEE intrinsic modules are illustrated for handling exceptions. The packaging includes a preprocessor flag that constructs a version of the function with and without support of the IEEE intrinsic modules.

Also included is a nonintrinsic implementation of the following IEEE modules: *IEEE_ARITHMETIC.f90*, *IEEE_EXCEPTIONS.f90*, and *IEEE_FEATURES.f90* for the Intel x86 and AMD architectures and intended for use with *gfortran*. There is an accompanying file of C source for functions that use machine instructions to manipulate the required flags, *c_control.c*. There is documentation for the package, *IEEE.pdf*, and a test program that exercises many of the features, *IEEE_gfortran.f90*.

Chapter10 Demonstrates standardized interlanguage calls between Fortran and C. Examples include a Fortran program that makes operating system calls for directory manipulation by calling a C routine, a C program that calls a Fortran

routine that calls another C routine, and a C routine that calls the Fortran
Level-3 BLAS routine *dgemm* for matrix products. Calls between the languages can be by reference or value. These examples illustrate basic exercises
of interlanguage programming.

Chapter11 Defined operations and overloaded assignment for solving square,
sparse matrix linear systems. An extended derived type is defined that contains the HB format sparse matrices and parameters associated with LU factorization performed by the SuperLU. The source for this library must be
downloaded and prepared by the user.

Solve and clearing operations are available using defined operations and overloaded assignment. The solve operations use the symbols **.ip., .pi.** for the
respective solves steps $Ax = b$ and $A^T x = b$. The underlying solver is implemented with Fortran standard interlanguage calls from Fortran to C. We
provide the C wrappers that call the library codes. The clearing and deallo-
cation operations use overloaded assignment with a right-hand side 0.

Chapter12 Defined operations developed for sparse matrices, and their specific
derived types, illustrate two applications. These are least-squares solutions
for a piecewise linear function used to fit a second function, t^2, $0 \le t \le 1$;
the second example uses a piecewise linear function to solve a boundary value
problem for Airy's equation. This latter sparse system is computed based on
finite element methods; both examples are solved using the tools of Chapters 4
and 11.

Chapter13 Direct interface to a core suite of the C library of MPI routines, thus
avoiding violation of the Fortran standards. A module provides a direct interface to the C versions using the Fortran and ISO standard interoperability
features. Examples are given for the numerical approximation to π by a
quadrature procedure, and work-sharing for computing a matrix-vector product, $y = Ax$.

Chapter14 Two examples using coarray Fortran. The examples are the approximate computation of π by a midpoint quadrature formula, and the partitioned
matrix-vector product, $y = Ax$ for an $m \times n$ matrix A.

Chapter15 Complete program units and subprograms illustrating the usage of
OpenMP directives.

Chapter16 Before and after versions of a sample Newton method program. The
"before" version contains withdrawn features. The "after" version has the
withdrawn features replaced by standard code, with "GO TOs" also removed.

Bibliography

[1] Milton Abramowitz and Irene Stegun. *Handbook of Mathematical Functions with Formulas, Graphs, and Mathematical Tables*. Dover Publications, New York, NY, USA, 10th printing, December 1972. ISBN 978-0-486-61272-0. URL http://www.cs.bham.ac.uk/~aps/research/projects/as/book.php. (Cited on pp. 30, 33, 77, 145)

[2] ACM. *Collected Algorithms from ACM*. Association for Computing Machinery, New York, NY, USA, 2011. URL http://calgo.acm.org/. (Cited on p. ix)

[3] Jeanne C. Adams, Walter S. Brainerd, Jeanne T. Martin, Brian T. Smith, and Jerrold L. Wagener. *Fortran 95 handbook: Complete ANSI/ISO reference*. The MIT Press, Cambridge, MA, USA, 1997. ISBN 0-262-51096-0. (Cited on pp. 102, 182)

[4] Jeanne C. Adams, Walter S. Brainerd, Richard A. Hendrickson, Richard E. Maine, Jeanne T. Martin, and Brian T. Smith. *The Fortran 2003 Handbook: The Complete Syntax, Features and Procedures*. Springer Publishing, London, 2009. ISBN 978-1-84628-378-9. (Cited on pp. x, 1, 119)

[5] E. Anderson, Z. Bai, C. Bischof, S. Blackford, J. Demmel, J. Dongarra, J. Du Croz, A. Greenbaum, S. Hammarling, A. McKenney, and D. Sorensen. *LAPACK Users' Guide*. SIAM, Philadelphia, PA, USA, 3rd edition, 1999. ISBN 978-0-89871-447-0. URL http://www.netlib.org/lapack/lug/. (Cited on p. 14)

[6] Deborah J. Armstrong. The quarks of object-oriented development. *Comm. ACM*, 49(2):123–128, 2006. ISSN 0001-0782. doi: 10.1145/1113034.1113040. (Cited on pp. 48, 49)

[7] John Backus. The history of Fortran I, II, and III. *IEEE Ann. Hist. Comput.*, 20 (4):68–78, October–December 1998. ISSN 1058-6180. doi: 10.1109/85.728232. (Cited on p. 209)

[8] David John Barnes and Michael Kölling. *Objects First with Java: A Practical Introduction Using BlueJ*. Prentice Hall, Upper Saddle River, NJ, USA, 5th edition, 2011. ISBN 978-0-132-49266-9. (Cited on p. 47)

[9] D. J. Barnes and T. R. Hopkins. The evolution and testing of a medium sized numerical package. In H. P. Langtangen, A. M. Bruaset, and E. Quak, editors, *Advances in Software Tools for Scientific Computing*, volume 10 of *Lecture Notes in Computational Science and Engineering*, pages 225–238. Springer Publishing, Berlin, 2000. ISBN 978-3-540-66557-1. (Cited on p. 195)

[10] Blaise Barney. *Message Passing Interface (mpi)*. Technical report, Lawrence Livermore National Laboratory, Livermore, CA, USA, 2012. URL `https://computing.llnl.gov/tutorials/mpi/`. (Cited on p. xiv)

[11] Blaise Barney. *OpenMP*. Technical report, Lawrence Livermore National Laboratory, Livermore, CA, USA, 2013. URL `https://computing.llnl.gov/tutorials/openMP/`. (Cited on p. xiv)

[12] Åke Björk. *Numerical Methods for Least Squares Problems*. SIAM, Philadelphia, PA, USA, 1996. ISBN 978-0-89871-360-2. (Cited on pp. 142, 147)

[13] Susan Blackford and Jack J. Dongarra. *Installation guide for LAPACK*. Technical report LAWN41, Department of Computer Science, University of Tennessee, Knoxville, TN, USA, June 1999. URL `http://www.netlib.org/lapack/lawnspdf/lawn41.pdf`. (Cited on p. 197)

[14] James L. Blue. A portable Fortran program to find the Euclidean norm of a vector. *ACM Trans. Math. Software*, 4(1):15–23, 1978. ISSN 0098-3500. doi: 10.1145/355769.355771. (Cited on pp. 104, 106)

[15] Clay Breshears. *The Art of Concurrency*. O'Reilly Media, Inc., Sebastopol, CA, USA, 2009. ISBN 978-0-596-52153-0. (Cited on p. 180)

[16] Ilene Burnstein. *Practical Software Testing*. Springer Publishing, New York, 2003. ISBN 0-387-95131-8. URL `http://en.wikipedia.org/wiki/Equivalence_partitioning`. (Cited on p. 198)

[17] Debra Cameron, James Elliott, Marc Loy, Eric S. Raymond, and Bill Rosenblatt. *Learning GNU Emacs*. O'Reilly Media, Inc., Sebastopol, CA, USA, 3rd edition, December 2004. ISBN 978-0-596-00648-8. (Cited on p. 225)

[18] Barbara Chapman, Gabriele Jost, and Ruud van der Pas. *Using OpenMP: Portable Shared Memory Parallel Programming*. Scientific and Engineering Computation. The MIT Press, Cambridge, MA, USA, 2007. ISBN 978-0-262-53302-7. (Cited on pp. 79, 169)

[19] A. C. Damhaug, K. Magne Mathisen, and K. M. Okstad. The use of sparse matrix methods in finite-element codes for structural mechanics applications. *Comput. Systems Engrg.*, 4(4–6):355–362, August–December 1993. ISSN 0956-0521. doi: 10.1016/0956-0521(93)90003-F. (Cited on p. 36)

[20] Akim Demaille and Miguel Santana. *a2ps*. Software download, 2007. URL `http://www.gnu.org/software/a2ps/`. Any to PostScript filter – gnu. (Cited on p. 225)

[21] J. J. Dongarra and A. R. Hinds. Unrolling loops in Fortran. *Software Practice Experience*, 9(3):219–226, 1979. ISSN 1097-024X. doi: 10.1002/spe. 4380090307. (Cited on p. 210)

[22] J. J. Dongarra, J. Du Croz, S. Hammarling, and R. J. Hanson. Algorithm 656: An extended set of basic linear algebra subprograms: Model implementation and test programs. *ACM Trans. Math. Software*, 14(1):18–32, March 1988. ISSN 0098-3500. doi: 10.1145/42288.42292. (Cited on p. 113)

[23] Jack J. Dongarra and Eric Grosse. Distribution of mathematical software via electronic mail. *Comm. ACM*, 30(5):403–407, May 1987. ISSN 0001-0782. doi: 10.1145/22899.22904. (Cited on p. 58)

[24] Iain Duff, Roger Grimes, and John Lewis. *User's Guide for the Harwell-Boeing Sparse Matrix Collection*. Technical report TR/PA/92/86, CERFACS, Toulouse, France, 1992. (Cited on p. 36)

[25] Victor Eijkhout. *Lapack Working note 50: Distributed Sparse Data Structures for Linear Algebra Operations*. Technical report 92-169, Computer Science Department, University of Tennessee, Knoxville, TN, USA, 1992. (Cited on p. 36)

[26] B. R. Fabijonas. Algorithm 838: Airy functions. *ACM Trans. Math. Software*, 30(4):491–501, December 2004. ISSN 0098-3500. doi: 10.1145/1039813. 1039819. (Cited on pp. xiii, 30, 31)

[27] B. R. Fabijonas, D. W. Lozier, and F. W. J. Olver. Computation of complex Airy functions and their zeros using asymptotics and the differential equation. *ACM Trans. Math. Software*, 30(4):471–490, December 2004. ISSN 0098-3500. doi: 10.1145/1039813.1039818. (Cited on p. 30)

[28] David Flanagan. *Java in a Nutshell*. O'Reilly Media, Inc., Sebastopol, CA, USA, 5th edition, 2005. ISBN 978-0-596-00773-7. (Cited on p. 182)

[29] George E. Forsythe, Michael A. Malcolm, and Cleve B. Moler. *Computer Methods for Mathematical Computations*. Prentice-Hall, Inc., Englewood Cliffs, NJ, USA, 1977. ISBN 0-13-165332-6. (Cited on p. 52)

[30] P. A. Fox, A. D. Hall, and N. L. Schryer. Algorithm 528: Framework for a portable library [Z]. *ACM Trans. Math. Software*, 4(2):177–188, June 1978. ISSN 0098-3500. doi: 10.1145/355780.355789. (Cited on p. 102)

[31] Alan George. Nested dissection of a regular finite element mesh. *SIAM J. Numer. Anal.*, 10(2):345–363, April 1973. ISSN 0036-1429. doi: 10.1137/ 0710032. (Cited on p. 36)

[32] The GCC Team. *GCC 4.7.1 Manual*. Free Software Foundation, Boston, MA, USA, 2011. URL http://gcc.gnu.org/onlinedocs/gcc-4.7.1/gcc.pdf. (Cited on p. 222)

[33] The GFORTRAN Team. *Using GNU Fortran*. Free Software Foundation, Boston, MA, USA, 2010. URL `http://gcc.gnu.org/onlinedocs/gfortran.pdf`. (Cited on pp. 14, 112)

[34] Gene H. Golub and Charles F. Van Loan. *Matrix Computations*. Johns Hopkins University Press, Baltimore, MD, USA, 3rd edition, 1996. ISBN 978-0-8018-5414-9. (Cited on p. 14)

[35] Fred G. Gustavson, John K. Reid, and Jerzy Waśniewski. Algorithm 865: Fortran 95 subroutines for Cholesky factorization in block hybrid format. *ACM Trans. Math. Software*, 33(1):8:1–8:5, March 2007. ISSN 0098-3500. doi: 10.1145/1206040.1206048. (Cited on p. 37)

[36] Richard J. Hanson, Clay P. Breshears, and Henry A. Gabb. Algorithm 821: A Fortran interface to posix threads. *ACM Trans. Math. Software*, 28(3):354–371, September 2002. ISSN 0098-3500. doi: 10.1145/569147.569152. (Cited on p. 180)

[37] Carsten Heinz and Brooks Moses. *The Listings Package*, 2007. Latex package for typesetting source code within a document. URL `http://www.ctan.org/tex-archive/macros/latex/contrib/listings/listings.pdf`. (Cited on p. 225)

[38] Nicholas J. Higham. *Accuracy and Stability of Numerical Algorithms*. SIAM, Philadelphia, PA, USA, 2nd edition, 2002. ISBN 978-0-89871-521-7. (Cited on p. 103)

[39] F. B. Hildebrand. *Introduction to Numerical Analysis*. Dover Publications, New York, NY, USA, 2nd edition, 1987. ISBN 0-486-65363-3. URL `http://store.doverpublications.com`. (Cited on p. 152)

[40] Michael D. Hirschhorn. When is the sum of consecutive squares a square? *Math. Gazette*, 95:511–512, November 2011. ISSN 0025-5572. URL `http://web.maths.unsw.edu.au/~mikeh/webpapers/paper173.pdf`. (Cited on p. 201)

[41] C. A. R. Hoare. Algorithm 64: Quicksort. *Comm. ACM*, 4(7):321, 1961. ISSN 0001-0782. doi: 10.1145/366622.366644. (Cited on p. 57)

[42] Roger W. Hockney. *The Science of Computer Benchmarking*. SIAM, Philadelphia, PA, USA, 1996. ISBN 978-0-89871-363-3. doi: 10.1137/1.9780898719666. (Cited on p. 197)

[43] T. R. Hopkins. Renovating the collected algorithms from ACM. *ACM Trans. Math. Software*, 28(1):59–74, March 2002. ISSN 0098-3500. doi: 10.1145/513001.513005. (Cited on p. 206)

[44] Marnie L. Hutcheson. *Software Testing Fundamentals: Methods and Metrics*. John Wiley, Indianapolis, IN, USA, 2003. ISBN 978-0471-43020-9. (Cited on p. 196)

[45] IEEE Task P754. *ANSI/IEEE* 754-1985, *Standard for Binary Floating-Point Arithmetic*. IEEE, New York, August 1985. A preliminary draft was published in the January 1980 issue of IEEE Computer, together with several companion articles. (Cited on pp. 20, 21, 101)

[46] ISO/IEC. *Programming Languages – FORTRAN (Withdrawn) – Fortran (ISO/IEC 1539:1980(E))*. ISO/IEC Copyright Office, Geneva, Switzerland, 1980. (Cited on pp. x, 2, 71)

[47] ISO/IEC. *Information Technology – Programming Languages – Fortran (ISO/IEC 1539:1991(E))*. ISO/IEC Copyright Office, Geneva, Switzerland, 1991. (Cited on pp. x, 13)

[48] ISO/IEC. *Information Technology – Programming Languages – Part 1, Base Language – Fortran (ISO/IEC 1539:2004(E))*. ISO/IEC Copyright Office, Geneva, Switzerland, 2004. (Cited on pp. x, 13)

[49] ISO/IEC. *Information Technology – Programming Languages – Part 1, Base Language – Fortran (ISO/IEC 1539:2010(E))*. Working Draft - ISO/IEC Copyright Office, Geneva, Switzerland, 2011. (Cited on p. 158)

[50] William M. Kahan. *Why Do We Need a Floating-Point Arithmetic Standard?* Technical report, EECS, University of California, Berkeley, Berkeley, CA, USA, 1981. URL http://www.cs.berkeley.edu/~wkahan/ieee754status/why-ieee.pdf. (Cited on p. 102)

[51] William M. Kahan. Mathematics written in sand. In *Proceedings of the American Statistical Association (Statistical Computing Section)*, pages 12–26, Alexandria, VA, USA, 1983. American Statistical Association, Alexandria, VA. URL http://www.cs.berkeley.edu/~wkahan/MathSand.pdf. (Cited on p. 101)

[52] William M. Kahan. *Kahan Summation Algorithm*. Technical report, University of California, Berkeley, Berkeley, CA, USA, 2013. URL http://en.wikipedia.org/wiki/Kahan_summation_algorithm. (Cited on p. 103)

[53] Donald E. Knuth. *The Art of Computer Programming, Volume III: Sorting and Searching*. Addison-Wesley, Reading, MA, USA, 2nd edition, 1998. ISBN 978-0-201-89685-5. (Cited on p. 57)

[54] F. T. Krogh. A Fortran Message Processor. *ACM Trans. Math. Software* (to appear). ISSN 0098-3500. (Cited on p. 222)

[55] Fred T. Krogh. 13.0 *Effective Use of the Quadrature Software*, 2009. URL http://mathalacarte.com/c/math77_head.html. (Cited on p. 94)

[56] C. L. Lawson, R. J. Hanson, D. R. Kincaid, and F. T. Krogh. Basic linear algebra subprograms for Fortran usage. *ACM Trans. Math. Software*, 5(3):308–323, September 1979. ISSN 0098-3500. doi: 10.1145/355841.355847. (Cited on pp. xiii, 103, 119)

[57] James R. Levine. *Linkers and Loaders*. Morgan Kaufman, Waltham, MA, USA, 2008. ISBN 978-1-558-60496-4. (Cited on p. 18)

[58] Xiaoye S. Li. An overview of SuperLU: Algorithms, implementation, and user interface. *ACM Trans. Math. Software*, 31(3):302–325, September 2005. ISSN 0098-3500. doi: 10.1145/1089014.1089017. (Cited on pp. xii, 131)

[59] Xiaoye S. Li, James W. Demmel, John R. Gilbert, Laura Grigori, Meiyue Shao, and Ichitaro Yamazaki. *SuperLU Users' Guide*. Technical report LBNL-44289, Lawrence Berkeley National Laboratory, Berkeley, CA, USA, 1999; updated 2011. (Cited on pp. xii, 36, 131, 133, 142)

[60] Wai-Hung Liu and Andrew H. Sherman. Comparative analysis of the Cuthill–McKee and the Reverse Cuthill–McKee ordering algorithms for sparse matrices. *SIAM J. Numer. Anal.*, 13(2):198–213, April 1976. ISSN 0036-1429. doi: 10.1137/0713020. (Cited on p. 36)

[61] Mark Lutz. *Learning Python*. O'Reilly Media, Inc., Sebastopol, CA, USA, 4th edition, 2009. ISBN 978-0-596-15806-4. (Cited on pp. 209, 225)

[62] Maplesoft. *Maple 17 User Manual*. Waterloo, ON, Canada, 2012. (Cited on p. 148)

[63] Robert Mecklenburg. *Managing Projects with GNU Make*. O'Reilly Media, Inc., Sebastopol, CA, USA, 3rd edition, 2004. ISBN 978-0-596-00610-5. (Cited on pp. 215, 216, 218)

[64] Michael Metcalf. convert.f90. Software download. 1997. Software package to convert between Fortran 77 and Fortran 90. URL `ftp://ftp.numerical.rl.ac.uk/pub/MandR/convert.f90`. (Cited on p. 223)

[65] Michael Metcalf, John Reid, and Malcolm Cohen. *Modern Fortran Explained*. Oxford University Press, Oxford, UK, 2011. ISBN 978-0-19-960141-7. (Cited on pp. x, 1, 10, 21, 55, 119, 164, 213, 218)

[66] Alan Miller. to_f90.f90. Software download, March 2000. Software to convert between Fortran 77 and Fortran 90. URL `http://jblevins.org/mirror/amiller/to_f90.f90`. (Cited on p. 223)

[67] Numerical Algorithms Group Ltd. *NAG Fortran Compiler*, 2010. URL `http://www.nag.com/`. (Cited on pp. 207, 218, 223, 225)

[68] Numerical Algorithms Group Ltd. *NAG Fortran Library*, 2010. URL `http://www.nag.com/`. (Cited on p. 58)

[69] OpenMP Architecture Review Board. *OpenMP Application Program Interface, Version 3.0*. Technical report, OpenMP Architecture Review Board, 2008. URL `http://www.openmp.org/mp-documents/spec30.pdf`. (Cited on pp. 169, 175)

[70] OpenMP Architecture Review Board. *OpenMP* 3.1 *Api Fortran Syntax Quick Reference Card, Version* 3.1. Technical report, OpenMP Architecture Review Board, 2011. URL http://openmp.org/mp-documents/OpenMP3.1-FortranCard.pdf. (Cited on p. 169)

[71] Charles Petzold. *Programming Windows.* Microsoft Programming. Microsoft Press, Redmond, WA, USA, 5th edition, 1998. ISBN 978-1572319950. (Cited on p. 18)

[72] R. Piessens, E. de Doncker-Kapenga, C. W. Überhuber, and D. K. Kahaner. *QUADPACK: A Subroutine Package for Automatic Integration.* Number 1 in Springer Series in Computational Mathematics. Springer Publishing, Berlin, 1983. ISBN 3-540-12553-1. (Cited on pp. xi, 51, 71, 90)

[73] C. Michael Pilato, Ben Collins-Sussman, and Brian W Fitzpatrick. *Version Control with Subversion.* O'Reilly Media, Inc., Sebastopol, CA, USA, 2nd edition, 2008. ISBN 978-0-596-51033-6. (Cited on pp. 215, 216, 219)

[74] *plusFORT (Version 6).* Polyhedron Software, Oxford, UK, 2012. URL http://www.polyhedron.com/pf-plusfort0html. (Cited on p. 223)

[75] Hugh Pumphrey. fmkmf. Software download, February 2006. Software to generate make file dependencies. URL http://www.geos.ed.ac.uk/homes/hcp/fmkmf/. (Cited on p. 225)

[76] Craig E. Rasmussen and Jeffrey M. Squyres. A case for new MPI Fortran bindings. In *Proceedings,* 12*th European PVM/MPI Users' Group Meeting,* Sorrento, Italy, September 2005. URL http://www.open-mpi.org/papers/euro-pvmmpi-2005-fortran/euro-pvm-mpi-2005-fortran.pdf. (Cited on p. 158)

[77] John Reid (ed.). *ISO/IEC TR* 15580(E) *Technical report: Information Technology – Programming Languages – Fortran – Floating-Point Exception Handling.* Technical report, ISO, Geneva, Switzerland, 2001. (Cited on p. 102)

[78] John Reid. Coarrays in the next Fortran standard. *SIGPLAN Fortran Forum,* 29(2):10–27, July 2010. ISSN 1061-7264. doi: 10.1145/1837137.1837138. (Cited on p. 164)

[79] John K. Reid and Robert W. Numrich. Coarrays in the next Fortran standard. *Scientific Programming,* 15(1):9–26, 2007. ISSN 1058-9244. (Cited on p. xiv)

[80] Arnold Robbins, Elbert Hannah, and Linda Lamb. *Learning the Vi and Vim Editors.* O'Reilly Media, Inc., Sebastopol, CA, USA, 7th edition, July 2008. ISBN 978-0-596-52983-3. URL http://shop.oreilly.com/product/9780596529833.do. (Cited on p. 225)

[81] Rogue Wave Software. *TotalView Fortran Debugger,* 2012. URL http://www.roguewave.com/. (Cited on p. 220)

[82] Youcef Saad. *SPARSKIT: A Basic Tool Kit for Sparse Matrix Computations.* Technical report, Center for Supercomputing Research and Development, University of Illinois, Urbana, IL, USA, 1994. (Cited on p. 36)

[83] Herbert Schildt. *The Complete Reference, C++.* McGraw-Hill/Osborne, Berkeley, CA, USA, 4th edition, 2003. ISBN 978-0-07-222680-5. (Cited on p. 10)

[84] Randal L. Schwartz, Brian D. Foy, and Tom Phoenix. *Learning Perl.* O'Reilly Media, Inc., Sebastopol, CA, USA, 6th edition, 2011. ISBN 978-1-4493-0358-7. (Cited on pp. 209, 225)

[85] Robert Sedgewick. *Algorithms in C - Parts 1-4: Fundamentals, Data Structures, Sorting, Searching.* Addison-Wesley, Reading, MA, USA, 3rd edition, 1998. ISBN 978-0-201-31452-6. (Cited on pp. xiii, 57, 58, 59)

[86] Marc Snir, Steve Otto, Steven Huss-Lederman, David Walker, and Jack Dongarra. *MPI-The Complete Reference, Volume 1, The MPI Core.* The MIT Press, Cambridge, MA, USA, 2nd edition, 1998. ISBN 978-0-262-69215-1. (Cited on pp. 157, 158, 163)

[87] Richard M. Stallman, Roland Pesch, and Stan Shebs. *Debugging with GDB: The GNU Source-Level Debugger.* Free Software Foundation, Boston, MA, USA, 9th edition, 2002. ISBN 978-1-882-11488-7. (Cited on p. 220)

[88] G. W. (Pete) Stewart. *Introduction to Matrix Computations.* Academic Press, London, UK, 1973. ISBN 978-0-126-70350-4. (Cited on p. 14)

[89] Gilbert Strang and George Fix. *An Analysis of the Finite Element Method.* Wellesley-Cambridge Press, Wellesley, MA, USA, 2nd edition, 2008. ISBN 978-0-9802327-0-7. (Cited on pp. 145, 146)

[90] Ruud van der Pas. *Memory Hierarchy in Cache-based Systems.* Technical report 817-0742-10, Sun Microsystems, Inc., Santa Clara, CA, USA, November 2002. (Cited on p. 37)

[91] Dimitri van Heesch. *Doxygen: Manual for Version* 1.7.5.1, 2011. URL `http://www.stack.nl/~dimitri/doxygen/download.html#latestman`. (Cited on pp. 216, 220)

[92] W. Van Snyder. Poor man's templates in Fortran 90. *SIGPLAN Fortran Forum*, 16(3):11, 1997. ISSN 1061-7264. doi: 10.1145/274104.274108. (Cited on p. 31)

[93] W. H. Vandevender and K. H. Haskell. The slatec mathematical subroutine library. *SIGNUM Newsl.*, 17(3):16–21, 1982. ISSN 0163-5778. doi: 10.1145/1057594.1057595. (Cited on p. 58)

[94] Michael Wester. makemake. Software download, February 1995. Software to generate make file dependencies. URL `http://www.fortran.com/makemake.perl`. (Cited on p. 225)

[95] Stavros A. Zenios. Network based models for air-traffic control. *European J. Oper. Res.*, 50(2):166–178, 1991. ISSN 0377-2217. doi: 10.1016/0377-2217(91)90239-R. URL `http://www.sciencedirect.com/science/article/pii/037722179190239R`. (Cited on p. 36)

Index

accessor-mutator routine
    example in a module, 7
    PUBLIC or PRIVATE
        components, 6
ACM, ix
    editors of CALGO, ix
Adams, Brainerd et al., *see* books,
    Fortran reference
Airy's equation
    boundary value problem,
        145–149
    connection formulas, 30
    $w'' - zw = 0$, 30
    Wronskian testing, 33
assignment overloading
    accumulating triplet list, 39
    accumulation
        data fitting, 142
        finite elements, 148
    clearing storage
        Harwell–Boeing (HB) format,
        137
    one-time LU factoring, 132
    saving LU factors, 132
    sparse matrix add, +, 44
ASSOCIATE symbol, =>
    example, in module, 6
Association for Computing Machinery,
    see ACM

benchmarking, 197
BLAS, 14,103,113,143,227
    called from C, 119–121, 129–130
    interface for, 25–27
    library building, 17–18

Blue's algorithm
    constants required for, 106
    l_2 norm, 105
book code on SIAM web site
    Airy functions, 29, 227
    BlasModule, 26
    C and Fortran
        interlanguage use, 117, 229
    c_dgemm, 121
    C_saxpy, 120
    cdgemm, 121
    classes, 47, 228
    coarray examples, 163, 168
    copyString, 122
    cSam, 125
    csaxpy, 119
    csaxpyval, 120
    csyscall, 127
    dfetrf, 14
    dfetrs, 14
    dgemm, 121
    dgemv, 26
    dnrm2, 26
    dnrm2_support, 106
    errnorm, 93
    exampleLapackInterface, 27
    exceptions, 101, 228
    funptrs, 125
    LAPACK example, 14, 227
    LapackInterface, 25
    MPI interface, 151, 229
    nonintrinsic modules
        IEEE_ARITHMETIC.f90, 228
        IEEE_EXCEPTIONS.f90, 228
        IEEE_FEATURES.f90, 228

normalPdf, 94
OpenMP examples, 169, 229
PtrArray, 123
qag, 51, 90
qag2003, 77, 89
qag2003s, 77, 90
qag2003v, 77, 90
qkgens, 90
qkgenv, 90
QUADPACK, 71, 228
QUADPACK documentation,
    89, 228
quadpack2003, 91
quicksort, 57, 228
saxpy, 119, 120
set_precision, 21
sparse defined operation, 35, 228
sparse matrix applications, 141,
    229
sparse system solves, 131, 229
syscall, 127
zeroin, 53, 55
books
    Fortran reference, x
        Adams, Brainerd et al., x
        Fortran 77 standard, x
        Fortran 90 standard, x
        Metcalf, Reid, and Cohen, x

C
    interoperability, *also see* Fortran, mod-
        ern features
        matching array indexing, 123
        matching data types, 119
        matching Fortran **COMMON**,
            C global data, 125
        matching pointers to C functions,
            125
        matching structs and derived
            types, 124
        name mangling, 120
        rationale, 117
        saxpy, C calls
            by reference, by value, 120
        string conversion, 122
    interoperability for MPI, 151

CALGO, *see* ACM
coarray, *see also* MPI
    allocatable arrays, 165
    codimensions, 164
    coindex, 164
    corank, 164
    critical {...} end critical, 168
    data communication,
        Fortran 2008 example, 164
    example of computing π
        with quadrature, 166
    example of matrix-vector products,
        167
    image_index, 166
    images, 163
    new convention for subscripts, 163
    num_images, 165, 166
    rationale, 163
    specifying data objects, 164
    sync all, 166
    this_image, 165, 166
code conversion
    regression testing, 182
Collected Algorithms from ACM
    (CALGO), *see* ACM
compiler options
    checking array bounds, 206
    checking deleted and obsolete
        features, 207, 213
    checking unassigned variables,
        206
    checking unused variables, 206
    deleted and obsolescent features,
        181
    optimization level, 209
    performance and debugging level,
        208
    performance and optimization level,
        212

data to user routines
    COMMON blocks, 51
    example, classes as arguments, 51
    example, *zeroin*, 55
    module variables, 51
    thread-safe, 51

defined operation
  .ip., .pi., superLU, solves, 132
  .p., .ip., assignment
    Airy's equation,
      boundary value problem, 145
    least-squares,
      piecewise linear, 142
  clearing storage
    interior of SuperLU , 137
  INTENT(IN), operands, 132
  parsing precedence, 42
    use of parentheses, 45
  sparse matrix add, +, 42, 43
  sparse matrix product, *, .p.,
    42, 45
  sparse matrix solve, .ip., .pi., 131
  sparse matrix transpose, .t.,
    42, 45
deleted features
  ASSIGN label,
    GO TO assigned label, 187
  END IF with label, 187
  nH or hollerith
    edit descriptors, 187
  PAUSE, 187
  REAL loop variables, 187
derived types
  class procedures, 63–64
  example, in module, 6
Dijkstra quote on testing, 193
documentation
  arguments
    input type, kind, and rank, 92
    output, 93
  example, *CALL qag2003()*, 95
  modules, derived types
    PUBLIC objects, 90
  QUADPACK use,
    example, 90
  routines called, 90
  user function
    interface, 91
    recommended packaging, 94
  variable dictionary, 89
  writing style, 89

equivalence partitioning, 198

Fortran
  statement functions, 211
Fortran development
  rationale, ix
Fortran optimization
  algorithm choice, 212
  memory access, 211
  MPI and coarrays, 212
  OpenMP, 212
Fortran standards, *see* books, Fortran reference
Fortran, modern features,
    see assignment overloading
    see data to user routines
    see defined operation
    see deleted features
    see derived types, classes
    see generic names, subprograms
    see IEEE standard
    see object-oriented
    see obsolescent features
    see procedures, type-bound
    see QUADPACK
    see recursion
  allocating with problem size
    example, 19
  ASSOCIATE symbol, 4
  avoiding name clashes, 27
  CASE statement
    computed-GO TO, 2, 184–185
  comments, inline, 2
    example, 3
  compilation units
    functions, 13
    main programs, 13
    modules, 13
    subroutines, 13
  compiler analysis, 210
  continuation lines
    use of symbol &, 3
  derived type, xi
    component separator, %, 5
    often a C structure, also a
      record, 5

PUBLIC or PRIVATE components,
  see modules, packaging
dusty decks, 212
early optimization, 209
gfortran, compiler, 14
INCLUDE
  file, 9–10, 32–33
  templates, 31–32
interfaces, 24
  defining a module procedure, 31
interoperability with C, ix, 117
intrinsic modules, 102, 119, 172
library, building, 18
modules, xi, *see also* modules,
    packaging
multiple statements per line
  avoid, 2, 4
name transformation
  dnrm2, locally called *l2norm*, 27
numeric inquiry functions, 102
optional arguments, 8
  example, 8, 11
  PRESENT intrinsic function, 8
pointer, 4
relational symbols, 5
source formatting, 2
timing routines, 10
  cpu_time, 10
  system_clock, 11
top 10 items, xi
use of symbol =>, 4
VOLATILE attribute, 173

generic names
  Airy functions
    example, 30
  packaging Airy functions
    example, 31
  subprograms
    advantages, 29, 30

IEEE standard
  floating-point exceptions, 102
    example, *d2nrm*, 103
  Fortran floating-point history,
    102

Fortran intrinsic modules
  IEEE_ARITHMETIC, 102, 111,
    113
  IEEE_EXCEPTIONS, 102, 111
  IEEE_FEATURES, 102, 111–112
  ISO_C_BINDING, 119–128, 136
Kahan, William, 102, 105
overflow and underflow
  setting flags, 109
setting IEEE halting mode, 107
underflow and denormalized results,
    113
intrinsic subprograms
  c_loc, 160
  cpu_time, 10
  huge, 104
  move_alloc, 41
  present, 8
  random_number, 141
  selected_real_kind, 21
  system_clock, 11
  tiny, 113
  transfer, 9

Kahan's algorithm
  constants required, 107
  l_2 norm, 108

LAPACK
  dgetrf, *dgetrs*, 14
  library building, 17
    ar, *ranlib*, 17
legacy code, restructuring, 188
legacy interfacing, 14
  BLAS, 14
  code bloat, 17
  compilation, linking, 17
  file suffix .*f*, 14
  LAPACK, 14
    timing, *dgetrf*, *dgetrs*, 15
  library building, 17
library, precompiled
  calls to module subprograms, 26
  calls, interfaces, 25
library, usage
  order, linker, 18

Maple version 11.02
    use of, 148
matrix, sparse, *see also* defined operation
    representation
        Harwell–Boeing (HB), 36
        triplet, 38
Metcalf, Reid, and Cohen, *see* books,
        Fortran reference
mistake, purposeful
    quicksort, correct coding, 60
modules, packaging
    derived types
        interfaces, subprograms, 6
        PUBLIC or PRIVATE
            components, 6
    KIND parameters, 20
    precision definition
        example, 21
        SELECTED_REAL_KIND, 21
    USE-association, 6
        example, 7, 8
MPI, *see* coarray
    c_loc, target attribute, 160
    core suite, 158
    module, *Fortran_to_MPI*
        interfaces, core suite, 160
    parameters, defining
        C provides values, 159
    routines, number of, 158

object-oriented (OO)
    accessor, mutator functions, 50
    class, 48
    inheritance, polymorphism, 49
    method, 48
    object, 48
obsolescent features
    alternate return, 183
    arithmetic-**IF** test, 182
    character function length, 186
    CHARACTER* declaration, 186
    computed-**GO TO**, 184
    DATA statements, scattered,
        185
    DO termination, 183
    fixed source format, 182

future obsolescence, 20
    one line functions, 185
OpenMP
    array update
        example, 171
    atomic, 175
    CHUNKSIZE, 180
    cons, 170
    critical, 175
    fragmentation, memory
        example, 178
    general models, *pthreads*, 180
    IEEE exceptions, 172
    input, output
        example, 173
    mutex, 180
    output only
        example, 172
    private variables, personal, 177
    pros, 170
    pthreads, 180
    race, deadlock, 170
    REDUCTION, example, 172
    SCHEDULE, 180
    subprograms, calling
        not thread-safe, 176
    thread-safe, 170
    thread-safe, tips, 176
    Windows threads, 180
operator overloading
    sparse matrix add, +, 42
optimization
    in-line calls, 62, 211, 212

packaging with modules
    features, 18, 19
precision, range
    IEEE floating-point, 21
procedures, type-bound
    CLASS versus TYPE declaration, 64
    example, 49
    FINAL, 54, 55
    NOPASS, PASS, example, 64
purposeful mistake
    C interoperability
        system calls, 127

QUADPACK,
  see also documentation
  derived TYPE (*quadpackbase*), 75
  enhancements, 73
    CLASS objects,
      abstract interfaces, 73
    generic names, 74
    procedure pointers, 74
    source conversion, 74
    vectorization, 74
  integrals
    complex, 72
      example, 85
    multiple, 72
    one-dimensional
      Bessel J_0, example, 77
      data passing, 77
    two-dimensional, 81
      compute recursively, 81
    vector, 72
  interface
    Fortran 77, *qag*, 75
    generic name, *qag2003*, 77
    scalar integrals, *qag2003s*, 77
    vector integrals, *qag2003v*, 77
  restrictions, Fortran 77, 73
    access to data, 73
    efficiency, 73
    integrals, multiple, 73
    vectorization, 73
quicksort, xiii, xv, 47, 57–70, 113
  algorithms, recursive definition, 58
  comparisons, 59, 60
  functions, in-lining of, 62
  in-situ sorting, 62
  operations, 59, 60

random numbers
  complex pairs, 8
  example, 8
recursion
  efficiency, reluctance, 57
  quicksort, 57
reverse communication
  example, Newton method, 188

SIAM, *see* book code on SIAM web site
solving least squares
  linear and sparse system, 142
    ill-conditioned or singular, 142
standard
  Fortran 2003, x
  ISO Fortran 90, x
SuperLU, C code
  clear_superlu, clearing storage, 137
SuperLU solving using C code
  SOLVE_with_SuperLU, 137

testing
  block coverage, 195, 202
  boundary values, 199
  decision coverage, 202
  equivalence partitioning, 198
  error logging, 196
  exhaustive, 194
  Lapack coverage, 195
  logging coverage, 195
  makefiles, 196
  metric, 195, 196
  oracle, 197
  regression, 196
  smoke, 201, 203
  soak, 196, 197, 203
  statement coverage, 195
  unit, 196, 197
  white box, 196
timing subprograms
  cpu_time(), 10
  system_clock, 10, 11
tools, software
  code coverage, 221
  code debuggers, 220
  code documentation,
    Doxygen, 219
  code profilers, 221
  editors, language aware, 215, 225
  error processors, 222
  make, 216
  Makefile, example, 217
  source formatters, 223
  text control, SVN, 219

x87 assembler, 104